The Golden Age of Amateur Basketball

The AAU Tournament, 1921–1968

Adolph H. Grundman

University of Nebraska Press
Lincoln and London

Library of Congress Cataloging-in-
Publication Data
Grundman, Adolph H.
The golden age of amateur basketball : the AAU tournament, 1921–
1968 / Adolph H. Grundman.
p. cm.
Includes bibliographical references
and index.
ISBN 0-8032-7117-4 (pbk. : alk.
paper)
1. AAU Tournament (Basketball—
History.   2. Basketball—United
States—History—20th century.
3. Amateur Athletic Union of the
United States—History.   I. Title.
GV885.49.A45G78 2004
796.332'06—dc22
2004007210

Set in Jansen by Kim Essman.
Printed by Edwards Brothers, Inc.

To my family:
Claudia, Sara, and Julie

Contents

Illustrations

Acknowledgments

In researching and writing this book I owe a great deal to a number of people who made it possible for me to complete this project. Vance Aandahl, who watched many of the tournaments before joining the English Department of Metropolitan State College, read the entire manuscript, offered encouragement, and strengthened the text with editorial comments. Norm Rosenberg of Macalester College read an early version of the manuscript and provided helpful observations. Sharon Porter transcribed many of my taped interviews with former players and, along with Gloria Kennison, Nita Froelich, and Sharon Roehling, provided valuable typing assistance. I owe a special debt to Marcellina Noth who patiently typed and retyped the final drafts of the manuscript. Professional development grants from Metropolitan State College of Denver made it possible for me to take several research trips that were extremely valuable.

My research of the aau tournament began with careful reading of accounts of the games in the *Kansas City Star*, the *Denver Post*, and *Rocky Mountain News*. An appreciation of the tournament and what the aau experience meant to the players rested on interviews with a host of aau veterans. While I have compiled a list of those interviews, I want to acknowledge several people who were extremely helpful. Bob Kurland allowed me to read his scrapbooks, which provided a quick overview of his career and the history of Phillips 66 between 1947 and 1952. Burdie Haldorson's scrapbooks provided similar information for Phillips between 1956 and 1960. Arilee Pollard shared her collection of scrapbooks and videos of her husband Jim Pollard and made my visit to Lodi, California, especially enjoyable. Warren Womble was generous in sharing his knowledge of the Peoria Caterpillars and Frank Fidler was equally gracious in discussing the history of Seattle's Buchan Bakers. Sally Habeeb, Vice President for Advertising at the Hillyard Chemical Company, made it possible for me to view the scrapbooks of the Hillyard basketball team. The archivists at the University of Kansas and the Phillips Petroleum Company were extremely helpful. Phillips Petroleum Company and the Basketball Hall of Fame generously provided me with a number of the photographs that appear in the book. Along the research trail, old friends like Randolph Hennes of the University of Washington and Bob and Cindy Hull of Wichita, Kansas, provided a home away from home.

The following players, coaches, and writers shared their stories with me and were indispensable in helping me understand the AAU experience. I want to thank all of them for their assistance. They are: Glendon Anderson, Ladell Anderson, Joe Belmont, Don Boldebuck, Bob Boozer, Dick Boushka, Jim Darden, George Durham, Floyd Burk, Chuck Darling, Hal Davis, John Dee, Dick Eicher, Frank Fidler, Ken Flower, Ben Gibson, Jack Gray, Alex Hannum, Frank Haraway, Fred Howell, Bud Howard, Fon Johnson, Bob Kurland, Ken Leslie, Albert "Cappy" Lavin, Cleo Littleton, Frank Lubin, Tom Meschery, Melvin Miller, Jimmy Reese, Willie Rothman, Russ Lyons, Kenny Sailors, Harv Schmidt, Dennis O' Shea, R. C. Owens, Terry Rand, Fred Scolari, Morris "Mushy" Silver, Bill Strannigan, Gary Thompson, Ron Tomsic, George Walker, Bob Wilson, Warren Womble, George Yardley, Larry Varnell, Phil Vukicevich and Jim Vickers. A number of these interviews are on cassette and will be deposited in the Basketball Hall of Fame in Springfield, Massachusetts.

Introduction

In the last thirty years there has been an explosion of academic interest in American sports. Colleges and universities offer courses in the history, philosophy, sociology, economics, and literature of sports. For twenty years I have taught a sports history class at Metropolitan State College of Denver. As I explored the scholarship of this burgeoning field and became familiar with Denver's sports history, it struck me that scholars had neglected an important part of the American basketball experience. A quick glance at the shelves of any library devoted to sports will reveal that basketball's literature is devoted primarily to the professional game, its greatest players, and some of the game's most successful college coaches. Most basketball fans born after 1960 would have no inkling that for the first sixty years of the twentieth century amateur basketball once competed with professional and college basketball for the attention of basketball junkies of earlier generations.

By amateur basketball, I mean the game governed by the Amateur Athletic Union (AAU), organized in 1888 to conduct athletic competitions and to monitor the amateur code. The leaders of the AAU believed that a sport played for its own sake rather than for profit was the purest form of athletic activity. It was this philosophy of sport that inspired Pierre de Coubertin to revive the Olympic Games in 1896. Historians have shown that amateurism had its darker side as it attracted elite sportsmen who thought that excluding professionals would preserve sports for the upper classes. Amateurism, whatever

the motivation of its adherents, faced an uphill battle, which it ultimately lost. The twentieth century saw sport become an important
form of entertainment for Americans who were prepared to pay top
dollar to see the nation's best athletes. It would, however, take time
for professionalism to assert its dominance in basketball. Before that
moment arrived in the late twentieth century, amateur sport struggled to keep its niche in American sports.

When James Naismith invented the game of basketball in 1891,
he did so for a class taught by Luther Halsey Gulick at the International Young Men's Christian Training School, now Springfield College, in Springfield, Massachusetts. Naismith's goal was to provide
a game that would teach teamwork and provide a laboratory for the
spiritual development of young men in the nation's YMCAS. In a classic example of the principle of unintended effects, he saw his game
transformed into one of the nation's major competitive sports, driven
by the forces of the economic market place rather than the values of
education. In 1896, as Naismith and Gulick turned their attention
to other challenges, they transferred the responsibility of governing
amateur basketball to the AAU. In 1897 the AAU conducted its first
national basketball tournament. The AAU basketball tournament had
the potential to offer competitive opportunities for athletes hoping
to play a game they enjoyed beyond their high school or college experiences. After 1897 the tournament was played intermittently by a
small number of teams and at changing locations. It did not generate
enough interest to merit much coverage by contemporaries or analysis by historians. This changed when the AAU moved the basketball
tournament to Kansas City in 1921, where it found its first home.
In 1935, when the tournament moved to Denver, it had established
itself as an important regional athletic event and remained so until
the early 1960s.

By reading accounts of all the tournaments in newspapers, yearbooks, and sports magazines, and interviewing AAU players and
coaches, I was able to find answers to the following questions:
Who sponsored teams and where did they come from? Who were
the players and coaches who generated fan interest? Why did the
tournament leave Kansas City for Denver in 1935? After years of

success, why did the tournament leave Denver in 1968 and what was its contribution to basketball history? Because the tournament enjoyed its greatest success in Denver, except for the first chapter, this book is about the AAU tournament in the Mile High City. Beginning in 1935, like clockwork, Denver's fans turned out to watch the old and new stars battle for a national crown and a spot on the AAU All-American team. Whatever the rest of the nation thought, for one week Denver believed it was the capital of basketball. The fans kept coming until the 1960s when television revenues and escalating salaries made it impossible for amateur teams to compete with the professional game.

There were several categories of teams that competed in the national tournament. A handful of athletic clubs sent teams to the tournament, the most successful of which were the Kansas City Athletic Club and the Olympic Club of San Francisco. They were able to recruit local college stars who received nothing more than club memberships at a reduced rate and the chance to continue playing basketball at a highly competitive level. For the wealthiest clubs basketball was just one of the many sports they sponsored in order to promote athletics in their communities. A larger number of teams were sponsored by medium-sized businesses who believed that sponsoring a basketball team was a good marketing device. Among the most competitive were the Wichita Henrys, the Oakland Bittners, Stewart Chevrolet of San Francisco, and the Buchan Bakers of Seattle. These programs had enough resources to hire a few players, subsidize a barnstorming schedule, or participate in a league. In most cases they competed for three or four years before the economic burden became prohibitive. World War II and the Cold War produced military service teams, a product of the Armed Services' belief that athletic competition boosted morale. There were numerous small businessmen who sponsored a team just for the tournament. Often these teams collected local university stars who had just completed their eligibility, and they occasionally made a serious run at the championship. Early in the tournament's history small colleges participated and some coaches used the promise of a trip to Kansas City or Denver as a recruiting device.

With time, the tone of the tournament was set by teams sponsored by large corporations. They saw their basketball teams as part of an overall activities program that would build company morale and market their company's products. Large companies recruited players by offering a program that mixed job training, basketball competition, and the opportunity of advancement in the corporation. The Phillips Petroleum Company set the standard for any corporation hoping to compete for a national title. While Phillips dominated the 1940s, the Peoria Caterpillar Tractor Company won five titles in the 1950s. Akron's Goodyear Tire and Rubber Company, which dated its basketball program to 1914, waited until the 1960s before it won an AAU championship.

Since the AAU governed the tournament, teams had to observe the amateur code. This meant that athletes could not play for pay or benefit in any way from their athletic fame. If basketball players played professionally, they permanently lost their amateur status. The programs developed by large corporations certainly blurred the distinction between amateur and professional athletes. Industry defended itself against charges of professionalism by documenting the high number of basketball players who remained with their companies. They pointed with pride to those who held high-ranking positions, including some players who rose to be presidents of their firms. If this was not the purest form of amateurism, as the purists argued, it was an accommodation that was crucial to the AAU tournament's success. It represented a form of pragmatism that some historians believe to be central to American culture.

The major impact of the industrial teams was to make the tournament more competitive. In the first three decades of the tournament, many teams made the trip to Kansas City or Denver with no expectation of surviving the week-long single elimination event. Many of the games had lopsided scores. By the 1950s the tournament committee became more selective and the field smaller. The emphasis was on excellence rather than participation. While some observers occasionally exhibited nostalgia for the more amateurish tournaments of earlier years, the tide ran in the other direction, toward an event that presented the audience with highly skilled players and disciplined teams.

In 1921 when Kansas City hosted its first tournament, it had no competition from professional basketball, which was concentrated in northeastern and, to a lesser extent, midwestern cities. Without the benefit of air travel, the long distances between cities from the Great Plains to the Pacific Coast discouraged the establishment of professional teams or leagues. Before World War II outstanding players of this region had little incentive to play professionally, since professional leagues were unstable, salaries low, and contracts not guaranteed, conditions that did not change significantly in the first decade after the National Basketball Association (NBA) was formed in 1949.

When the national AAU tournament moved to Denver in 1935, the United States was in the depths of a terrible economic depression. It had lost its Western League baseball team in 1932, but still had the *Denver Post* baseball tournament. The national AAU basketball tournament offered another opportunity for the city to boost its attractions if only for a week, in difficult economic times. In some ways the timing could not have been better. By 1935 basketball rule changes made the game faster and more entertaining. Players were becoming more creative, shooting with one hand and, within the decade, utilizing the jump shot. Moreover, universities and colleges in the Great Plains, the Southwest, and the West had outstanding coaches and players. Kansas's Forrest "Phog" Allen, Oklahoma A&M's Henry Iba, Wyoming's Everett Shelton, and Utah's Vadel Peterson were among the most successful, each coaching a National Collegiate Athletic Association (NCAA) champion.

As a spectator event, the tournament's popularity rested on a number of familiar themes in America's past. Its drama required rivalries, which sports journalists exploited to heighten fan interest. In the 1920s it was the Hillyards of St. Joseph, Missouri, or the Wichita Henrys against Kansas City's best; in the 1930s and 1940s the Denver-Phillips rivalry electrified the fans; and in the 1950s the Peoria Caterpillar and Phillips games had a special edge.

Fans found heroes to cheer and villains to boo. In the Kansas City tournament Forrest "Red" DeBernardi was a perennial AAU All-American and a fan favorite in the 1920s, while Melvin Miller and Chuck Hyatt were popular and innovative players of the early 1930s. When the tournament moved to Denver, the Mile High City's sports fans idolized Jack McCracken, a poker-faced guard, and Robert "Ace" Gruenig, a tall center with a sweeping hook shot. They led Denver to three national titles. The Phillips 66ers were the villains. Like baseball's New York Yankees, especially in the 1940s, Phillips had the resources and players that were the envy of their competitors. The 66ers received more than their fair share of jeers from Denver's rabid fans.

Also enhancing the stature of the AAU tournament was its connection to the Olympics, which added basketball to its program in 1936. In that year and the next three Olympiads, the coach and at least half the players were from AAU teams. The privilege of representing the United States was a much-coveted honor for those who competed during these years. The selection of the Olympic team also became part of a larger dispute between the AAU and the NCAA over which institution governed amateur sports in the United States.

Along with heroes, villains, rivalries, and the chance for Olympic gold the tournament had tradition. Jack McCracken, Ace Gruenig, Melvin Miller, Chuck Hyatt, Omar "Bud" Browning and others played and/or coached for over a decade. Denver sports journalists such as Jack Carberry, Frank Haraway, Chet Nelson, and Leonard Cahn watched the event in Denver from its beginning in 1935 to its end in 1968. They saw basketball evolve as a game and made the inevitable comparisons between generations of players that are so much a part of American sports culture. The event had the elements of a reunion as players, writers, and fans exchanged memories, evaluated new talent, and soaked up the atmosphere of another tournament.

For over four decades AAU basketball gave highly skilled athletes an opportunity to extend their playing careers and, if they played for a large corporation, to develop skills and careers that would provide economic security. Around 1960 the NBA began to offer salaries that were difficult for industrial teams to match. After Denver washed its hands of the tournament in 1968, the AAU's contribution to American basketball and Denver sports history gradually faded. By 1968 Denver had an American Basketball Association team that joined the NBA in 1976. Although there were a variety of reasons why Denver succeeded in supporting a professional team, one is that, because of the AAU tournament, Denver thought of itself as a basketball town. With this book, I hope to have recaptured an important part of America's basketball history before basketball became a big business.

PART I

A BASKETBALL TRADITION IS BORN

The first three chapters place the national AAU basketball tournament in its historical context. From 1921 through 1934 the tournament found a home in Kansas City. By the early 1930s a number of teams had earned reputations for basketball excellence and produced AAU All-Americans such as Forrest "Red" DeBernardi, Melvin Miller, and Chuck Hyatt. To boost interest in the tournament, promoters also focused on intercity rivalries pitting teams from Kansas City, Missouri, St Joseph, Missouri, and Wichita, Kansas. Teams like the St. Joseph Hillyards and Wichita Henrys also regularly barnstormed to California, stopping at cities along the way to promote basketball. As the event became more attractive, Denver sportswriters and AAU officials were successful in their bid to bring it to Denver in 1935. If only for a week, Denver hoped the tournament would place the Mile High City on the sports map. AAU basketball brought to Denver two of its early sports legends: Jack McCracken and Robert "Ace" Gruenig. In 1936 the significance of the tournament soared as it became an integral part of the process to select America's first Olympic team. When the stakes became higher, the competition between the AAU and the NCAA grew more intense as each organization asserted its claim to represent the United States in international competition.

Between 1921 and 1936 there was no collegiate national basketball tournament. Basketball played second fiddle to football on most college campuses. Almost all the professional leagues were composed of teams from New York, New Jersey, and Pennsylvania and small cities in the Midwest. Salaries were low and the leagues unstable. The best known teams of the period were the barnstorming teams like New York's Original Celtics and two African American teams: New York's Renaissance Big Five (the Rens), and the Harlem Globetrotters, founded in Chicago. Whether it was the AAU, the colleges, or the professionals, changes in the rules and new styles of play made the game faster and more exciting. By the end of 1936 basketball was about to enter a phase of its history that would eventually make it one of the world's most popular games.

ONE

Everything Is Up-to-Date in Kansas City

The 1920s witnessed the first Golden Age of Sport in America. Professional baseball, boxing, and college football drew huge crowds and produced celebrities like Babe Ruth, Jack Dempsey, and Harold "Red" Grange; but basketball, whether professional or amateur, failed to generate competitions of national significance. As far back as 1897 the Amateur Athletic Union (AAU) had sponsored a national basketball tournament, but it was held sporadically, drew few teams, and its sponsors regularly took a bath in red ink. This began to change in 1921 when Kansas City won the right to hold the national (AAU) basketball tournament. For fourteen consecutive years, Kansas City hosted this event. Then it moved to Denver in 1935. By the mid-1930s basketball's popularity was soaring, and the AAU benefited from the growing interest in basketball as a spectator sport.[1]

By 1921 exactly three decades had elapsed since James Naismith formulated the first rules of basketball at the Young Men's Christian Association (YMCA) training school in Springfield, Massachusetts. His game had spread throughout the nation and, aided by the YMCA, to the world. In America's crowded cities reformers, according to historians, utilized basketball as one of the techniques of assimilating new immigrants who played the game in settlement houses, church leagues, and high schools.[2] Following the example of football, colleges added basketball as still another activity to entertain students and alumni. In the Northeast the first professional leagues emerged as early as 1898–99, as well as barnstorming teams like the Buffalo Germans (1895–1926) and New York's Original Celtics (1914–36).[3] Therefore, when Kansas City decided to host the AAU tournament, basketball was widely played but its coaches and players had not yet discovered the style of play that would make it appealing to spectators.

There were a variety of reasons for basketball's lack of popular appeal. Foremost among them was that the games were low-scoring and often boring. The ball, leather with seams and laces, was more difficult to shoot and dribble than today's slightly smaller molded ball. A shooter's repertoire was limited to a two-handed set shot or an underhanded shot. One-handed shots were reserved for lay-ups or other opportunities under the basket. Finally, the rules encouraged coaches to assume a defensive mentality. Since the ten-second line was not adopted until 1932, teams used the entire court to protect a lead by stalling. The defensive team could not regain control of the ball by fouling, because the team with the ball could waive its free throws and take the ball out of bounds, a rule enforced until 1953. The absence of a shot clock also meant there was no penalty for holding the ball. The rule requiring a center jump after every field goal or free throw interrupted the rhythm of the game and favored the team that controlled the jump, until eliminated in 1937.[4] Forrest "Phog" Allen, the University of Kansas's successful coach, spoke for many of his colleagues when he wrote: "Possession of the ball is the main object of the game."[5] Sports writers and fans found little entertainment in this style of play. In 1934, after watching a typical ball control game between two AAU teams, Howard "Ham" Beresford, of the *Rocky Mountain News*, made a modest proposal: take the baskets down "so they won't be in the way and allow the lads to run all over the building playing hide-and-seek with the ball."[6] Chet Nelson, also of the *Rocky Mountain News*, agreed and wrote that fans craved "scoring and a quantity of action" and grew tired of watching players "flinging the ball around out in the center of the floor."[7] A few years after Beresford and Nelson offered their criticism of basketball, fans, writers, and players would see basketball transformed by a combination of rule changes, mentioned above, and new offensive techniques and strategies.

In the 1920s and 1930s basketball was also a pawn in the battle between the AAU and the NCAA, founded in 1906, for control of amateur sports in the United States. Founded in 1888, the AAU initially was part of an effort to use sport as an instrument for promoting such values as teamwork and discipline. At the heart of the amateur ethic was the belief that athletes engaged in competition for the sheer love of sport rather than for its financial rewards. While the AAU and NCAA preached the gospel of amateurism, it was riddled with contradictions. Historians have amply documented the rise of professional college coaches in the 1890s, the lure of gate receipts, and the "under-the-table" payments to athletes that permeated collegiate and AAU competition. Nonetheless, the ideology of amateurism was very attractive, and American sports fans continually displayed a remarkable facility to overlook the commercial underpinnings of amateur sport.[8]

In the first two decades of the twentieth century the prestige of the AAU rested on its domination of the American Olympic Committee (AOC). When Baron Pierre de Coubertin masterminded the revival of the Olympic Games in 1896, track and field were the most prominent events. Since the AAU controlled amateur track and field competition in the United States, by 1900 it had assumed the responsibility for selecting the U.S. Olympic team and raising the funds so that it could compete. AAU officials also represented the United States on international sports federations that established rules for international competition in the respective sports. The AAU exercised its power over American amateur sport by registering athletes and sanctioning competitions. Following the 1920 Olympics the NCAA publicly criticized the AAU's management of the Olympic program, marking the beginning of a long bureaucratic struggle for control of the Olympic movement in the United States.[9] When basketball became an Olympic sport in 1936, it immediately served as another source of tension between the two organizations. In 1921, however, basketball had not yet established any traditions worthy of a fight.

Between 1897 and 1912 the AAU conducted seven national tournaments. In reality the tournament was quite regional as the contestants were usually from cities and towns in the vicinity of the tournament site. Sometimes a tournament had only four teams and never more than sixteen. The AAU tried different sites for the tournament, including New York and Chicago, as it searched for a suitable home. Beginning in 1913 the tournament was held yearly, except for 1918, when it was not held because of the World War. The teams that competed were usually sponsored by athletic clubs, men's clubs, and less frequently a college or university.[10]

Kansas City argued that its geographic location and outstanding basketball fans made it an ideal location for a national basketball tournament. In 1905 the Kansas City Athletic Club (KCAC) had defeated the Buffalo Germans, who claimed the world championship by virtue of having won the basketball championship at the St. Louis World's Fair in 1904. One of the stars of the Kansas City team was Forrest "Phog" Allen, who by 1921 had just begun his long and distinguished career as the basketball coach of the University of Kansas Jayhawks. The Blue Diamonds of KCAC had also earned a third place finish in the 1920 AAU tournament held in Atlanta.[11]

The driving force behind the Kansas City tournament was Dr. Joseph A. Reilly, director of athletics for the Kansas City Athletic Club. A native of Boston, Reilly played football, ran track, and studied medicine at Georgetown University in the first years of the twentieth century. After completing his athletic eligibility, Georgetown hired Reilly to coach its football and track teams. Reportedly he resigned when Georgetown declared that students from the law and medical schools were ineligible for varsity athletic competition. Reilly planned to practice medicine in Boston until the Kansas City Athletic Club recruited him to serve as its director of athletics. By the 1930s, in addition to successfully fulfilling his responsibilities with the KCAC, Reilly had won a reputation in amateur athletics as a football, wrestling, and boxing official and "the man who put national basketball tournaments on a paying basis."[12]

According to the *Kansas City Star*, the thirty-two teams that met in 1921 made this tournament "the largest in history" and brought with them "the cream of the nation's court talent."[13] Teams representing Brooklyn College, the Los Angeles Athletic Club, and the Atlanta Athletic Club made the tournament draw truly national. Almost half of the teams came from Missouri, Kansas, and Oklahoma. While a majority of the teams represented athletic clubs, small businesses, and a few large corporations, college teams also competed in the tournament. Almost all the college teams were from the state college conferences in Oklahoma, Kansas, and Missouri. During the fourteen years of national tournament play in Kansas, two college teams, Butler College and Washburn College, won the national tournament. Three others, Southwestern College of Winfield, Kansas, Maryville State Teacher's College of Maryville, Missouri, and the University of Wyoming, lost in the championship game.

The tournament's format was very demanding. To win the championship a team had to win five games in six days. The first round was played on Monday and Tuesday with games scheduled for the entire day. As the tournament became more popular and the draw expanded to forty teams or more, the committee scheduled games for the Saturday before the normal Monday opener in order to narrow the field to thirty-two teams.

Given the episodic history of the tournament before 1921—its failure to draw many teams or to make money—Dr. Reilly and KCAC faced a serious challenge. The key to success was to field strong Kansas City teams that could attract local fans to Convention Hall for the duration of the weeklong event. The tournament committee's worst nightmare was that all of the home teams would suffer an early defeat and leave the local fans with nobody to root for and no reason to attend games in the later rounds. KCAC clearly hosted the tournament in the belief that its club team could compete for the national championship. The reliance of promoters on a strong local entry to attract local fans to a national tournament was not unique to Kansas City. Ned Irish, who made Madison Square Garden into a basketball mecca, relied on powerful local teams including Long Island University, the City College of New York, New York University, and St. John's University to attract fans to his college doubleheaders beginning in 1934. When Madison Square Garden hosted the first National Invitational Tournament in 1938, sponsored by the Metropolitan Basketball Writers Association, none of the six teams were from the South or the Pacific Coast. Between 1939, the first year of the NCAA basketball tournament, and 1951, the field was limited to eight teams. It was not until 1952, when sixteen schools were invited to play, that the semifinals and finals were played at the same site.[14] What made the AAU tournament unique was its week-long format, large field, and mixture of club, college, and industrial teams.

In 1921 the KCAC assembled an outstanding team. The Blue Diamond's most celebrated player was Forrest "Red" DeBernardi, who starred at Westminster College in Fulton, Missouri. One writer commented that "there is nothing he can't do on a basketball court. The game just comes natural with the 'red head,'" who sported a bristling red mustache in the 1920s.[15] Although only two inches over six feet, he was described as "the best frog that every leaped in the court circle." In the 1921 tournament this same writer observed that "few times during the week's play has a rival center got the tip off on DeBernardi."[16] This was especially important at a time when a center jump followed every basket. Two other notable players on the Blue Diamonds included Milton Singer, whose 21-point average led the tournament, and Arthur "Dutch" Lonberg, a University of Kansas (KU) All-American, who subsequently coached basketball at Washburn College and Northwestern University in Evanston, Illinois, before returning to KU, where he directed athletics from 1950 to 1964. Led by the combination of DeBernardi, Singer and Lonberg, the KCAC won the championship game by beating South-western College of Winfield, Kansas. The tournament committee reported that 16,300 people paid $13,241 to watch the tournament, a response that was judged a success.[17]

This and subsequent tournaments also served as a stage for Ernie Quigley, one of the most colorful basketball officials of this or any era. A major league baseball umpire and a popular football official, Quigley was a showman on the basketball court. Quigley's trademark was to bellow, "You can't DOOO THAT!" to a player caught committing a foul. Frequently, Quigley followed this admonition with a lecture that ended with, "Young man, do you understand me?"[18]

In 1922, led by Milt Singer and "Red" DeBernardi, the KCAC easily advanced to the championship game where they were upset by a team sponsored by Lowe and Campbell, a Kansas City athletic store. George and Fred Williams, brothers who starred at the University of Missouri, led the champions. Despite claims by C. E. McBride, sports editor of the *Kansas City Star*, that "Kansas City had established itself as the basketball center of the world," only six thousand fans were in attendance for the title game at the Convention Hall, which could have accommodated fourteen thousand.[19]

Coverage of the tournament included some commentary on strategy and style of play. One article reported that fans booed when two teams decided to protect close leads by stalling. When this strategy did not work, one writer attributed its failure to pressure from the fans. This writer also observed that "nothing can retard a basketball game so quickly as a succession of long shots which fall far from their mark. On the other hand, long shots from the middle of the court that 'ring the bell' will do much to create intense interest in the game."[20]

The Hillyards Polish the Opposition

In 1923 the Hillyard Chemical Company of St. Joseph, Missouri, made its first serious bid for a national AAU title. The Hillyard Chemical Company had dominated town ball in St. Joseph, Missouri, but had never advanced beyond the second round in Kansas City. N. S. "Pop" Hillyard, the founder and president of the company, had built a business that sold disinfectants and stain removers for national and even international markets. Before the First World War Hillyard sponsored church teams and watched his son, Marvin, star for Central High School. Although Marvin died during the flu epidemic that struck the United States during the war, "Pop" Hillyard remained a patron of the game. In the fall of 1922, Hillyard built a fifteen-hundred-seat basketball facility on the second floor of his factory for thirty thousand dollars. This new facility, according to the *St. Joseph Gazette*, would make St. Joseph "a place of real importance in middle-west basketball circles." Besides providing a home for his basketball team, the new floor gave the Hillyard Company the opportunity to experiment with basketball floor finishes, which became another important product for the firm. The combination of a successful business and a promising basketball team made Hillyard one of the Missouri River town's leading citizens.[21]

Employing the model used by industrial teams, the Hillyard Company recruited players by offering them jobs as well as an opportunity to play basketball. The team's biggest new name was the charismatic "Red" DeBernardi. Others stars were Pete Reif, a burly forward who had starred at Southwestern College in Winfield, Kansas, and George Rody, captain of the Kansas Jayhawks in 1921–22.[22] The *St. Joseph News Press* reported that an evening of basketball at the Hillyard Gym attracted St. Joe's high society and leading politicians. It also observed that basketball crowds were no longer "lady-like" but "borrowed the choicest expressions from the baseball and football fields. And the fun is more acute because in an enclosed space like a basketball court you can call the referee a robber and the chances are he will hear you." As if it feared that it had gone too far in emphasizing the rowdy aspects of the game, the *News Press* reassured its readers that "basketball is a stable sport, which has taken its place with other amusements that have come to stay."[23]

Since their team was undefeated in the regular season, Hillyard basketball fans looked forward to the 1923 national AAU tournament with great anticipation. The *St. Joseph News Press* urged city fans to charter a train for the championship night and reminded its readers "that encouragement from friends has given more than one athlete the necessary punch."[24] St Joe's fans were not disappointed as the Hillyards advanced to the championship game against the Kansas City Athletic Club. Prior to that game, the *St. Joseph Gazette* reported that five hundred Hillyard fans planned to take a train to Kansas City and that more was involved than bragging rights, as Hillyard fans wagered anywhere from two thousand to four thousand dollars on their team.[25] Since DeBernardi had jumped to the Hillyards from the KCAC, Kansas City fans were eager to see the Blue Diamonds dump the high-flying Hillyards. To compensate for DeBernardi's loss, the KCAC had recruited George Williams and George Reeves from Lowe-Campbell's 1922 championship team. In the championship game, before eight thousand fans the Blue Diamonds held

DeBernardi to four points and handed the Hillyards their first loss of the season.[26]

In their quest for the 1924 AAU championship, Hillyard added "Long" John Wulf, a six-foot-six all-conference center from the University of Kansas, and George Starbuck, an AAU star from Indianapolis. Despite a star-studded cast, the team attracted small crowds, and by January of 1924 the *Gazette* predicted that the team would "disband, if attendance did not pick up."[27] Disappointment deepened when Butler College of Indianapolis edged the Chemists in the semifinals of the national tournament. The loss so frustrated the Hillyards that the *St. Joseph Gazette* reported that "the players are going to give up the game and enter their respective business careers."[28] Butler then stunned Kansas City partisans, when it nipped the KCAC to win the championship.[29]

Kansas City took its loss before ten thousand fans philosophically and with some evidence of humor. Since a Kansas City team had won the first three titles, the *Kansas City Star* wrote: "We thought it natural that the title rest with us. Basketball as it is played in other parts of the country was all right, but quite some better here, we thought."[30] While Butler had two players on the all-tournament team, its coach, Pat Page, received the most ink. The Helms Basketball Player of the Year in 1910, Page had led the University of Chicago to two mythical national championships in 1908 and 1909 before embarking on a long career in coaching.[31]

To prove that a victory by a collegiate team was no fluke, Washburn College of Topeka, Kansas, surprised the experts by winning the 1925 national tournament. Arthur "Dutch" Lonberg, who starred on the KCAC's championship team in 1921, coached the Washburn five. To win the championship Washburn stopped the Hillyards and denied the Chemists a victory in their second chance in the championship round. The star of the Washburn team was its center, Gerald Spohn, who scored 62 points in five games to make him the tournament's scoring leader.[32] Rumors spread that "Pop" Hillyard, disappointed by another loss, considered dropping his sponsorship. Leading businessmen and the *St. Joseph Gazette*, who ranked him "among the cleanest and best sportsmen and boosters for his home town," persuaded him to persevere.[33]

Before the 1925 tournament, "Pop" Hillyard hired George Levis to coach his team and bring him a much coveted but elusive national championship. As the Helms Player of the Year in 1916, when he led the Western Conference in scoring, Levis played at the University of Wisconsin under Dr. Walter Meanwell, one of the nation's pioneer basketball coaches.[34] Despite the setback in the 1925 championship game, the press and players praised Levis's coaching. For the next three years he would take a leave of absence from the University of Wisconsin to coach the Hillyards during the tournament.[35]

With daily attendance averaging between two and three thousand, Dr. Reilly reported that the tournament lost money. If the tournament was not yet turning a profit, Reilly wrote, it had "created interest in other sections of the country." The San Francisco Olympic Club and the Bay City's Young Men's Institute represented San Francisco, and Southern California sent the Hollywood Athletic Club. The national tournament, Reilly continued, had been "somewhat of a joke" but now with the prospect of a truly national championship, the caliber of AAU play was improving as teams prepared to compete in Kansas City.[36]

In the 1925–26 season the Hillyards had a veteran team that included John Wulf, Bob Mosby, George Starbuck, George Rody and "Red" DeBernardi. George Levis, like most of his peers, believed that: "A well drilled team aims at all times to control possession of the ball." Since Wulf controlled most jump balls, the Hillyards, according to Levis, were able to maintain possession of the ball for thirty of the forty minutes of each game in the 1925–26 season.[37]

Although the Hillyards had already put together a powerhouse team in an effort to win the national championship, they picked up Harold Hewitt just before the tournament, an addition that proved critical to the team's tournament success. Hewitt had led Rosendale High School to the Missouri State Championship in 1924 and played with Platte Commercial College in the 1925 tournament. The Hillyards were very familiar with his skills, because Platte Commercial College practiced at the Hillyard gym.[38]

The 1926 AAU tournament attracted forty teams and set new attendance (27,000) and box office ($18,428) records.[39] The championship game pitted the Hillyards against their in-state rival, the Kansas City Athletic Club. During the regular season the Hillyards edged the Blue Diamonds in their first meeting but, just before the tournament, the KCAC clobbered the Chemists before ten thousand at Convention Hall.[40] The Blue Diamonds were a formidable team led by Tus Ackerman, a former All-American at the University of Kansas, and ten thousand fans poured into Convention Hall to watch these great rivals play. Gabe Kaufman, Convention Hall's manager, reported that this was the largest crowd ever to see a basketball game in Kansas City. The crowd included "high school kids, collegians, men in dark suits, and women in colorful hats." For those not in the Convention Hall, WDSF, a radio station owned by the *Kansas City Star*, carried the play-by-play. A writer with a gift for hyperbole compared Convention Hall to "the battlefields of the Medes and Persians" and "the gladiatorial arena of old Rome." On that March night there was no basketball "better played anywhere in the world than here in Kansas City." In basketball, he concluded, "ten men struggle with a speed and deadly frenzy no Roman populace ever witnessed."[41]

When the final gun marked the end of the game, the Hillyards owned a hard-fought victory. Hewitt with ten points and DeBernardi with eight points led the way for the Chemists. A writer for the *Kansas City Star* thought Hewitt "performed like a satellite of years standing, cool and steady in this court crisis. When he left the game . . . the crowd of one accord paid him tribute."[42] "Pop" Hillyard was so happy that he threw the team's warm-ups into the crowd and yelled, "We'll buy new ones now."[43] Joseph Reilly summed up the game for the disappointed Blue Diamonds in this way: "When any basketball team can go into a contest with a center that towers into empyrean like a mountain (John Wulf) and takes the tip off most of the time; when to these advantages is added a bundle of steel springs named Hewitt, with an uncanny eye for the basket—well, that team is simply unbeatable."[44]

The Hillyards were the talk of St. Joseph's as 380 fans turned out for a banquet at the Hotel Robidoux to honor their team. Judges, ministers, and politicians praised "Pop" Hillyard and the team as the "greatest advertising medium St. Joseph has." City boosters pointed to the team as proof that "There is nothing in the United States that any other city has done that we cannot do if we all cooperate and go after it in the right manner."[45]

Eight months after winning its first championship, N. S. Hillyard denied charges that the Hillyard players were professionals masquerading as amateurs. These claims were originally made in *Collyer's Eye*, a Chicago sports weekly, and republished in the *Kansas City Star*. Hillyard said he welcomed an investigation and declared that "Every member of the Hillyard basketball team is employed by this concern—in the factory, office, or as a salesman, and they receive their pay for this work." Unnamed college coaches reported that Hillyard's players received hefty bonuses for playing basketball. Moreover, Pete Reif, a former Hillyard, agreed and stated that Hillyard players were getting rich. Other reports alleged that John Wulf and Forrest DeBernardi had turned down offers to play professionally, with the implication that their financial package with Hillyard was pretty sweet. In his defense, Hillyard argued that if his players were getting rich, they would not have left for better jobs as George Rody and Bob Mosby did after the 1926 season.[46] While this controversy blew over, charges of professionalism remained a continuing problem in amateur basketball. Too many stories have survived to dismiss the charges that star players received special treatment from their companies. Harold Slater, retired city editor of the *St. Joseph News Press*, recalled that "DeBernardi had a desk down at the Hillyard office . . . but I never saw him sitting at it."[47] Jim Houck, who played in the 1920s, remembered asking DeBernardi why he never played professionally and he replied, "Because I make more money playing amateur."[48]

The controversy between Kansas City and the Hillyards heightened local interest in the 1927 national AAU tournament, as fifty-three teams competed for the championship. To prepare for the tournament, the Hillyards played twenty-three games, fourteen against college competition. Two players from the 1926 championship team,

George Rody and Bob Mosby, were replaced by Jimmy Loveless, who had starred for Emporia State College, and Babe Mitchell, a six-foot-four center who had played for the Southside Turners of Indianapolis in the 1926 tournament.[49]

Obviously eager to recapture the AAU title, the KCAC was essentially a collection of Kansas University stars. Forrest "Phog" Allen, who had led KU to six straight Missouri Valley championships, agreed to coach the Blue Diamonds in this tournament. Allen, well on his way to establishing himself as a basketball legend, took this tournament very seriously. Three weeks before play began, Allen wrote a four-page letter to Tus Ackerman, one of his former stars who was the captain of the Blue Diamonds. After commenting on the KCAC's poor play against the University of Missouri, Allen wrote, "If I were you fellows, I would eat together, sleep together, talk basketball, and shut out every interest of my life until that National Tournament is over." If Allen's letter so inspired the KCAC that it even beat his KU team in the game they were scheduled to play on February 28, Allen added that "I would be willing to stand a defeat so that these Kansas trained boys can win the National title." Allen concluded his letter, "I take it that basketball is now one of your first concerns because you are representing a great Club in a great city in the best section of the United States."[50] Prior to the competition Allen bolstered his squad by adding Gale Gordon and Al Peterson, two stars from his 1927 KU team. After two easy victories, the KCAC was upset by Ke-Nash-A of Kenosha, Wisconsin, a team that played a ball control game.[51]

The Hillyards were more fortunate. After two easy wins, they squeezed out victories against Goodyear Rubber, Phillips University, and Washburn College. In the championship game the Hillyards crushed Ke-Nash-A, as the Wisconsin team's deliberate style of play proved inadequate in a game where they fell behind by fourteen points in the first half.[52] In the second half the Hillyards held the ball for sixteen minutes as the fans booed in the background. When the crowd began to leave Convention Hall, George Levis reported that "Doctor Reilly, the general manager of the tournament, came to me with tears in his eyes and begged us to make a ball game out of the affair."[53]

After capturing two successive national titles, the Hillyards' rivalry with Kansas City intensified. On the eve of the 1928 tournament, C. E. McBride, *Kansas City Star* sports editor, once again leveled charges of professionalism against the Hillyards. Jerry Thrailkill, sports editor of the *St. Joseph Gazette*, replied that McBride's "unusual powers of discrimination in separating the good in sport from the evil" should focus on Kansas City basketball. The *Gazette* sports editor recommended that McBride examine the roster of a new Kansas City team sponsored by the Cook Paint Company of Kansas City, which included former Hillyards players Bob Mosby and "Red" DeBernardi. According to Thrailkill, the owner of Cook Paint Company, Charles Cook, "sang a siren to DeBernardi that caused this venerable star to fairly bolt out of the Hillyard plant." Then, just before the tournament, the Painters added two University of Oklahoma stars, Vic Holt and Roy Lecrone, as well as Hugh McDermott, their coach. "Certainly all of these young men, many of whom are college graduates," Thrailkill wrote, "do not want to become paint salesmen or shipping clerks."[54]

While the Hillyards lost the charismatic DeBernardi, and John Wulf retired, they picked up Jerry Spohn, the Washburn College star, who led his college team to the 1925 AAU championship. In 1928 the Hillyards took a western trip in which they compiled a perfect 13–0 record against teams in Colorado, Wyoming, and California. In addition the Hillyards played in the Missouri Valley League with other AAU teams. On the eve of the tournament, however, a series of illnesses hit key players and weakened the team's chances for the championship.[55] In the semifinals Cook Paint crushed the Hillyards in a grudge match that pitted former teammates against each other.[56] The following evening eight thousand fans watched as the Painters dumped the KCAC for the championship.[57]

The 1929 tournament was the last for the Hillyards. During the 1928–29 season, "Pop" Hillyard did not sponsor a team until weeks before the tournament. In February Hillyard announced that he would back a team composed of players from the Sterling Milk Company of Oklahoma City and the St. Joseph Cardinals. Since St. Joseph had become "the basketball center of the United States," and Hillyard's "trade territory should be represented by a good team in the tournament," Hillyard believed it was important to compete in Kansas City. While this team lost in the second round, it had two men who would make basketball history. The coach of this makeshift team was Everett Shelton, who had guided the Sterling Milks to a third place finish in 1928 and remained as Sterling's coach until it disbanded in February of 1929. Shelton would lead Denver to its first AAU championship in 1937 and then move on to the University of Wyoming, where he would enjoy great success and win an NCAA championship in 1943. One of Shelton's players on the Sterling Milks–Hillyards was Henry Iba, who would eventually win two NCAA championships at Oklahoma A&M and coach three United States Olympic teams. The Hillyards' loss in 1929 marked their last AAU tournament appearance.[58]

HERE COME THE HENRYS

The end of the Hillyard era barely overlapped with the emergence of the Wichita Henrys, a new AAU basketball powerhouse from southern Kansas. Henry Levitt, the team's sponsor, owned a clothing store in downtown Wichita and sponsored his first team in the 1928–29 season. Although Levitt did not have a sports background, he provided the team with generous support. Melvin Miller, one of Levitt's stars, recalled: "When we went on the road, we stayed in the best hotels and ate at the best restaurants." When the team traveled by train, Levitt "chartered a Pullman with no one but us. When we got to our destination, they set the car on a siding and we lived there." While Levitt could not employ all of his players, he helped them find positions with other Wichita businesses.[59]

The genesis of the Henrys can be traced back to 1925 when Wichita High School won the national high school basketball championship sponsored by the University of Chicago. Two members of that team, Barry Dunham and Ross McBurney, along with Harold Davis, played at Wichita University, which finished third in the 1927 AAU tournament (as McBurney made the All-America team) but lost in the third round of the 1928 tournament. To this nucleus the Henrys added Jerry Spohn, former Washburn and Hillyard star, and several others. During the 1928–29 season, the Henrys won the Missouri Valley AAU league and barnstormed as far as Miami, Florida. Prior to the tournament Henry Levitt hired "Dutch" Lonberg, who had just finished his second year at Northwestern University, to guide the Henrys at Kansas City.[60]

In Kansas City, the Henrys won five games and the right to play in the title game against Cook Paint Company, the defending champion. The Painters returned DeBernardi, Gail Gordon, Vic Holt, and Al Peterson and added Harold Hewitt from the Hillyards, Floyd Burk, a classy guard from Southwestern College in Winfield, Kansas, and Frank Harrigan, a deadly shot from the University of Michigan. The six-foot-six-inch Holt consistently controlled the center jump so that the Cook Painters controlled the ball for three quarters of the game and dominated the Henrys.[61] The next three titles, however, would belong to Wichita.

By the end of the 1929 season J. Lyman Bingham, chairman of the AAU Basketball Committee, reported that about five thousand basketball teams competed in AAU-sanctioned events and that the national AAU basketball tournament was "one of the major events on the calendar of amateur sport." While pleased with this activity, Bingham stressed that the AAU "must not lose sight of the necessity of exercising proper control over this sport and maintaining the true spirit of amateurism." The threat to amateurism came from industrial teams that were "springing up everywhere." Bingham worried about businessmen who organized "a team from the basketball stars of the community where, in a great many cases, the object is either to advertise a certain business or commodity or to seek personal gain" rather than "to provide a healthy program of recreation" for their employees. He reported, with some chagrin, that he saw teams "on the basketball floor attired in uniforms advertising everything from pink pills to real estate."[62]

Bingham also criticized independent teams who recruited college stars just prior to the event. He thought this practice gave the independents a competitive edge over the college teams, who could not make these last-minute additions to their rosters. If the tournament director placed all college teams in one bracket and all the independents in another, Bingham believed, this problem would be remedied. By adopting this format, the national tournament would produce a college champion, an independent champion, and, after they played each other, a national champion.[63]

In 1930 the Wichita Henrys won their first of three consecutive national titles. During the regular season the Henrys compiled a 22-4 mark that included eight victories during a ten-game road trip in California. Levitt recruited Harold Hewitt, Floyd Burk, and George Starbuck, three former AAU All-Americans, and John "Tex" Gibbons of Southwestern College in Winthrop, Kansas, to his Wichita nucleus of Ross McBurney, Harold Davis, and Barry Dunham. Prior to the tournament Wichita added two McPherson College stars, Melvin Miller and Ray Nonken, and called upon Gene Johnson, the fiery coach of the University of Wichita, to direct the team. After an overtime win against Ke-Nash-A and a hard fought victory against East Central Teachers of Oklahoma, the Henrys cruised by the Olympic Club of San Francisco in the championship game.[64] In the third-place game, East Central Teachers of Oklahoma belted Bethany College. The game was noteworthy only because the center jump was abandoned in the game's first half. A *Kansas City Star* writer remarked that this "made for much faster play and if it is adopted it will mean a basketball squad must contain twice as many players as at present."[65]

The Depression and the failure of a Kansas City team to reach the semifinals hurt attendance as fewer than seven thousand fans turned out for the championship game. The KCAC did not field a team during the regular season, which made the tournament, according to the *Kansas City Star*, "one of the least interesting in years."[66] Cook Paint Company dropped its sponsorship of basketball and joined the Hillyard Company on the sidelines. Twenty years later "Red" DeBernardi recalled that after two consecutive championships, the owner of the Cook Paint Company figured that the team could not do much better. He told DeBernardi, "Well, let's forget all about it now. It's just too much trouble."[67]

In the summer of 1930, as the United States sank deeper into economic depression, the Wichita Henrys and the Phillips Petroleum

Company engaged in a battle for the services of Melvin Miller, one of Wichita's stars in the 1930 tournament. Incorporated in 1917, Phillips sponsored its first team in the 1920–21 season and made its first Kansas City appearance in 1922, losing in the first round. One of the players on these teams was Kenneth S. "Boots" Adams who would ultimately serve as the company's president (1938–51) and the basketball team's major benefactor and fan. Phillips did not go to Kansas City again until 1929, two years after it entered the retail service-station business. In 1929, as part of an advertising strategy, Phillips hired Louis G. Wilke, a successful college coach at Phillips University in Enid, Oklahoma, to coach the 66ers. While the 66ers compiled a 47-5 record in their first season, they lost in the second round at Kansas City.[68] As the 66ers looked to strengthen their team, they successfully recruited Floyd Burk, John "Tex" Gibbons, and Harold Hewitt from the Henrys. One of the major problems faced by Henry Levitt was that his clothing store was too small to successfully employ a basketball team. While Levitt did not object to losing Burk, Gibbons, and Hewitt, perhaps because they were not from the Wichita area, he drew the line with Miller. When Wilke asked Levitt if he would release Miller, Levitt replied that "Wichita has ceased to be a basketball farm for Phillips."[69]

The bidding over Miller illustrated the elasticity of the amateur code. Wilber Cooper, the Kansas chairman of the AAU, admitted there was no rule that prohibited player raiding, but he considered this practice distasteful and urged Kansans to rally around Levitt. Phillips Petroleum did not take kindly to this attack on its ethics. On August 24, 1930, the oil company bought a full page in the *Wichita Eagle* to explain its conduct. The position taken by Phillips, as articulated by Louis G. Wilke, was that Miller had made the initial contact when he wrote Phillips that he wished "to use my basketball ability as the opening edge to a business career." For Phillips the question was, "shall a boy play basketball after he is out of college just for the interest of some individual or firm which exploits him to its own advantage without regard to his own best interests or should he be allowed to use his playing ability as a means to secure a job that would mean something for his future?"[70] Phillips lost this battle as Miller returned to Wichita, where he played on two more championship Henry teams. After the 1930–31 season, because of the Depression, Phillips did not sponsor a team again until 1936.

In 1931 Henry Levitt selected George Gardner, Washburn College's coach, to direct his team in the tournament. In the semifinals the Henrys soundly defeated the Los Angeles Athletic Club, which featured Chuck Hyatt, a former college All-American at the University of Pittsburgh. The Californians had beaten the Henrys twice during the season by comfortable margins and were favored to do so again. Instead, Johnny Callahan limited Hyatt to eight points and Merle Alexander dominated L.A.'s tall center, Tom Pickell, as the Henrys won comfortably.[71] In the championship game the Henrys faced the KCAC, a team that had captured the Missouri Valley AAU crown and owned two victories over the Wichita five. Playing with great confidence, the Henrys routed the Blue Diamonds before ten thousand fans. Since Merle Alexander, a new player from the University of Indiana, dominated the center jump, the Henrys controlled the ball for about 80 percent of the game, one of the keys to victory. One sportswriter thought the Blue Diamonds played like they were under the spell of the "occult" and "black magic." They played like they were "afraid," moved "indecisively," and "fought for the ball sheepishly." Continuing with this psychological analysis, the writer described the "the Henrys' bench silently exultant, the Henrys' players masterfully dominant." The Henrys' uniforms were "red, white, and blue, were starred and striped and had 'champions' writ large across them." The worst part of the KCAC's defeat was "the dismal prospect of seeing the Wichita team next winter in uniforms of disagreeable flamboyance."[72]

Not surprisingly, Wichita now claimed that it was the basketball capital of the nation. In the 1931–32 season the team's nucleus remained fixed with Dunham, McBurney, Miller, and Callahan. In place of Merle Alexander, Wichita recruited center Tom Pickell, who had played previously with the Los Angeles Athletic Club and Phillips 66. Since Phillips had decided against sponsoring a basketball team, Floyd Burk and John "Tex" Gibbons returned to Wichita, where they had played on the 1930 national championship team. Despite the economic hardship in the United States, thirty-five teams congregated in Kansas City for the national tournament. West Texas Teachers College from Canyon, Texas, brought Joe Fortenberry, a six-foot-eight center, playing in his first of many AAU tournaments. The Texans eliminated the KCAC in the first round of the tournament, the earliest exit in Blue Diamond history.[73] Frank Lubin, who would join Fortenberry on the first U.S. Olympic basketball team in 1936, also played in his first AAU national. After leading the Pasadena Majors to a first-round win, the six-foot-six Lubin was described by a writer "as one of the great centers of the tournament. He has fine height, is a strong scorer, and aggressive on defense."[74] Neither Fortenberry nor Lubin, however, could lead their teams to the quarterfinal round in this tournament.

In the championship game, Wichita faced Maryville State Teachers of Maryville, Missouri, one of the most interesting college teams of this era. Directing the Bearcats was Henry "Hank" Iba, affectionately call the "Iron Duke" by his players. By 1932 Iba had taken his first steps toward building a legendary coaching career. In 1930 Iba's first Bearcat team registered a perfect 31-0 record. Going into the championship game against the Henrys, the Bearcats were 24-0, which included a win over Wichita in Maryville. Iba's coaching style featured tough man-to-man defense and a ball control offense that produced low scoring games but also great success. The star of the Bearcat team was Jack McCracken, who had played for Iba at Classon High School in Oklahoma City, where they won a state championship and a second-place finish in the University of Chicago's national high school tournament.[75] Although only six feet two inches tall, McCracken, nicknamed "Jumping Jack," played center and was strong enough to defend against taller centers. Writers and spectators were particularly impressed with his effortless and expressionless play, which caused one writer to describe him as "wonderfully rhythmic" and "something of a mystic figure."[76] Iba's Bearcat team also included such future AAU stars as Robert "Duck" Dowell, Herman Fisher, and Tom Merrick.

Before the championship game, the Bearcats were the favorites of the Kansas City crowd. A writer for the *Kansas City Times* reported that a Missourian and Kansan had decided years ago that it "would be everlasting disgrace to permit the other to defeat him in any contest requiring strength and skill."[77] The *Wichita Eagle* reported that Kansas City fans "boo and hiss every time they [the Henrys] have the ball. They razz every minor misplay and spur the opposing players on to greater fight."[78] In the title contest Iba's Bearcats controlled the tempo of the game and limited Wichita to a mere four points in the first half as the Bearcats scored nine. Wichita narrowed the gap in the second half and won the game 15–14 on a shot with twenty seconds left in the game by Mclvin Miller. Wichita controlled the center jump after this basket, and the game ended without the Bearcats having another ball possession. Pete Lightner, sports editor of the *Wichita Eagle*, who covered the Henrys during their championship years, wrote that the final game "was no stalling battle at all. It was just a fine exhibition of defensive work and probably the greatest game of its kind ever played in the tourney here."[79] No team had ever won the national tournament three times before Wichita notched its third consecutive triumph. Several days after the championship game the Henrys and Maryville played for the third time in three weeks, before an overflow crowd of 4,500 fans at the Wichita Forum. This time the Henrys won 21–10, the largest margin of victory in the series and the first game in which either team scored more than 16 points.[80]

In 1933 the national tournament coincided with President Franklin D. Roosevelt's decision to impose a bank holiday on the financial community. C. E. McBride, sports editor of the *Kansas City Star*, reported that "the entire city looked on the tournament as a sort of civic proposition."[81] Hotels offered special rates and the auditorium management lowered its rent. Tournament officials also reduced tournament ticket prices to attract fans. Forty teams from fifteen states showed up to battle for the national championship, adding to the satisfaction of producing a successful tournament during difficult economic circumstances.

The Henrys' three-year reign as national champions came to an end in 1933. Wichita failed to add a significant player and relied on Miller, Dunham, Pickell, McBurney, and Callahan to bring the city a fourth championship. By the tournament the Henrys were a tired team, having played over fifty games. In the semifinals the Tulsa Diamond DX Oilers, coached by William Miller, trounced the Henrys.[82] The floor leader of the Oilers was Chuck Hyatt, who in his second year with Tulsa, was described as "the nearest approach to a perfect player."[83] Carl Larson, a six-foot-five center from Bethany College in Kansas, and Bart Carlton, a rugged guard from East Central State of Oklahoma, were other stars on Tulsa's team.

In the championship game Tulsa escaped with a two-point victory over Chicago's Rosenberg-Arvey. Sponsored by two Chicago politicians, the Rosenberg-Arveys did not even own team uniforms a month before the tournament.[84] They were just a bunch of kids from Chicago who wanted to test their skills in Kansas City. One of the Rosenbergs was six-foot-three Joe Reiff, an All-American forward at Northwestern who had just led the Western Conference (later Big Ten) in scoring. One of Reiff's teammates, Robert Gruenig, was an all-state player at Crane Tech in Chicago who played some freshman ball at Northwestern. Gruenig, a six-foot-eight center who would become a ten-time AAU All-American, immediately caught the eye of basketball writers. In the championship game Pete Lightner of the *Wichita Eagle* observed that Reiff and Gruenig took every one of the Rosenbergs' shots. In addition Gruenig won the tip more than half the time, which prompted Lightner to write, "some team is going to be lucky to get him."[85]

Despite the misfortune of having scheduled the tournament during the same week that President Franklin Roosevelt chose to declare a bank holiday, the tournament was a success. Although Dr. Joseph Reilly continued to serve as the tournament director, the Kansas City Athletic Club neither sponsored the tournament, a task performed by Rockhurst College, nor entered a team in the tourney. The Blue Diamonds, however, had made a significant contribution to AAU basketball.

After the 1933 tournament Henry Levitt dropped his sponsorship of the Wichita Henrys. Evidence of dissatisfaction with the team appeared in the *Wichita Eagle* at the end of the 1933 season. One of the problems, according to Pete Lightner, was that basketball attendance "has slumped here badly the past two years."[86] If Wichita had a team, Lightner wrote, "there should be about half the games played this year; regular practice and a regular coach." While Lightner thought Wichita's fans deserved "high grade basketball," he concluded, "it can't be played on a strictly commercial basis."[87] As the owner of a clothing store, Henry Levitt did not have the resources to sponsor a championship team indefinitely. The evidence suggests that in 1932–33 the Henrys played a much expanded schedule hoping that ticket revenues would meet expenses, a formula that obviously did not work.

In 1934 Kansas City hosted the national AAU tournament for the last time. Fifty-four teams participated, and the tournament earned $16,399.16 from ticket revenues.[88] The University of Wyoming Cowboys were the surprise of the tournament. Prior to the opening day of play the *Kansas City Star* observed that: "The National AAU basketball tournament has become almost exclusively an affair to be settled among independent teams and of these those representing the Missouri Valley still predominate."[89] In the third round of play the Cowboys became the sentimental favorite of the Kansas City fans when they overcame a 31–11 halftime deficit to edge Utah's Ogden Boosters 39–35.[90] The Boosters were a team made up of stars from the Wichita Henrys and West Texas State, including Melvin Miller and Joe Fortenberry. In the next two games Wyoming knocked off two Missouri Valley AAU independents, the Wichita Gridley Chieftains and the Hutchinson, Kansas, Reno Creamery.[91] Governor Leslie A. Miller of Wyoming flew to Kansas City for the championship game, which impressed Kansas City fans, but his team was no match for the Tulsa DX Oilers, led by Chuck Hyatt, Bart Carlton, and Tom Pickell.[92]

Between 1921 and 1934 the Kansas City tournament had become a mecca for basketball players, coaches, and fans. The most significant development during this period was the emergence of businesses as sponsors of championship caliber basketball teams. Before 1921 the tournament champion was usually an athletic club. After 1921 businesses of various sizes backed the most successful teams by offering a job to skilled players. With this arrangement businessmen advertised their product and earned some civic recognition, while the players extended their careers and gained some business experience. As evidenced by the Hillyards, Cook Paint Company, and the Wichita Henrys, the investment in basketball by business was for a relatively short term. When these teams folded, the best players moved on so long as their skills were in demand. While the players did not get rich, they were not amateurs, if an amateur is defined as an athlete who does not profit from his athletic ability. By 1934 the AAU tournament was a well-established event, which regularly attracted teams that spanned a geographic area from California to Indiana. Because the best teams took annual barnstorming tours, players like "Red" DeBernardi, Marvin Miller, Barry Dunham, Chuck Hyatt, and Frank Lubin were widely known and popular gate attractions.

The one missing ingredient was the African American athlete. There is no evidence of African American players competing during the Kansas City period. Although several African Americans played in Denver in the 1930s and 1940s, it was not until the late 1950s that black players played a more prominent role in the AAU tournament.

Reflecting on the tournament's history one columnist wrote, "Kansas City doesn't feel that it is the only place the National AAU Basketball tournament may be held successfully, although the sentiment is well rooted here that Kansas City has done right well by it . . . and no doubt will be able to do so again in the event the tournament returns there at some future date."[93] Kansas City lost the tournament, in part, because of the Depression. After the tournament lost money in 1933, the AAU awarded the tournament to Kansas City in 1934 to give Dr. Reilly one chance to recover his losses. The AAU expected to earn a profit from the tournament and Denver promised it a bigger payday. One measure of Kansas City's success was that, after the AAU awarded the tournament to Denver, local sportswriters immediately declared "Denver one of the leading basketball centers in the country." They saw the tourney as a good business investment that would bring to the city "advertising which could not be bought for any amount of cash."[94]

TWO

The AAU Tournament in Denver

Before Denver could host an AAU tournament, it had to have its own quality basketball team. The first steps in that direction were taken by William Haraway, vice president and Denver divisional manager of the Piggly Wiggly Safeway stores. Jack Carberry, the influential sports columnist of the *Denver Post*, wrote, "Bill Haraway formed the Denver Pigs largely to be able to hold his spot on the throne where his kids have placed him."[1] While Carberry's claim had the ring of an insider's joke, there was a certain truth to it. One of Haraway's boys, Frank, lost the movement of his legs when he was stricken by tuberculosis of the hips at the age of six. As a boy, Frank became an avid sports fan and firmly believed that his father developed the team because of Frank's interest in sports.[2] Haraway's Pigs made their first trip to Kansas City in 1932 but fell to Brown Paper Mill of Monroe, Louisiana, in the first round.[3]

For the 1932–33 season Haraway recruited three stars from Maryville State Teachers College, runner-up in the 1932 AAU tournament. Joining the Pigs were Robert "Duck" Dowell, Tom Merrick, and, most important, "Jumping" Jack McCracken, who gave up his senior year of college for a steady job in Denver.[4] Haraway named Glenn Jacobs, a former star at Colorado Teachers College in Greeley, Colorado, to coach his rebuilt team. Jacobs coached Greeley Teachers High School to the Colorado State title in 1926 and then coached basketball, football, and track at New Mexico College in Las Vegas, New Mexico. Denver sportswriters had high expectations for their new players and coach, who, they predicted, would produce "one of the toughest and trickiest quintets in the nation." They promised that Denver's fans would see "big-time basketball, just as champions play it."[5]

The aggressive development of a basketball team immediately raised questions of professionalism. The press assured its readers that "All members of the team and the coach are employed in the Piggly Wiggly organization either in the store or traffic division." Jack McCracken worked in the warehouse, "where he is . . . mastering the problems of merchandising, as he expects to make this his life's work." Displaying some diplomatic skills McCracken declared that basketball was only "incidental to the larger problems, which I am mastering." William Haraway praised the young men for "donating their time to the . . . development of the outstanding basketball team for the Rocky Mountain region, and we hope of the entire country." He insisted that basketball was not "a part of their duties" and that they were "playing for the love of the game."[6]

Denver's plan to win national basketball recognition gained credibility in January of 1933 when the Pigs beat the powerful Wichita Henrys. Five thousand fans poured into City Auditorium to watch the contest, which, according to Chet Nelson, was "the largest crowed to watch a basketball game in years." After Denver's victory the excited Nelson wrote, "Don't be surprised if Denver has a national champion this year."[7] While the Pigs were good, succeeding weeks demonstrated that they were not invincible as they suffered losses to the Henrys (in a rematch), the Southern Kansas Stage Lines, and Tulsa's Diamond DX Oilers. When they lost at Phillips University, a *Rocky Mountain News* headline joked, "Our Pigs Are Just Ham Now."[8] The season ended in Kansas City when in the third round of the national AAU tournament Denver fell to Rosenberg-Arvey of Chicago.[9]

In the 1933–34 season the Piggly Wigglys' biggest addition was Ernie "One Grand" Schmidt from Pittsburg Teachers in Kansas. A six-foot-four center who had scored a thousand points as a collegian, thus earning his nickname, Schmidt played the pivot, which allowed McCracken to move to the backcourt.[10] While the Pigs had strengthened themselves, their claim to basketball dominance was challenged by the Denver Athletic Club (DAC), which decided to sponsor a team with national championship aspirations. The team included stars from the Rocky Mountain Athletic Conference such as Elwood Romney of Brigham Young University and Jerry Campbell of the University of Utah.[11] While the Pigs were considered the class of Denver basketball, their late season tailspin and 1933 tournament flop left fans disappointed. Howard "Ham" Beresford, *Rocky Mountain News* sports columnist, suggested that a breakdown in training habits accounted for the team's misfortunes in 1933. Beresford assured his readers that Haraway had warned his players that "late night visits to 'grog shops'" would have a "deflationary effect on their paychecks." If the "eight little Pigs" avoided the "Big Bad Wolves which run wild after sundown," Beresford thought Denver's basketball fortunes were bright.[12]

After posting a solid 27-9 record, the Pigs played a two-game series in March with the Denver Athletic Club, which had won 20 of 29 games.[13] Both Denver newspapers played up the rivalry and suggested a feud existed between the players. In preparation for this series and the AAU tournament, the Pigs hired Coach Henry Iba, the University of Colorado basketball coach and former Maryville State College mentor, as an advisory coach to Glenn Jacobs.[14]

In the first game Schmidt and McCracken led the Pigs to a victory that included a fight between Robert "Duck" Dowell and Jerry Campbell. Leonard Cahn wrote that after the first fifteen minutes, "General McCracken took charge and the pyrotechnics started. His passing was perfect, his left-hand pivot shot a revelation and his generalship without fault."[15] On the next night the Pigs swept the series in a game that the *Denver Post*'s Robert Gamzey described as "one of the most vicious court battles of the winter."[16] While these hard won victories raised hopes for a national championship in Kansas City, the goal eluded the Pigs once again when they lost a tough quarterfinal game to the Olympic Club of San Francisco, 31–30, as Frank Lubin led the victors with 13.[17]

After the tournament *Denver Post* sports editor C. L. "Poss" Parsons reported that Denver had an excellent chance of hosting the

1935 tournament. As far back as 1924 Denver had made a bid to host the tournament. In November 1933 Denver had mounted a strong effort to hold the tournament in 1934, but Dr. Joseph Reilly, the director of the tournament during its fourteen years in Kansas City, reported that the tournament had lost money in 1933 and that Kansas City needed another tournament to recover its losses.[18] Parsons explained that the Kansas City hosts had to pay $3,500 to rent Convention Hall for the week. In 1934 the net profit for the AAU was $3,200. If the Denver AAU committee used City Auditorium on a cost basis, a benefit already extended to the officials of the high school tournament, Denver would begin at $3,000 ahead of its Kansas City rivals.[19] Parsons generally praised Kansas City's management of the tournament, but favored rotating this event among various cities, a view he quickly abandoned after the AAU moved the tournament to Denver. The most annoying feature of the Kansas City tournament to Parsons was that fans were allowed to smoke in their seats. "By the time the finals were played Saturday night," he wrote, "the smoke was so thick it could be cut with a knife. It is tough enough playing in a championship game, or any other game for that matter, without having to breathe such foul air." In Denver, smokers had to satisfy their habit in the lobby or outdoors.[20]

Previously two arguments had been used against the Denver promoters of the tournament. One was that Denver's altitude proved a tremendous disadvantage for visiting teams. The other was that Denver lacked an adequate facility. Although Denver overcame both objections, the facility issue was a touchy one. Denver did not have a first-rate basketball arena, and its biggest games and high school tournament were played at City Auditorium, which seated about 5,500 fans. The games were played on the auditorium stage, which inspired Ham Beresford to write that "the crowds expect some sort of coloratura soprano, ballet, historic pageant or pipe organ solo." Many fans were so far away from the stage that they could not "be sure whether it is Ruth St. Dennis or Jack McCracken out there." While City Auditorium lacked elevated seating for basketball, Beresford amusingly concluded that the Auditorium's "grandiose Burning of Rome canvas should inspire big, strong men to mighty feats."[21]

In December of 1934 J. H. K. Martin, president of the local AAU district, and Willard "Bill" Greim, an AAU official and director of health education for the Denver Public Schools, traveled to the AAU convention in Miami, Florida, and secured the national AAU tournament for Denver. Chet Nelson declared that this made Denver "one of the leading basketball centers in the country. I can see no reason why the national tournament wouldn't be an immense success if staged here."[22] John M'Manmon, another *Rocky Mountain News* sportswriter, echoed Nelson's views and saw the award as "a tribute to their city's—and this section's—standing in the sports world." So excited was M'Manmon about the news that he elevated Denver from one of America's basketball centers to the "leading basketball center of America." For him the tournament's real payoff was the people it would draw to Denver and the advertising it would generate for the city because of telegraphic descriptions of the games. "It is advertising which could not be bought for any amount of cash." He congratulated Greim and Martin "for their work and for their civic pride."[23]

Despite all the enthusiasm for the tournament and the desire to make basketball a crowd-pleasing spectacle similar to football, Denver sportswriters expressed reservations about basketball as a popular spectator sport. In February of 1934, after Denver beat the Southern Kansas Stage Lines 15-10, Ham Beresford dissected basketball's flaws. In describing this game Beresford wrote: "It was a smokeless, almost shootless tussle, in which both sides were so cautious with the ball that they nearly put the goodly crowd of spectators at the City Auditorium to sleep."[24] Two days after the game Beresford expanded upon basketball's shortcomings, particularly as played by AAU teams, in a clever column entitled "So You Don't Like Good Basketball?" While Beresford appreciated ball handling, he thought the Pigs–Stage Line game was "like watching a champion boxer clinch and stall his way through 10 rounds of an exhibition." Beresford had no objection to what writers were already calling the "Iba style" of basketball, but he criticized teams like the Stage Lines who refused to shoot the ball. When Beresford watched the University of Colorado, coached by Iba, play Denver University the night after the Pigs–Stage Lines game, he declared there was more excitement in ten minutes than forty minutes of the AAU games. The difference was that the college players tried to score. While purists might object that Beresford did not appreciate "the fine arts of caging," he thought that if the AAU style did not change, "fans will turn to college games or stay home and play cribbage." It was foolish, he thought, to argue that basketball was "going through some new vision and dream into a higher and more intellectual plane."[25] In December of 1934, as the new season was unfolding, Chet Nelson joined Beresford in condemning Piggly Wiggly's emphasis on the more scientific phases of the game. Fans craved "scoring and a quantity of fast action" and grew tired of watching players "flinging the ball around out in the center of the floor."[26]

Whatever the limitations of the game, which was about to become faster and more exciting, or the venue, the prospect of a national tournament offered a welcome and inexpensive diversion in Depression Denver, where a fourth of the working population was umemployed.[27] Therefore the fans followed closely Denver's preparation for its first national tournament. Piggly Wiggly's major acquisition for the 1934–35 season was Robert Gruenig, a six-foot-eight center from Chicago's Crane Tech High School, where he was the public league scoring champ for three years. After two disappointing tournaments, William Haraway recognized that his team could not win a national championship without a big center. Haraway spotted Gruenig, who left Northwestern University after his freshman year, at Kansas City, when the former Crane Tech star played with Rosenberg-Arvey in 1933 and Lifshultz Fast Freight Company in 1934.[28] According to Frank Haraway, when his father recruited Gruenig, the latter's only condition was that his high school buddy and AAU teammate, Werner Frank, accompany him to Denver with a chance to make the team.[29] Gruenig, known to all as "Ace," arrived in Denver amidst great fanfare. John M'Manmon placed him alongside Jack McCracken "as the biggest box office attraction of the year" and reported that Gruenig wanted his Denver fans to know that he was now a citizen of Colorado and intended "to stay as long as possible."[30] When Gruenig married Helen Berce of Wheat Ridge in January of 1935, it was front-page news and suggested that Ace was in Colorado to stay.[31] Chet Nelson shared this high opinion of Gruenig and thought Ace was the key ingredient in Denver's bid for a national championship.[32]

Although impossible to predict at the time, the relationship between Jack McCracken and Ace Gruenig became one of the most celebrated in Denver sports history. After watching him for two years John M'Manmon described McCracken as "the most versatile player that ever stepped on a local floor . . . the idol of every Colorado youth, from the rough-and-ready newsie on the street to the pampered lads of private prep schools."[33] McCracken's teammates and opponents agreed that he controlled the tempo of the game and remained under control in all situations. This discipline was most likely the result of his emotional makeup and the influence of Henry Iba, his coach for six years. As a player and a coach, the evidence suggests that McCracken's approach to basketball rested on sound fundamentals and a clear understanding of each player's role. When Dick Wells joined the team in 1937, McCracken told him, "Dick, it's your job to get the rebounds, pass the ball to me, and I will get it to 'Ace.' "[34] Occasionally, McCracken would mix in a two-handed flip shot, which he shot from his waist with great accuracy and from long distance. For his part, Gruenig immediately acknowledged McCracken's skills, which he had witnessed in Kansas City. He told Denver's writers that "There and then I was sold on McCracken" and added, "I'd like to be able to play the game like that guy."[35] Because their roles complemented each other, there was little friction between the two players, who became close friends. Eventually the names McCracken and Gruenig became inseparable to basketball fans from the Missouri Valley to the Pacific Coast and especially in Denver.

In 1934–35, the Pigs prepared for the national tournament by playing about forty games against college and company teams and won all but one of the contests.[36] The highlight of the pre-tournament season, for the Pigs, were three games with their city rival, the Denver Athletic Club. The first of the confrontations with the Denver Athletic Club produced a 33–31 victory for the Pigs with

McCracken's 13 points topping all scorers.[37] With 3,500 rabid fans shaking City Auditorium, the players, Chet Nelson wrote, put on a performance "that contained everything from the finest in expert basketballing to scenes that touched upon a battering battle royal." After the game Chet Nelson reported that the town was buzzing over the officiating and rough play. This led Nelson to recommend that the two teams hire Ernie Quigley, one of the nation's best-known officials, to blow the whistle for the next game. With Quigley the game would be basketball, not a "combination wrestling match, prize fight and rodeo."[38]

Three days before the rematch on February 6, the Denver papers began to promote the game and focused on themes like "bad blood" and "revenge." Quigley was not hired to officiate the game, so instead the two teams secured two Missouri Valley officials, John Wulf and Ed Halpin.[39] On the morning of February 7, the *Rocky Mountain News*, on its front page, reported that the largest crowd in Denver basketball history, 5,500, saw the Pigs take another two-point victory, 38–36. The fire department closed all doors thirty minutes before the game, which left a thousand disappointed fans on the streets. Ernie "One Grand" Schmidt scored the winning basket with seconds left and Ace Gruenig led all scorers with fourteen points. The players avoided dirty play in a game that offered, in Chet Nelson's view, "as great a hand-to-hand combat as the cage court offered in the modern era of the sport."[40] The two teams played their third game on February 27. Anticipating another great battle, the Greater Denver Basketball Tournament called a one-day moratorium and John M'Manmon recommended that Denver fans get to the game early.[41] Before 5,200 fans, the Pigs laced the DAC 48–24 and securely established themselves as Denver's top team.[42]

Denver now turned all its attention to the tournament, and sportswriters wrote as if Piggly Wiggly mania had consumed the city. In 1935 and thereafter the tournament acquired a certain rhythm. First there were daily reports from Bill Greim on the number and identity of tournament entries. Usually the number of entries ranged from forty-five to fifty-five teams. The entry fee for the first tournament was ten dollars. Sportswriters looked for the unusual and interesting. One of those teams in 1935 was Southern Oregon State Normal, coached by Howard Hobson, whose University of Oregon team would win the first NCAA title in 1939. Black players were never numerous in the Denver tournament until the 1960s, and Southern Oregon's Charles Patterson was the first African American to play in the Denver tournament.[43] Nineteen other college teams were in the first tournament, including Denver University, Colorado College, and Greeley Teachers. Some of the teams, like the St. Louis Pabs and Jones Store from Kansas City, had to fight through the great dust storms of 1935 to reach Denver. The Pabs had to leave their cars and hitchhike on a freight train.[44] When the teams arrived, they usually stayed at the Shirley-Savoy, the Cosmopolitan, or the Brown Palace, which was the tourney headquarters in 1935.

In 1951 the *Denver Post*'s Harry Farrar described the AAU tourney "as a combination of state fair, southern social, and fish fry."[45] All these elements were already present in the 1935 tournament. "Frankenstein" would be at the tournament blared the *Denver Post*, as it reported that Jack Pierce, manager of the team sponsored by Universal Pictures and its head makeup man, planned to put Frank Lubin in costume on Monday night.[46] Along with Frankenstein, Farrar observed that Denver fans would see "drawling boys from Arkansas and the fast-talking lads from Chicago and points east . . . the groggy all-day patrons red-eyed from overexposure to afternoon versions of basketball."[47] During the Depression, it was tough for kids to pay for a ticket, so they found ways to sneak into the auditorium. Sixty years after the tournament came to Denver, Jack Gray, who later played for Denver's American Legion and Nuggets, remembered that he and his buddies would go down the Auditorium coal chute, or catch a team coming in to play and masquerade as their managers by grabbing their towels and water bottles.[48] In its heyday the tournament always began on Sunday afternoon, and the schedule called for games all day on Monday and Tuesday. Wednesday's games began in the afternoon and, beginning with the quarterfinals on Thursday, all remaining games were in the evening. On Monday night, play was temporarily interrupted as city and AAU officials greeted all the teams, who marched by the reviewing stand in their uniforms, and then honored some notable athletic hero of the present or the past.

On the eve of the 1935 tournament, the *Denver Post* urged the fans to do "their part in supporting this world series of basketball." If they did, Poss Parsons—the tournament manager—predicted, "Denver can be host to the nation's basketball teams for a period of years." Parsons reminded his readers that "You asked for the best and we delivered it to you so get behind the tourney and BOOST."[49] A *Rocky Mountain News* editorial argued that "Denver's invigorating climate makes for top speed performance" (conveniently omitting the effects of high altitude) and thought that "if the basketball championship is to be determined here, why not other championships as well."[50]

A key to the tournament's success was the play of the Denver Pigs, who had compiled a 34-1 record during the season that included victories over the Tulsa Oilers and Universal Pictures. Chet Nelson warned that "we're going to have a tournament with the best teams in the country performing. Favorites have been beaten before in countrywide conclaves."[51] Unfortunately disaster struck in the quarterfinals for Denver when the Pigs squandered a lead against the Southern Kansas Stage Lines and lost 30–28. Leonard Cahn wrote that the Kansas City team had left "the largest crowd to witness a basketball game in Denver . . . stunned and awe-stricken." Frank "Buck" Weaver, the coach of the Stage Liners and a former AAU All-American with the Kansas City Athletic Club, used a press in the second half that completely upset Denver's attack. Cahn observed that "[i]n the final analysis the Pigs lacked a versatile attack. They could only play deliberate ball and when the Liners started pressing on defense and mixing their slow game with a fast break the locals had nothing to counter." Since this was the Pigs' only loss on its home court, Cahn also suggested that "[a] jinx seems to hover over them. In three tournaments they never have been able to get beyond the quarter-final round."[52] Since the DAC lost to the Tulsa Oilers, Denver was not represented in the semifinals. The other semifinalists were the McPherson, Kansas, Globe Refiners and Universal Studios."[53]

The most interesting of the semifinal contests saw the McPherson Globe Refiners edge Universal Studios. McPherson's Gene Johnson, one of the most innovative coaches of the era, favored such a fast-breaking offense that the Oilers were called the "fire department team." Universal had Chuck Hyatt, Frank Lubin, Carl Knowles, and Art Mollner, all of whom had long and illustrious AAU careers. Down 36–28 with eight minutes left in the game, the Refiners scored the last twelve points of the game. In the other semifinal game Herman Fisher and Omar "Bud" Browning led the Southern Kansas Stage Lines over the Tulsa Oilers. In the final the Stage Liners swamped McPherson as Browning and Ray Piper scored half of Kansas City's points.[54]

Despite the gloom that followed the Pigs' defeat, the tournament's net receipts of $6,500 had never been approached by Kansas City in fourteen years.[55] Moreover there was a sense of satisfaction that Denver had successfully conducted one of "the nation's major sporting events."[56] While the AAU selected the location of the tournament at its yearly convention in December, Poss Parsons thought Denver's fans deserved a "return engagement."[57] Although deeply disappointed by his team's defeat, Bill Haraway dispelled any rumors that he was throwing in the towel and declared that his coach, Glenn Jacobs, would return despite some criticism from local fans.[58]

As the 1935–36 season opened, the Denver press announced that the Pigs had been transformed in more ways than one. T. W. Henritze, general manager of Safeway, announced that the team would be known as Denver Safeway Stores, although sportswriters still referred to the team as the Pigs.[59] More important, Chet Nelson announced that the Grocers had adopted the "fire department" style of play. He gave personal testimony that upon a visit to the YMCA he saw "McCracken, Dowell, Merrick, Schmidt and all the rest—racing up and down the floor at breakneck speed—just fast-breaking all over the place." Nelson approved of this change and thought it virtually mandated by passage of the three-second rule, which limited an offensive player to three seconds in the free-throw area or key. Rules makers also eliminated the center jump after made free throws although it was still retained after made baskets.[60] Also, the Grocers entered the Missouri Valley League for the first time in Denver history. Two other important changes were the Rocky Mountain

Athletic Conference's ban on playing AAU basketball teams and the Denver Athletic Club's decision to drop its team.[61] Finally, Safeway added Jack Ozburn, a high-scoring forward who played with the Hunt Oilers of Tullos, Louisiana, in the 1935 tournament and Johnny Edwards, a guard with McPherson in 1935.[62]

Safeway struggled in its first year in the Missouri Valley League. When the McPherson Oilers drubbed the Grocers by twenty points, the licking prompted Chet Nelson to confirm rumors of dissension on the team. Nelson thought: "The Grocers have the best personnel in the league . . . but personnel doesn't win ball games if all hands are not in the right frame of mind."[63] The *Rocky Mountain News* sports editor also observed that the absence of a city rivalry and competition with college teams had dampened interest in basketball. He hoped that a team sponsored by Kansas City Life Insurance of Denver and composed of players from the DAC might supply some local competition for the Grocers.[64]

In late January Denver suffered back-to-back home losses to the Globe Refiners, which dumped more cold water on Denver's season. In his defense of the Safeways, Chet Nelson argued that "the Grocery Boys grew up on basketball the 'slow way' . . . and this surging, speed thing that they call the fast-break is one that's hard to put into their heads with effective results forthcoming immediately." To those who urged the Safeways to return to their set plays and deliberate style, Nelson responded by arguing that new rules made the old game "passé." More important, the deliberate style of play "isn't the people's choice." Nelson argued that "the fast game provides the excitement and sensationalism. And apparently the faster you are the more popular you're going to be." Since Denver had never won the national AAU tournament by employing "scientific basketball," Nelson counseled his readers to exercise patience until the Safeways figured out the "fire department" style.[65]

When the Kansas City Philcos—led by Paul Burks, "Long" Tom Pickell, and Bill "Skinny" Johnson—gave the Safeways another sound beating on the Auditorium floor, the great experiment was over. In this loss Denver was taken to task for "fumbling the ball, and showing absolutely no signs of a functioning offensive attack."[66]

Three nights later the Safeways returned to the deliberate style of play and beat the Hutchinson Reno Transits in back-to-back games.[67]

The Denver Safeways finished the Missouri Valley in third place with a 9-7 record.[68] The national AAU tournament remained as the last opportunity for Denver to salvage its season. Because basketball was an Olympic event in 1936, the first time in Olympic history, the tournament took on greater importance since the top two teams qualified for the Olympic tournament scheduled for New York's Madison Square Garden in April and the chance to play in the Berlin Olympics. In an effort to break 1935's attendance mark the AAU planned to open the tournament with a spectacular program that Poss Parsons promised would be "the most colorful athletic event ever offered to Rocky Mountain sports lovers." In following the Olympic model Parsons explained that the AAU recognized that such pageantry "appeals to the people more than the actual competition." The centerpiece of Denver's program was Dr. James Naismith, the inventor of basketball. He would review all the players, who would march by him as a tribute to the game's inventor. Naismith would then proclaim the opening of the games and make a speech on basketball's origins. The ninety-minute program included remarks by Mayor Ben Stapleton and Governor Ed Johnson. In a strange promotional twist, the night of the official opening was designated "society night" so that "Denver's elite could honor the only living inventor of a major sport."[69] Four thousand fans poured out to see the seventy-four-year-old Naismith, who was visibly moved by the event.[70]

The pressure on the Safeways to overcome their tournament woes was enormous. Poss Parsons announced that during the tournament the team would stay in a mountain cabin and would "be permitted to see their wives and sweethearts only at the auditorium door." Parsons speculated that "the respite from the backslapping of their friends and the hysteria around town will do much to keep them from choking as they did last year."[71]

The tournament experts picked the McPherson Globe Refiners, the 1935 runners-up, to win the national crown. Before organizing the Globe Refiners in 1934, Gene Johnson coached successfully at Wichita University between 1930 and 1933 and also guided the Wichita Henrys to a national AAU title in 1929. Johnson favored a fast-breaking offense and some credited him with introducing a full-court press.[72] Just before the Denver tournament, the Globe Refiners traveled to New York City to play the Metropolitan College All-Stars coached by Clair Bee. Billed as the tallest and best basketball team in the world, the Globe Refiners attracted the attention of the New York press. Sportswriters were particularly impressed by McPherson's lay-up drill in which the players, according to Arthur J. Daley, "pitched the ball downward into the hoop, much like a cafeteria customer dunking a roll in coffee." When asked to compare his team to the best college clubs, the cocky Johnson replied, "We could spot either Notre Dame or Purdue 10 or 12 points."[73] After the Oilers beat the Metropolitan College All-Stars 45–43, Arthur J. Daley called the contest "the most brilliantly played and spectacular game that Madison Square Garden ever has seen." Daley thought Francis Johnson, the coach's brother, "the best amateur forward ever seen in New York."[74]

On quarterfinal night basketball fans jammed City Auditorium as several thousand disappointed latecomers hovered around the Auditorium outside. When the evening ended, the disappointment of those without tickets did not match those Denver fans in the Auditorium as Universal Pictures dropped the Safeways, 31–30, on a Carl Knowles free throw without any time left on the clock following a foul by Duck Dowell. Leonard Cahn called the infraction committed by Duck Dowell the most costly foul in the history of the national AAU basketball tourney, "because it shattered the city's dream of a championship and representation in the Olympic games. For the fourth straight year, Cahn lamented, "the best team ever assembled in this city failed to reach the semifinals." The margin of defeat was so close that Cahn thought "it's no wonder the town is saying: It isn't in the cards."[75] Disputing all the talk about jinxes, Chet Nelson thought it time to find a new coach. "Glenn Jacobs is a fine fellow," Nelson wrote, but "new leadership is needed if the team is to scale the heights."[76] The next day Jacobs announced his resignation and Ernie Schmidt, a three-year veteran, retired to take a job with General Motors Acceptance Corporation.[77] While the Safeways sorted out their future, Gene Johnson's McPherson Refiners came back from a 20–15 deficit to defeat Universal Pictures in the championship game, 47–35. The coach's younger brother, Francis Johnson, led all scorers with fifteen points.[78] The finalists had won the right to compete in the Olympic tournament in Madison Square Garden.

Financially the tournament fell short of the 1935 figures. The tournament's gross of $18,167 was about $500 below the 1935 figure. But expenses jumped by $1,450 so the net profits dropped from roughly $6,800 to $4,700.[79] While Poss Parsons claimed these profits exceeded many conventions attracted to the city, he recognized that the local AAU committee might not bid for the tourney because of these figures. The greatest disappointment for the promoters was the drop in attendance on the last two nights of the tournament. The failure of a Denver team to reach the semifinals clearly affected attendance. To make the tournament a bigger financial success Denver promoters could only hope for greater tournament success from the Safeways, although Parsons thought civic groups might underwrite the prices of tickets to encourage attendance on the final two nights.[80] The fight for control over the 1936 Olympic basketball program and its budgetary negotiations, however, quickly eclipsed the budgetary problems of the Denver tournament.

THREE

Forrest C. Allen and the
Politics of Olympic Basketball

When basketball was added to the Olympic program, not surprisingly, it became another battleground between the AAU and the NCAA.[1] One of the major players in this bureaucratic squabble was Dr. Forrest C. "Phog" Allen, the legendary basketball coach of the University of Kansas Jayhawks. By 1936 Allen's teams had already won eighteen conference titles, produced several All-Americans, and trained a number of distinguished coaches, including John Bunn, Arthur "Dutch" Lonberg, and Adolph Rupp. An admiring biographer called Allen America's "first great basketball coach."[2] Indeed Allen, who was born in 1885, had grown up with basketball, which he played at the University of Kansas under James Naismith, who subsequently would be his friend and colleague. Allen was clearly a person with enormous ability and ambition. It was no surprise that in 1928 he led an effort to persuade the International Olympic Committee (IOC) to place basketball on the Olympic program in the 1932 games in Los Angeles.

One of the major obstacles faced by Allen was the widespread belief that basketball was exclusively an American game. Using information collected by James Naismith to correct this misunderstanding, Allen wrote an article entitled "The International Growth of Basketball," which asserted that "eighteen million people from every part of the globe played basketball."[3] While his evidence impressed Avery Brundage, president of the AAU, and others, they cautioned Allen against expecting a positive response because the IOC was inclined to reduce rather than to increase the athletic program in 1932. Because the United States was the host country in 1932, the U.S. Olympic Committee had the authority to place a demonstration sport on the program. Brundage warned Allen that the Los Angeles Olympic Committee (LAOC) would favor the sport likely to produce the most revenue.[4] The LAOC thwarted Allen's efforts when it chose to use football as a demonstration sport because of the expectation that it would draw larger crowds.[5] Despite these disappointments, Allen and others campaigned for the addition of basketball to the Olympic program in 1936. Their hard work paid off when Germany agreed, in October of 1934, to include basketball as part of the 1936 Olympics.[6]

Once basketball was an official Olympic sport, American athletic officials turned their attention to the issue of selecting a team and coaches for the Berlin games. To perform these responsibilities, an Olympic Basketball Committee (OBC) was formed that included six representatives from the AAU, four from the NCAA, two from the American Olympic Association, and one selected by the committee. Although basketball was not a marquee international sport, it was a key element in the fund-raising strategy of the U.S. Olympic Committee (USOC). In the midst of the Depression, the USOC worried about raising the money, estimated at $350,000 by Brundage, to send American athletes to Berlin. The OBC believed that a national basketball tournament would raise anywhere from fifty thousand to two hundred thousand dollars for the Olympic fund.[7] The OBC decided to hold an eight-team tournament in Madison Square Garden to determine the composition of the Olympic basketball team. After an all-day meeting on October 14, 1935, the Olympic Basketball Committee decided to allocate five tournament slots to the colleges, two to the AAU and one to the YMCA. A number of participants objected to the allocation of one spot to the YMCA, since they considered "Y" teams to be much inferior to those of the colleges and the AAU. Following much debate, the YMCA won representation in the tournament as compensation for its work in planting basketball in foreign countries. Colleges received the most representation because of the expectation that their district tournaments to determine the final five would raise enough money to send the team to Germany. While the AAU wanted four teams, the expectation was that at least one of its two teams would make it to the finals.[8]

Coach Allen was deeply interested in these negotiations because he was lobbying to either coach or otherwise lead the basketball team to Berlin. There were different scenarios discussed by Allen and his friends about how the Kansas coach could achieve his goal. Allen concluded that the coach of the team that won the tournament in New York deserved to coach the Olympic team. While the coach handled the players on the floor, the team needed a person to supervise "its conduct and its relationship with the other teams." Allen was not sure what title to give to this position, a problem he proposed to leave to the "administration bright-lights." Because of his "effort in getting the game included in the Olympic competition," Allen expected some recognition from the OBC, but wanted something more substantive than an honorary position. He offered evidence to convince his friends that he would not use his position to subvert the basketball coach in Berlin. Instead, Allen wanted a position that would allow him to boost the game, to represent the team in dealings with officials from other countries, and to protect the image of the American team.[9]

There was considerable support for Allen on the OBC. Major John L. Griffith, president of the NCAA, supported Allen, and Griffith controlled four votes on the OBC. In addition, the National Basketball Coaches Association and the National Basketball Rules Committee endorsed Allen's candidacy to serve as Olympic basketball coach.[10] On February 2, 1936, the OBC met and decided to recommend to the United States Olympic Committee that it send eighteen people to Berlin. They included fourteen players, the director of basketball, the head coach from the winner of the Madison Square Garden tournament, an assistant coach from the second-place team, and a manager. The OBC recommended that Allen serve as the director of basketball. One of the difficulties faced by these general recommendations was that Avery Brundage, who was president of the U.S. Olympic Committee, president of the AAU, and chairman of the American Olympic Finance Committee, thought that a party of eighteen was too large to send to Berlin.[11]

At this point bureaucratic politics took a backseat to basketball. While McPherson and Hollywood prepared for the Olympic tournament, the Olympic dreams of the Denver Safeways unexpectedly were not yet dead. In what the *Denver Post* described as a "magnanimous act," Safeway decided to send the team, all of whose players were YMCA members, to the national YMCA tourney in Peoria, Illinois, the winner of which would receive a berth in the Olympic tournament.[12] A triumph in Peoria would not be easy, however, since another disappointed AAU loser, the powerful Kansas City Philcos led by Chuck Hyatt, were also in the tournament. In three days the Denver team won three games including a tense 23–20 victory over the Philcos and a 47–45 nail-biter over the Wilmerding, Pennsylvania, YMCA team.[13]

Although Denver fans were ecstatic, three days before the first Olympic tournament, the YMCA banned the Denver entry. The national secretary of the YMCA, Dr. John Brown, ruled that Denver had violated a rule that prohibited a team playing under another name in another tournament from playing in a YMCA tourney until ninety days after its previous competition. In other words the Denver team was not a legitimate YMCA team. Denver argued unsuccessfully that the identities of the Denver and Kansas City teams were known prior to the Peoria event and that they had been included in order to build up attendance.[14]

The colleges, meanwhile, were participating in a national tournament to determine the five college teams that would compete in Madison Square Garden. The director of the tournament was Arthur A. Schabinger, athletic director at Creighton University. The tournament committee divided the United States into ten districts. After the ten district finalists had been determined, the five teams that survived interdistrict play would go to New York City. For a variety of reasons several outstanding teams chose not to compete in the Olympic tryouts. Long Island University (LIU), coached by Clair Bee, declared that it "would not under any circumstances be represented in Olympic games held in Germany." LIU had won thirty-three consecutive games but joined those Americans who favored a boycott of the Berlin Olympics because of Nazi laws discriminating against German Jews. To participate in the tournament, LIU feared, "would be indirect, if not direct, contribution to the raising of funds to finance participation" in the Berlin Olympics. New York University and the City College of New York, like LIU, had a large number of Jewish players and they also elected against playing in the tournament. Notre Dame said that its players could not afford the missed class time, so it did not enter the tournament. The South, which was in District Three, did not hold a tournament because of the expense and conflict with spring football.[15]

Only thirty-eight colleges competed for a chance to represent the United States in Berlin. The five college teams that survived this tournament format were Temple University, De Paul University, the University of Arkansas, Utah State, and the University of Washington.[16] The Utah State Aggies defeated Phog Allen's Kansas Jayhawks in a three-game series played at Convention Hall in Kansas City. Prior to this playoff, KU had won twenty-two consecutive games and the Big Six Conference championship. Nonetheless, Utah State denied the Jayhawks a place in the Olympic tournament.[17] KU's failure also ended Phog Allen's chances to coach the Olympic basketball team and meant his role was now solely in the hands of the Olympic Basketball Committee.

In early April eight teams gathered at Madison Square Garden to determine the composition of the first U.S. Olympic basketball team. Arthur J. Daley of the *New York Times* wrote that this tournament would give "local fans their opportunity to view a cross-section of the court game as it is played throughout the country."[18] The tournament directors, as in Denver, invited James Naismith to open the tournament. On the first evening of play twelve thousand fans watched as four of the five college teams were eliminated from play. Francis Johnson, described "as the perfect basketball player," led the McPherson Globe Refiners to a victory over Temple, while Sam Balter scored eleven points to lead Universal Pictures over Arkansas. In the biggest surprise of the tournament the Wilmerding, Pennsylvania, YMCA team set a Madison Square Garden scoring record when it crushed Utah State, 62–48. Equally stunning was Washington's romp over De Paul, 54–33. "As a spectacle," Arthur J. Daly wrote, "the affair even surpassed expectation. There was better basketball than ever before in the Garden."[19]

In the semifinals, before seven thousand fans, the Globe Refiners ran the University of Washington off the Garden floor, and Frank Lubin's 18 points helped to give Universal Pictures a win over Wilmerding YMCA.[20] Although McPherson seemed invincible, it lost the championship to Universal Pictures, 44–43. The Globe Refiners' chances suffered a severe blow when they lost Francis Johnson to fouls with only three and one-half minutes gone in the second half.[21] As a result of the victory, Universal Pictures placed Frank Lubin, Carl Knowles, Art Mollner, Carl Shy, Duane Swanson, Don Piper, and Sam Balter on the Olympic team. Sam Balter was Jewish, one of six Jewish Americans on the United States Olympic team.[22] Universal's victory also meant that the Olympic Basketball Committee made Jimmy Needles the head coach of the team. Gene Johnson, McPherson's coach, served as the assistant coach, and six of his players—Francis Johnson, Joe Fortenberry, Tex Gibbons, Jack Ragland, Bill Wheatley, and Willard Schmidt—played on the Olympic team. Ralph Bishop, a center from the University of Washington, was the only college player named to the team.[23]

While the OBC managed to select a basketball team, revenues from the tournament were far below expectation. Madison Square Garden collected gross receipts of $14,961 rather than the $60,000 it had anticipated. After paying the travel expenses of the eight teams, the OBC pocketed a disappointing $6,740.[24] Instead of a "cash cow" that enriched the American fund-raising effort, the OBC had failed to raise enough money to send the American basketball team to Berlin.

In addition to financial disappointment, the OBC had an embarrassing public relations problem. At the center of this storm was Phog Allen. By the end of April, Dr. Allen had decided not to pursue the directorship of the Olympic basketball team and "to give the AAU a good blast and refuse to have anything to do with the outfit."[25] There were a variety of reasons for Allen's displeasure with the AAU.

One was that some of the AAU leaders expressed displeasure with the poor financial showing of the college tournaments. While Major John L. Griffith, president of the NCAA, was surprised that the college games failed to draw, he thought that "[t]he college coaches could have helped by not scheduling such long schedules of college games but as it was their men were tired of basketball when their college season ended and so many of the teams that should have entered the sectional tournaments did not do so." Avery Brundage was one of these critics. According to Griffith, "I sat in his office one day when he spoke his mind very freely and sharply criticized certain of our college men." The combination of the poor payout and the AAU teams' "marked superiority over the college teams," Griffith wrote Allen, encouraged the AAU to seek more patronage.[26]

In Allen's letter of resignation to Dr. Walter E. Meanwell, chairman of the Olympic Basketball Committee, Allen condemned "the unsportsmanlike attitude of the AAU members of the Olympic Basketball Committee" and "their deceitful political bartering." The Kansas coach described the leaders of the AAU as "Quadrennial Oceanic Hitch-hikers" who "chisel their way across the oceans every four years on the other fellow's money." As evidence, Allen submitted that he "managed and promoted the Kansas–Utah State series in Kansas City which proved to be the financial gravy wagon on which the Olympic Basketball contingent will travel to Berlin." As Allen saw it, he raised eight thousand dollars for the Olympic basketball team, while the Missouri Valley AAU "grossed less than $700 on three nights thereby showing the difference in public favor between college and independent basketball." Although the national AAU tournament in Denver netted six thousand dollars, Allen noted that all the money was spent to pay the administrative expenses of the AAU in New York and Chicago.[27]

Allen also took a swipe at Dr. Joseph A. Reilly, the athletic director of the Kansas City Athletic Club, who was named the manager of the Olympic basketball team. Reilly had directed every national AAU basketball tournament that was held in Kansas City between 1921 and 1934. In the bureaucratic struggle for the appointment of manager of the Olympic team, Reilly had paid his dues, but he also was a beneficiary of the AAU's domination of the Olympic tryout at Madison Square Garden. Reilly was not Allen's first choice as manager, and the Kansas coach criticized Reilly for leaving Kansas City to officiate in the Golden Gloves Tournament in New York City while Kansas and Utah State played their interdistrict tournament. The implication was that Reilly was an AAU freeloader.[28]

Dr. Joseph A. Reilly and Avery Brundage responded immediately to Allen's attack. Reilly declared that he had been in New York for two days, but returned to Kansas City "a day before the tournament opened here." While Allen claimed credit for raising eight thousand dollars for the Olympic team, Reilly charged that Allen was "talking through his hat." Reilly said: "I made the arrangements for the hall, sent Utah State money to get here and took care of other things. Allen didn't do any more managing of the tournament than did Dick Romney, Utah State coach. All they did was bring their teams here to play."[29] Brundage and J. Lyman Bingham, his assistant and secretary of the Olympic Basketball Committee, found Allen's resignation letter presumptuous, since he had never been appointed director of the U.S. Olympic team. They stressed that Allen's appointment had been merely recommended. They called Allen the real "hitchhiker," since he sought a position as "an extra and unnecessary official." For good measure, Bingham added that "Allen went to the AAU tournament at Denver and deducted his expenses from the money taken in at the Kansas City Olympic tournament." Finally, Bingham reported "that Mr. Brundage, instead of spending Olympic money, paid his own expenses to the winter games at Garmisch-Partenkirchen. I think he would do the same thing again this summer if there is a shortage of money."[30]

Allen's letter to Meanwell was disingenuous in three respects. First, Allen stated that he "found satisfaction enough" in getting basketball on the Olympic program "without thought of personal award." In fact, he had lobbied diligently for the position of director of Olympic basketball. Second, Allen joined critics of the AAU when he "emphasized how precarious is the position of the Olympic Basketball, when left in the hands of technical amateurs but actual semi-professionals."[31] The inspiration for this blast was "[t]he disgraceful—post Olympic Tournament—exhibition game at Topeka, Kansas." On April 10 the *Topeka Daily Capital* reported that the McPherson Globe Refiners defeated Universal Studios in a "Farcical Contest." Topeka writers scolded the Universals for only suiting up five players and reported that Frank Lubin played until he had eight fouls. Moreover the Topeka writers and fans charged that the Universals showed little interest in the outcome of the game because the gate, in this case eight hundred dollars, went to the Olympic Committee. Topeka gave the Globe Refiners "a clean bill of health" and attributed the Universals' poor play to the handicap of growing up in California where the athlete "expects to be paid."[32] By 1936, however, only a partisan could see any difference between college and AAU basketball players. Finally Allen concluded his resignation letter by stating that he wrote "as an individual and not as a member affiliated with the National Collegiate Athletic Association."[33] Allen's subsequent attack on the AAU and his close relationship with leaders of the NCAA did not make this claim very credible.

One of the consequences of the process of selecting the Olympic team was that, in effect, the United States had two Olympic teams: McPherson's Globe Refiners and Hollywood's Universal Pictures. The two teams never practiced together in the United States and were individually responsible for finding a way to New York City, where they boarded the ship carrying American athletes to Berlin. Because Universal Pictures won the Olympic tournament, Olympic officials determined that getting the Californians to Berlin was their first responsibility. One unnamed official said: "Then, if we get enough money, we will add as many players as possible to the squad. If we get more funds we will send an assistant coach."[34] Nonetheless the players on the Universal team had to get to New York. While they thought Universal Pictures would pay their expenses to New York, Universal dropped its sponsorship of the team because of the treatment of German Jews by the Nazis. To help the Olympians, Braven Dyer Sr., sports editor of the *Los Angeles Times*, organized a team of college all-stars to play Universal Pictures at the Olympic Auditorium in Los Angeles. Although the Universals lost, they made enough money to start the trip to New York. Exhibition games along the way made it possible for the Californians to complete the trip.[35]

The McPherson Globe Refiners faced the same predicament as Universal Pictures. In June Coach Gene Johnson made a personal appeal to the people of McPherson to raise one thousand dollars in solicitations so that all six of McPherson's players could play in Berlin. He hoped that every basketball fan would contribute anywhere from one to twenty-five dollars.[36] As late as June 26, players were selling tickets for the "Dollar Donation Fund."[37] On July 11, 1936, the *McPherson Daily Republic* reported that two cars were driving to New York with Gene Johnson, six players, and two wives. At this late date the *Daily Republic* wondered if the players from Universal Pictures would even make it to New York before the uss *Manhattan* left for Hamburg, Germany.[38]

Of course, all players and coaches made it to New York on time for the eight-day trip across the Atlantic. There was no place to practice on the uss *Manhattan*, but the players did run, stretch, and pass the basketball. The voyage also gave the coaches an opportunity to prepare the players for the international rules that would govern the Olympic tournament. Perhaps the most important was a rule that allowed each team to suit up only seven players for each game. Also, when a player was replaced, he could not return unless a player was injured or fouled out. While the players wanted the Universals and the Refiners to alternate, one team playing the first round, the other playing the next round and so on, Coach Needles chose to integrate the players of the two teams. Sam Balter, one of the Olympians, reported that the fourteen men were divided into "Sure-Passers," mostly Universal players, and "Wild Men," primarily Globe Refiners.[39] With fourteen men eager to play, one of the most disappointing aspects of the tournament was that the United States drew Spain, which boycotted the Olympics because of the Spanish Civil War, in the first round, and then drew a bye in the third round.[40]

Consistent with international rules, the entire tournament was played on five outdoor courts composed of compressed clay and sand. There were other annoyances. The International Federation of Amateur Basketball (FIBA) adopted the Berg, a German product, as the official game ball of the tournament. The Berg was slightly lop-sided and smooth so that dust and mud stuck to its surface, making it difficult to handle. After the United States had crushed Estonia, the Philippines, and Mexico, the International Basketball Federa-tion passed a rule that limited future international competition to players under six feet three inches tall. While this rule was never implemented, it was an amusing reaction by other nations to the height of the United States team.[41] Finally, some Americans com-plained that the U.S. Olympic Committee had not done enough to honor Dr. James Naismith, who traveled to Berlin on funds raised by the United States Basketball Association. Jim Tobin, a New Yorker who officiated some of the Olympic basketball games, reported that some of Naismith's friends secured a pass for him and then arranged an impromptu ceremony for him.[42]

When the tournament was over, the United States claimed Olympic basketball's first gold medal by compiling a perfect 4-0 record, including a 19–8 victory over Canada in the championship game, a contest marred by a driving rainstorm, which turned the court's surface to mud. It is difficult to disagree with Sam Balter's conclusion that the Olympic tournament was "a sandlot affair."[43] It confirmed that American basketball was decades ahead of the rest of the world. The American delegation to Berlin, nonetheless, made history and helped to make basketball an international game.

After the Olympics, Dr. Allen renewed his attack on the AAU. In a post-Olympic statement, Allen compared AAU administrators to "Chicago racketeers who do not create a business or industry but who step in and tell those who did build up an establishment that they are going to help run it." Allen contended that "NCAA members, coaches, and directors of athletics" had more integrity than their AAU counterparts, because they were "paid their annual salaries by their respective schools and they draw no monies from outside sources."[44] In his indictment of the AAU's conduct of the Olympics, Allen cited the treatment of Naismith and also Jesse Owens. In the latter's case, the AAU suspended the star of the Berlin Olympics when he failed to complete a post-Olympics barnstorming tour of Europe to raise funds for the American Olympics Committee.

While the AAU was exploiting Owens, so was everybody else. Ohio State had shielded Owens from classes required for graduation in order to insure his athletic eligibility. L. W. St. John, Ohio State's director of athletics, wanted Owens to return to Columbus for his senior year so that Ohio State could capitalize on his fame. While the AAU was excessively harsh on Owens, the latter's decision to forego European barnstorming was motivated primarily by his eagerness to capitalize financially on his fame after receiving advice from NCAA men who despised the AAU. There was an ironic twist to Allen's critique of the exploitation of Owens. In fact Owens found it difficult to capitalize on his fame until the Republican Party paid Owens ten to fifteen thousand dollars to campaign for its presidential candidate, Alf Landon, the governor—of all places—of Kansas.[45] Allen assured sports fans that if the NCAA represented the United States in Olympic competition, "the necessary funds would be safe in a bank vault" months before the Olympics and "there would be no post-Olympic barnstorming on the part of any athlete not wishing to compete."[46]

Because of the success of the AAU teams in the 1936 Olympic tournament, John L. Griffith, president of the NCAA, believed in 1940 that "the AAU will insist on running . . . Olympic basketball, maintaining that their brand of basketball is superior to the college brand and further maintaining that we fell down on the job this year. This will mean that the colleges that want to try out will have to enter the AAU tournament."[47] World War Two, of course, intervened and there were no Olympics in 1940 and 1944. When the Olympics resumed in 1948, the method used for selecting the Olympic basketball team was modeled on the 1936 format. Four years later, in 1952, Coach Allen represented the United State Olympic Basketball team as its assistant coach. He missed his chance to serve as the head coach when the Peoria Caterpillars, coached by Warren Womble, edged the University of Kansas in the final game of the Olympic tournament at Madison Square Garden.[48]

The ramifications of launching Olympic basketball were not all contentious. While walking the streets of Berlin, representatives of the Lithuanian government approached Frank Lubin, whose parents were Lithuanian, and invited him to tutor their countrymen on the techniques of this new American game. Lubin accepted the offer and embarked on a three-year adventure as the player-coach of the Lithuanian national team. Playing under his Lithuanian name, Pranas Lubinas, the Californian scored the winning basket for Lithuania in the title game of the 1939 European championships. For his efforts Lithuania remembered Lubin as "the Godfather of Lithuanian Basketball," which in 1988 placed four players on the Soviet team that defeated the United States on its way to a gold medal in Seoul, South Korea.[49]

PART 2

A DYNASTY IS CREATED

The next twelve years were golden for the AAU tournament in Denver. In these twelve years Denver came to see itself as a basketball town. From 1937 through 1942, Denver teams, led by Jack Mc-Cracken and Robert "Ace" Gruenig, won three national championships and were runners-up twice. This period also witnessed the emergence of the Phillips Petroleum Company as the model industrial basketball team. The 66ers won their first national AAU championship in 1940 and added a record six consecutive titles between 1943 and 1948.

These years were also significant in college basketball. Stanford's Angelo "Hank" Luisetti used a one-handed shot to establish new scoring records in the 1936–37 season. After the 1937–38 season Madison Square Garden held its first National Invitational Tournament (NIT), which was won by Temple University. Edward "Ned" Irish, a sportswriter turned promoter who directed the NIT, had introduced college basketball doubleheaders to Madison Square Garden in 1934, and they had become a popular event soon copied by other major cities. In March of 1939 the University of Oregon won the first NCAA national basketball tournament. Until the revelations of a point-shaving scandal in 1951, the most successful college teams annually played in both the NIT and the NCAA tournaments.

Because of World War Two, the Olympic Games of 1940 and 1944 were not held. The tournament to select the American Olympic team resumed in 1948 in preparation for the London games. When Phillips 66 defeated Adolph Rupp's Kentucky Wildcats in the championship game of the Olympic tournament, it firmly established the 66ers as the dominant amateur team of the era.

During this period professional basketball struggled. The American Basketball League folded after the 1945–46 season. Most of the teams in the National Basketball League, in business between 1937 and 1949, played in small midwestern cities. It was not until after the war that these teams played more than thirty games a season. In 1946 the Basketball Association of America, with franchises in larger cities, played the first of its three seasons. There were no professional teams west of St. Louis. Between 1939 and 1948 the *Chicago Herald American* sponsored a World Professional Basketball Tournament at the Chicago Stadium, which usually included the New York Rens and the Harlem Globetrotters.

FOUR

Gruenig and McCracken Triumphant

In an effort to win the 1937 title, William Haraway of the Denver Safeways tried unsuccessfully to recruit Henry Iba, McCracken's coach at Classen High School in Oklahoma City and Maryville State Teachers. Although he turned Haraway down, Iba recommended Everett "Ev" Shelton for the Safeway job. Iba claimed that he "had learned much of his famed scientific system from Shelton when he played under Ev on the Sterling Milk's AAU semifinalist team in 1927."[1] Shelton had been a three-sport star between 1919 and 1923 at Phillips University in Enid, Oklahoma, where he coached for several years in the mid-1920s. In addition to coaching several AAU teams in the late 1920s and early 1930s, Shelton coached Christian Brothers High School in St. Joseph, Missouri. The thirty-eight-year-old Shelton was about to begin the most productive years of a coaching career that would lead to induction into the Naismith Memorial Basketball Hall of Fame in 1979.[2] The nucleus of Shelton's team was still Gruenig, Dowell, and McCracken. The most important addition was Jack "Tex" Colvin, an AAU veteran who played college ball at West Texas State.[3]

During the regular season, the Safeways once again played in the Missouri Valley League. While the McPherson Globe Refiners decided against sponsoring a nationally competitive team, the Phillips Petroleum Company returned to AAU competition. Because of the Depression Phillips had not sponsored a team since the 1929–30 season, but rising profits and the enthusiastic support of Kenneth S. "Boots" Adams, the company president, combined to revive 66er basketball.[4] Two Globe Refiners, Joe Fortenberry and Jack Ragland, both Olympians, joined Phillips. They teamed up with four other established AAU stars—Chuck Hyatt, Tom Pickell, Jay Wallenstrom and Bud Browning. Ray Ebling, Big Six scoring champion from the University of Kansas, and Dave Perkins, a Phillips University star, were the team's freshmen.

The Safeways played well during the regular season and finished in second place behind Phillips. Denver approached the tournament with a cautious confidence. Given its disappointing tournament record, fans took solace in the view that the squad "is capable and has, above all else, a great spirit and excellent coaching in the person of Ev Shelton."[5] In the 1937 national AAU tournament, Denver breezed through the first two rounds, but before its quarterfinal game against Long Island University, coached by Clair Bee, the "tension was nerve-wracking . . . as the 'jinx' superseded all thoughts," according to the *Denver Post*'s Robert Gamzey. After the Safeways trounced Bee's team, Gamzey triumphantly declared: "The jinx is buried. The dreaded quarterfinal hoodoo that killed off every local tournament team in history was dealt a death blow before 7,500 cheering supporters who jammed the auditorium to the roof."[6]

As the Safeways approached the semifinal game, the *Denver Post*'s Leonard Cahn observed that "[b]asketball hysteria gripped Denver as the zero hour approached. The town was plum loco."[7] Denver's semifinal opponent, Hollywood's Laemmle Stars, was almost the identical team that had beaten Safeway by one point in the 1936 AAU tournament before winning the Olympic tournament and a gold medal in Berlin. The star of the Hollywood team was Frank Lubin, a six-foot-seven center, who had outplayed Gruenig the previous year. Before the largest crowd ever to witness a semifinal game, Denver dominated Lubin's Stars as, Tex Colvin's 15 points led all scorers.[8] To win the championship game Denver had to beat what Leonard Cahn described as a "dream team" assembled by Phillips Petroleum Company of Bartlesville, Oklahoma.[9] In a brilliantly played game, Leonard Cahn wrote that "six men of iron, shuffled about by the magic hand of Coach Everett Shelton, literally beat the Phillips all-star cast into the ground" for a 43–38 victory.[10]

Chet Nelson called it "the greatest game Rocky Mountain fans ever witnessed." The six who carried the Grocers, in Nelson's words, were "lanky Gruenig and cocky Werner Frank; cool McCracken and hard-working Colvin; busting Duck Dowell and shy Jimmy Bauer. They played their roles flawlessly." Dowell led a balanced attack with eleven points. Tex Colvin, Bob Gruenig, and Jack McCracken made the first team AAU All-American team for the Safeways.[11] According to Frank Haraway, Willard N. "Big Bill" Greim said that when he made the All-America presentation to Jack McCracken it was his greatest sports thrill and that "the sustained outburst of the crowd sent shivers up and down my spine. . . . My Adam's apple was bobbing up and down until I thought I might not be able to finish the presentation. Never did I dream that one athlete could so endear himself to a crowd of sports fans."[12]

Robert Gamzey of the *Post* gave Shelton much of the credit for Denver's success, especially his work with Ace Gruenig. In the previous two tournaments Gruenig had been a disappointment, and some questioned his competitiveness. According to Gamzey, Shelton "spent countless hours improving his pivot shot, his defense, and other fundamentals but primarily Shelton worked on Gruenig's mind, preparing him for the role of being America's best center. Gruenig began to believe in himself."[13] Chet Nelson seconded Gamzey's assessment and called Shelton "the best coach in independent basketball, or, in any basketball for that matter."[14]

Denver's national championship not only was the talk of the town, but a financial success. For the first time in AAU basketball history gross profits exceeded twenty thousand dollars.[15] Poss Parsons declared that Denver could not afford to let the tournament slip away since it was "one of the most colorful events of the year." He added that "Mayor Benjamin Stapleton is sold on the national and he wants Denver to bid again next year." Excited by the response, local AAU officials announced that they would seek the tournament for the fourth time.[16]

As the Safeways prepared for the 1937–38 season, the additions of Ralph Bishop and Dick Wells strengthened the team. Bishop, a graduate of the University of Washington and the only collegian on the 1936 Olympic team, was a forward with excellent offensive and rebounding skills. Wells, a native of Hutchinson, Kansas, had been a three-year starter for Forrest "Phog" Allen at the University of Kansas. A fierce defender and rebounder, Wells's talents were familiar to Denver fans, since he had played with the Kansas City Philcos and Denver's Kansas City Life. The 1937–38 season was also the first without the center jump after each made basket.[17]

As the season evolved, it became clear that Shelton had put together a formidable team. James Naismith, the inventor of basketball, thought the Safeways were the "greatest team I have ever seen." While impressed with Denver's size, he described the Safeways as "so smart they don't have to rely on height alone to win games." Like so many fans and writers Naismith singled out McCracken as "one of the finest players I have ever seen."[18]

The Safeways did not lose a game until January 3, 1938, when Phillips 66 edged them at Tulsa, Oklahoma, in a nonleague exhibition, ending a twenty-nine-game winning streak that stretched back to February of 1937. A night later Gruenig scored 25 points as Denver won a measure of revenge by beating Phillips in Bartlesville.[19] Two weeks later over four thousand fans watched the Safeways squeak by Phillips in City Auditorium, a crowd that suggested the birth of a new basketball rivalry.[20] This was confirmed in early February when Phillips turned the tables on Denver and won before four thousand at City Auditorium. Chet Nelson thought the game a "brilliant exhibition" of basketball and believed that "if there are better teams in the country, they haven't been exposed."[21]

The 1938 tournament drew fifty-four teams from over twenty states. Enhancing the tournament's diversity were the Chicago Collegians, the first African American team to compete in the national AAU tourney, and the Crow All-Stars from the Crow Indian Agency in southern Montana, the first and only Native American team in Denver.[22] The Crow All-Stars fell in the first round to the Studebaker Athletic Club from South Bend, Indiana, but Ed Old Crow impressed spectators with 23 points.[23] The Collegians lost in the third round to the Colorado Antlers Hotelmen.[24]

For the first time in four years of tournament play in Denver, all seats for the quarterfinal games were sold by reservation.[25] In the semifinals the Safeways defeated the Wichita Gridleys, and the Kansas City Healey Motors surprised Phillips.[26] In the title game before seven thousand fans, Fred Pralle, a Kansas All-American picked up for the tournament, drove in for a bucket with twenty seconds left to give the Healeys a two-point victory over Denver, 40–38.[27]

However disappointing the results, more shocking was the announcement made by T. W. Henritze, divisional manager of Safeway Stores, that the company was dropping its sponsorship of basketball because of the new state tax on chain stores, which cost Safeway sixty-eight thousand dollars. The baffled fans also wondered if Safeway's decision threatened Denver's claim to host the tournament. Coach Shelton and his players promised to find a Denver sponsor in order to keep basketball and the tournament alive.[28]

William Haraway and Tom Butterworth, president of the Junior Chamber of Commerce, found a solution for the orphaned team's members. Instead of one sponsor, they found employment for each player with a local business such as the Brown Palace Hotel, the Public Service Company, Capital Chevrolet, and Providence Mutual Insurance Company.[29] The team also had a new nickname, the Denver Nuggets, which according to the *Post* was the invention of Ray McGovern of the *Post* sports department.[30]

Denver's sports community heaved a sigh of relief when basketball was saved. The 1938 tournament had broken all attendance records as thirty-five thousand attended games during the week. On three nights City Auditorium sold out and turned away unlucky fans.[31] Gross receipts jumped by $4,000 to $24,827 and the national and local AAU pocketed record amounts of money.[32] Since Denver had been without professional baseball since 1932, and, as Chet Nelson observed, other professional sports had been "null and void for the last half-dozen years," AAU basketball was the biggest form of sports entertainment in Denver and its only source of recognition in the national sports community.[33] Denver did not want to lose its major claim to athletic distinction.

As the Denver Nuggets prepared for the 1938–39 campaign, Jack McCracken assumed the role of player-coach. Under the new sponsorship, Ev Shelton had been unable to work out a satisfactory arrangement and in January moved to Colorado Springs, where he coached a team sponsored by the Antlers Hotel. McCracken's team was virtually intact from the previous season, with the exception of guard Jim Bauer, a valuable sixth man, who joined the Antlers. The most important addition was Tee Connelley, a stocky, square-jawed guard who played at the University of Oklahoma for three years and spent the 1937–38 season with Oklahoma City Parks in the Missouri Valley League. Bill Ogle from Montana State and Haskell Leuty, who played with Denver in 1934 and 1935, rejoined the team and provided depth.[34] Just before the season began, tournament officials learned that the AAU had elected to award the national tournament to Denver for the fifth time.

In 1938–39 the Nuggets schedule called for sixteen games in the Missouri Valley League and fourteen exhibition games. The Nuggets offered a season ticket package of eight home league games and two exhibitions for $5.50 with children under twelve admitted free.[35] The composition of the Missouri Valley League changed slightly as the Wichita Gridleys and Kansas City failed to enter teams. They were replaced by the Tulsa Fruehaufs and the Chicago LaSalle Hotelmen, a team that included Ray Meyer, who later distinguished himself as the coach of DePaul's Blue Demons. Denver won the first half of the Missouri Valley League and tied Phillips in the second half of the season. In the playoff game to determine the champion of the second round, Denver topped Phillips and reigned as undisputed Missouri Valley champion. Chuck Hyatt, who coached Phillips in 1938–39, ranked Denver "with all the great amateur basketball teams in history."[36] Gruenig led all scorers in the Missouri Valley League with a 13.9 average, and along with McCracken made first-team All Missouri Valley.

Before the tournament, the so-called experts established the 29-3 Nuggets as a heavy favorite to win the national crown. Poss Parsons

described the Nuggets as "a murderous, almost unbeatable quin-
tet that spread terror in the league and its opposition."[37] In anticipation of a strong Denver finish, for the second straight year,
the tournament was sold out for its last three nights. According to
form Denver advanced to the Saturday night championship game
against Phillips 66, which had picked up Fred Pralle, the Kansas All-
American, who had starred in the 1938 tournament for the Healey
Motors; Fred Troutwine, a six-foot-nine center from Warrensburg
Teachers in Missouri; and Don Lockard, an All-Southwest Conference star from the University of Arkansas. Since the Nuggets had
beaten Phillips in four of five meetings, were undefeated on the City
Auditorium floor, and were the tourney favorites, the pressure on
them was enormous. The Denver press already called this "one of
the most hostile rivalries in sport" and spiced up the confrontation
by adding that, "the players had little regard for each other on or off
the court."[38] Denver prevailed 25–22 in a cautiously played game,
with pressure, according to Chet Nelson, "hanging over the arena
so thick it seemed you could slice it with a dull blade." At one point
in the second half neither team scored for seven minutes and forty
seconds. Nelson thought that Dick Wells was Denver's outstanding
player that night "as he was all over the floor, driving hard, clearing
rebounds and feeding his mates."[39] Leonard Cahn lavished praise
on Tee Connelley, "who covered the dangerous Fred Pralle like a
tent and did not yield a single basket to the most valuable player of
last year's tournament." Ace Gruenig, who scored 9 points, limited
"College" Joe Fortenberry to one basket.[40]

The victory was particularly sweet for McCracken, who was in his
first year as a player-coach. Unlike Shelton, who had a reputation as
a rigid disciplinarian, McCracken was seen by the press as a new kind
of coach. McCracken gave no pep talks and inflicted no harangues
upon his team. McCracken reported, "I never said anything to them
all season outside of just talking things over at different times with
all of us giving ideas."[41] In 1939 McCracken owned Denver and had
won, the *Post* reported, "an everlasting place in the hearts of Denver
Sports lovers."[42] Sportswriters named McCracken the tournament's
Most Valuable Player and placed him along with Gruenig and Wells

on the AAU All-American first team. Characterizing McCracken as unselfish and brilliant, one writer described him "as one of the greatest players the game has ever known if not the greatest."[43]

The linkage between Denver sports, business, and politics was clearer in this tournament than in any of its predecessors. Before the final, Tom Butterworth, president of the Junior Chamber of Commerce, who coordinated the effort to find jobs for the players, announced that there would be a team in 1939–40. He added that in seeking jobs for new players he "found Denver businessmen in a much more responsive mood than last year, when we worked most of the summer on finding jobs."[44] Henry Meier, the team's business manager added, "AAU players have told me they are satisfied with the civic sponsorship plan. It worked very nicely through the past campaign for all concerned, and we don't intend to throw it over."[45] When Butterworth received the championship trophy following the game he, in turn, presented it to Mayor Ben Stapleton and commented, "Because Denver has given this team such wholehearted support, the trophy belongs to the city."[46] Although tournament attendance and profits dropped slightly, they were healthy enough to make another tournament bid inevitable. The *Rocky Mountain News* reported that, for the year, the team's gate receipts balanced expenses.[47]

In the 1939–40 season Tex Colvin, William Ogle, and Haskell Leuty did not return from the championship team. Their places were taken by two popular local players, Art Unger and Bob Marsh. During the early 1930s Unger had won all-state honors at Manual High School in basketball, baseball, and football. Unger grew up near Denver's stockyards in a family that included six brothers and six sisters. All of his brothers were athletes, and one of Denver's basketball traditions of the 1930s and '40s was the annual exhibition game between the Ungers and the Allens (another Denver family with a batch of athletic sons), played at the Trinity Church Invitational basketball tournament. At a time when athletic scholarships were unavailable, Unger enrolled at the University of Colorado in the fall of 1934 subsidized by a dollar-a-day job provided by the National Youth Administration. At six feet four inches and broad shouldered, Unger earned ten letters at Boulder in baseball, basketball, and football.[48] Bob Marsh, a star at North High School and one of the Denver Prep League's most highly regarded basketball prospects in the mid-1930s, never played college ball. Instead, he played in the Denver city league until 1938 when he joined the Antlers Hotelmen of Colorado Springs. A tenacious defensive player, Marsh always drew the opposition's best offensive player.[49]

In 1939–40 the Missouri Valley shrank to a mere four teams— Phillips, Denver, Oklahoma City, and St. Louis. Since each team played a home-and-away series, the league schedule amounted to a mere six games. Denver, with a 3-3 record, came in second to Phillips 66, which lost one league game to Denver. Bob Gruenig was the leading scorer in the league with a 12.6 average. Exhibition games absorbed most of Denver's pre-tournament campaign.

As the season evolved, evidence mounted that, as a civic enterprise, the basketball operation was about to unravel. When the Nuggets were short of money, the Denver Tourist and Convention Bureau helped to subsidize the team. On February 3, 1940, the Nuggets embarked on a seventeen-day road trip that included three Missouri Valley games and a number of exhibition contests. As they left Union Station, the players unfurled a large sign, at least twenty yards long, with the words "Come Up To Denver" painted upon it.[50] Wherever the Nuggets played or stayed, the sign was exhibited in an attempt by the team to persuade Denver of its value to the community. As the players barnstormed across the Midwest, Poss Parsons used his column to propose that the fans of Denver congregate at Union Station to welcome the team upon its return. Parsons explained that in 1937 the champions had been honored at a testimonial dinner but had not been after the 1939 championship. He thought that Denver's fans were much too apathetic and that the Nuggets deserved "the admiration of the hometown."[51] This effort to boost the team's morale was directly related to some player dissatisfaction resulting from the Junior Chamber of Commerce's inability to find jobs for two (Unger and Marsh) of the team's eight players.[52]

Members of the business community supported the idea of a

homecoming, and one, H. J. Palmatier, wrote, "the advertising we get from them [Nuggets] is of untold value. Let any other city have the array of basketball talent that the Denver Nuggets represent and it would take a great deal to get them discouraged, so let's do it here."[53] Since the idea caught fire, Tom Butterworth, chairman of the Junior Chamber of Commerce, arranged for a special greeting, which included a police escort to city hall where Mayor Ben Stapleton would welcome the team, a ceremony to be broadcast over a local radio station. Several hundred fans greeted the players, each of whom spoke to their well-wishers before dutifully meeting with Mayor Stapleton.[54]

As the national tournament approached, Poss Parsons stressed the immediate necessity of resolving the problem of sponsorship rather than running the risk of losing key players. He wrote: "The Denver Nuggets and the national AAU tourney are two of this city's greatest assets, it would be a shame to lose either of them, but one is contingent upon the other." Chances of hosting the tournament, he explained, hinged on having a strong local team to generate attendance.[55] Just before the tournament Clarence V. Beales, commander of the American Legion Leyden-Chiles-Wickersham Post No. 1, announced that his organization had voted to operate the Nuggets for the next season. The plan was to have each of Denver's service clubs assume the responsibility of finding a job for one player. Beale explained that the Legion's decision rested on the belief that "[m]uch beneficial publicity comes to a city having a team the caliber of the Nuggets, and their presence satisfies a need for winter sports entertainment."[56]

The 1940 tournament opened on St. Patrick's Day and a *Rocky Mountain News* writer reported that the first patrons were an elderly couple, with a lunch basket, who bought their tickets forty minutes before the 10:00 a.m. tipoff. By the time of the first jump ball, about three hundred people had joined them. Thirteen hours later the final gun brought the eleven-game program to an end as approximately four thousand spectators wandered in and out of City Auditorium.[57] If those fans purchased a general admission ticket, it cost fifty-six cents. Those who preferred a reserved seats paid $1.12, or $1.68

to sit on the stage.[58] In honor of St. Patrick the Catholic Youth Organization team from Butte, Montana, coached appropriately by Pat McCarthy, came out in green jerseys and, instead of warm-up suits, wore green-and-white boxing robes. Their opponents, Allen-Bradley of Milwaukee, decked out in orange uniforms, eliminated them in the first round.[59]

To reach their fourth consecutive championship game, the Denver Nuggets registered victories over Cincinnati Gymnasium, University of Montana, University of Idaho, Southern Branch, and in the semifinals one of the most interesting teams in the tournament, Golden State Creamery. The Oakland team's roster included Bill Wheatley, an Olympian in 1936; Melvin Miller, a former star for the Wichita Henrys; and Jim Pollard, a seventeen-year-old Oakland Technical High School graduate, who was playing in his first AAU tournament and was at the beginning of a Hall of Fame basketball career. Phillips, Denver's opponent, reached the finals with easy wins over Edentide Club of Louisville, Kentucky, and United Service Car of St. Louis, but had tougher contests against Twentieth Century Fox and S. L. Savidge of Seattle.[60]

Prior to the championship game, the Denver press joined forces in promoting this duel between the two "titans" of basketball. The *Denver Post* saw the game as "another enactment of the bitterest rivalry in basketball."[61] In a game that matched expectations, Phillips won its first national AAU championship, 39–36, before seven thousand mostly partisan spectators. Denver papers praised the play of both teams and tournament officials rewarded them with nine of the ten All-American slots.[62]

Ironically the tournament's very success opened it up to mild criticism. J. Lyman Bingham, assistant president of the national AAU, wished that City Auditorium had a greater seating capacity. "If we had Madison Square Garden we could fill it for the quarter-finals, semi-finals, and finals." As Bingham scrutinized the "bottom line," he added that he hoped "Denver fans appreciate the attractions they are getting at half the cost they would pay in many other cities."[63] Bingham, however, failed to understand that the AAU tournament benefited from the regional traditions that had evolved over the years, beginning with the Kansas City tournament, and meant little in New York City.

For the 1940–41 season the Denver Legion added Jack Harvey and Don Thurman, two stars from Forrest "Frosty" Cox's University of Colorado team, which won the 1940 NIT championship. After three years of service Ralph Bishop, one of the team's steadiest players, decided not to play. There was no Missouri Valley League so the team's schedule was limited to exhibition games with Phillips and various all-star teams. By March of 1941, the Legion had played only sixteen games, winning thirteen of them.[64]

The focal point of the 1941 national tournament was Angelo "Hank" Luisetti, perhaps the most famous basketball player of the late 1930s. Generally regarded as the player who perfected the one-handed shot, Luisetti was a three-time All-American at Stanford University between 1936 and 1939 and the first college player to score fifty points in a game. Like most great players Luisetti was much more than a scorer. At six feet three inches he was a skilled playmaker and an outstanding defender.[65] Because he had appeared in a movie, the AAU had suspended Luisetti in 1940, so 1941 was his first national tournament. Luisetti came to Denver with San Francisco's Olympic Club, which had won the AAU national championship in 1915 and consistently sent strong teams to Kansas City and Denver. The Olympic Club won the right to a free ticket to Denver by winning the very competitive Pacific Athletic Association's tournament for Northern California. San Francisco was a hotbed of basketball from the 1930s through the 1950s, and Luisetti, a graduate of Galileo High School, was the city's most celebrated player. His presence had a dramatic impact on fan enthusiasm. One San Francisco columnist wrote: "He is responsible for club basketball crowds which jumped from 300 to 3,000 persons like magic when he had returned to the court."[66]

The biggest surprise of the tournament's early rounds came on Wednesday night when lightly regarded James K. Wilson of Dallas, Texas, a team of collegians from Southern Methodist University, stunned Denver, 31–30.[67] As second-guessers analyzed the Legion's fate, there was a consensus that the Legion had played an inadequate season schedule and were not ready to compete against first-rate opponents. The dismal tournament performance and concern about future support left the future of Denver basketball in doubt. Chet Nelson remarked that Denver basketball had been "our biggest sports institution, valuable and wholesome."[68]

Contrary to received wisdom, Denver's early departure did not dampen attendance or profits. Gross profits increased by more than $3,000 to a record high of $26,752. The same was true for net profits as both the national and local AAU walked away from the tournament with record shares.[69] Thirty-five thousand fans attended the week-long tournament, which exceeded the 1939 record year by five thousand fans.[70]

Part of the tournament's appeal was the play of Hank Luisetti, who scored 17, 28, and 22 points in his first three games and impressed everybody with his passing skills and jumping ability. Chet Nelson reported that Denver's fans "seemed to be playing with him" and when he left the court "they beat applause back and forth against the arena walls."[71] Luisetti was mystified by the interest in him and was reported to say: "I don't get it. I came here just as a basketball player and I found people staring at me and making comments— well, it's kind of amusing."[77] Although limited to 11 points in the semifinals, Luisetti's teammate, Ralph "Toddy" Giannini, a Santa Clara star, tallied a game high 16 to eliminate the Athens Athletic Club of Oakland. On the other side of the bracket Twentieth Century Fox stunned Phillips, 27–24. Hollywood's starting five— Les O'Gara, Ed McGrath, Frank Lubin, Carl Knowles, and Art Mollner—played the entire game for the winners.[73]

For the first time in AAU history two California teams faced each other in the championship game. Before a packed auditorium Twentieth Century Fox, led by Frank Lubin's 20 points, overwhelmed the Olympic Club, 47–34. Los Angeles was rather blasé about Fox's triumph. Paul Zimmerman of the *Los Angeles Times* argued that basketball had not yet caught fire in Southern California. Corporations were not supportive of amateur basketball, and the "colleges never thought it essential to spend much for the cage game because football was much more profitable."[74] Tournament officials chose five

Californians to the first team All-America—Lubin and his team-mate Carl Knowles (they both graduated from UCLA in 1931), Hank Luisetti and Ralph "Toddy" Giannini from the Olympic Club, and Chet Carlisle, the star of Oakland's Athens Club.[75]

J. Lyman Bingham, assistant to the president of the Amateur Athletic Union, was overjoyed with the tournament, which he thought "the greatest ever staged by the AAU." Besides the record breaking gate, Bingham stressed that California's success built "confidence in the minds of teams throughout the country that they have a chance to win the national." Bingham relieved any fears that Denver would lose its tournament and the American Legion announced it would sponsor a Denver team in 1942.[76]

In the summer of 1941 the challenge of rebuilding the Legion team took a nosedive when Dick Wells retired and Tee Connelley moved on to Oakland's Golden State Creamery. By the end of July, Chet Nelson reported that the team still needed three jobs. The players wanted jobs with "normal starting salaries and jobs with promotion advantages." Nelson thought the team's future was in jeopardy and made the familiar arguments for retaining it in Denver. He hoped that "businessmen [would] listen to Legion enthusiasts and Mayor Stapleton to clear away employment difficulties."[77]

The Denver Legion managed to sustain the basketball operation but made no glittering additions to the team. The most intriguing was Jack Gray, who was a product of Denver's amateur basketball leagues and had played in the national tournament with the Denver Red Shield Boys Club in 1941. More than fifty years later Gray recalled that Denver East's Clarence Whipple cut him twice during high school tryouts. Not discouraged, he worked out his schedule so that he could hustle over to the YMCA, where the Legion practiced. Since the AAU limited teams to nine players, a tenth was needed for scrimmages and Gray made himself available. In 1941 Gray not only had the skills to play AAU ball, but he already had a job with Public Service, so finding employment for him was not a problem.[78]

The biggest game of the pre-tournament schedule matched the Legion against the University of Colorado. For several years the Big Seven had prohibited conference teams from playing AAU clubs.

In the late 1930s and early 1940s Forrest "Frosty" Cox built several outstanding teams in Boulder, and the Denver sports community thought a CU-Legion match-up a natural. The Buffs had three All–Big Seven players—Pete McCloud, George Hamburg, and Bob Doll. With all the proceeds going to the Mile o' Dimes infantile paralysis fund, 6,500 fans poured into City Auditorium and raised four thousand dollars for this charity. In a hard-fought game the Legion prevailed 38–32 and handed CU its first loss of the season. The game was a vehicle for embellishing the reputation of Ace Gruenig, who scored a game high 23 points, which prompted the *Denver Post*'s Ray McGovern to write, "There may never be another Gruenig."[79]

Despite the unsettled wartime conditions, forty-seven teams from twenty states entered the national tournament in March. While Chet Nelson did not consider Denver a "soft touch," he wrote, "It is with a touch of sadness that I recognize the rocky road ahead for Denver's American Legion ball club." Reflecting popular opinion, Nelson added, "[W]e know they're not quite the team so proudly hailed on the eve of previous tournaments."[80] Recognizing his team's limitations, Jack McCracken called Ev Shelton at the University of Wyoming for help and recruited All–Big Seven guard Bill Strannigan for the tournament. A native of Rock Springs, Wyoming, Strannigan was one of the state's most gifted athletes, all-state in multiple sports and the holder of Wyoming's pole vault record. In 1938–39 Strannigan played on Colorado's conference basketball championship team, but returned to Wyoming after his father's death so that he could assist his mother. In 1940–41 Wyoming won the conference title and lost to Arkansas in the NCAA regional at Kansas City. In the 1941–42 season Wyoming was even stronger, but a couple of early conference losses left Wyoming in the runner-up spot to Colorado. Because of Big Seven rules Wyoming could not play in the AAU tournament, but individuals were free to hook up with interested teams. Three days before the tournament, Strannigan practiced with the Legion for the first time.[81]

Each tournament seemed to bring forward a new twist, a new story, and a new star. In 1942 the Salesian Boys Club of San Francisco's predominantly Italian American North Beach and their star,

Fred Scolari, were the early talk of the town. Chet Nelson described Scolari as "a carbon copy of Hank Luisetti" and "as loose as a feather bed and as full of fakes as a con man."[82]

Scolari was born in 1922 and attended San Francisco's Galileo High School, the same school where Hank Luisetti perfected his one-hand shot. Unlike Luisetti, he never played on Galileo's varsity but made an All City team composed of smaller and lighter players than those on the varsity. After leading the University of San Francisco (usf) freshman team in scoring, Scolari left the university when he received little playing time as a sophomore on the varsity. He got a job with Bank of America and played on its aau team, which oddly enough was coached by Wally Cameron, who recruited him to usf before being replaced. Scolari, however, credited Angelo Fusco, the director of the Salesian Boys Club, for advancing his basketball career. Fusco regularly opened the church gym and turned on the lights for Scolari so that he could work on his game. In 1942 Fusco raised the money and organized the trip to Denver.[83] In his first game Scolari scored 34 points as the Salesians walloped a team from Green Mountain, Iowa.[84] In the second round Denver ended the club's hope for advancement, when Bob Marsh held Scolari to 6 points and Gruenig scored 27 points against the shorter opponents.[85] Fifty-five years later Scolari remembered Marsh and the game well. He recalled: "They had a fellow named Bob Marsh; boy did he jam it on me. He didn't play offense. He guarded me whenever they had the ball." Scolari continued to play aau ball until 1946, when the Washington Capitals drafted him. He played professionally with Washington, Baltimore, Fort Wayne, and Boston before retiring in 1955.[86]

While the Salesian boys pleased Denver's Italian American fans, Chicago's Division Street ymca Clippers surprised a 1941 quarterfinalist, Morris Dickson of Shreveport, Louisiana, to the delight of Denver's Polish Americans. Most of their team had played at Wells High School and their high scorer, Ed Bagdanski, was a regular at De Paul. Joe Myers, who did the radio play-by-play, cried "frame-up", according to Chet Nelson, when asked to handle such "tongue-twisters as Zmudski, Padraza, Rybicki, Bagdanski, Kardzionsk, and

Stargyk."[87] The Clippers had won the National "Y" championship in 1941 and the Central AAU tournament in 1942, so they were no fluke. When the Chicagoans were short of money to make a trip to Denver, they thought of financing their trip by giving blood at ten dollars per head. When a benefit game produced enough money, the Clippers announced that they would then donate blood at Cook County Hospital upon their return to Chicago.[88]

Behind Bill Strannigan's 15 points, Denver marched into the quarterfinals as it clobbered Bradford Clothiers of Portland.[89] The following night, a standing-room-only crowd witnessed the quarterfinals and shook City Auditorium with cheers as Denver trounced the Los Angeles Cliftons. In other games Twentieth Century Fox breezed by the San Francisco Athletic Club as Frank Lubin scored 23 points. Phillips crushed the "Y" Clippers and Golden State Creamery blasted Seattle's Alpine Dairy.[90] In the semifinals Jack McCracken, the "Old Man," guided Denver to a well executed 38–31 triumph over Twentieth Century Fox, the defending champions. An injured finger had limited McCracken's play but, against Hollywood, Chet Nelson wrote that Jack was "his old time self as he flipped in his wrist-action long shots, alternately spread and tightened the defense and directed virtually every maneuver of his men." Nelson believed that "the Denver Star" was on the verge of bowing out and he was out to make this "one last fling in the big time a memorable one." Thus his story line was about a great warrior "who gathered all the strength and savvy in his ancient basketball frame and exposed it in one of the grandest of his many displays."[91] In the other semifinal game Hank Luisetti, though hampered by a knee injury, scored 13 points and led Phillips to a convincing victory over Golden State Creamery. Phillips had recruited the Stanford star after his outstanding performance in the 1941 tournament. For the fourth time in six years the tournament had produced a Denver-Bartlesville final and expectations of a great championship game. The Legion was the underdog as Phillips carried a 49-5 record into the game.

For its fans the championship game had a storybook ending as Denver blew open a tight game in the second half and romped to a 45–32 victory. A jubilant Chet Nelson wrote: "The team that was supposed to be old, too dull from lack of competition and lacking in necessary reserve strength smacked the experts right between the eyes."[92] There were plenty of heroes to go around. Ace Gruenig's stature soared to new heights as his 20 points earned game high honors and made him the tournament's scoring champion and its Most Valuable Player. Leonard Cahn called Gruenig's performance "the masterpiece of an amazing ten-year career." Bob Marsh, named second team All-American, held Luisetti to 4 points as he continued to set the standard for defensive excellence. Joining Gruenig on the first team All-America were Bill Strannigan, who sparkled for the entire tournament, and Jack McCracken, who in Denver's eyes was "the greatest ever." Finally, former University of Colorado star Jack Harvey won a place on the second All-America team.[93] McCracken played only five players until Harvey fouled out with only a few minutes left in the game. Frank Haraway called the players "the greatest athletic heroes in Denver's history," and reported that "the thunderous ovation" tendered Strannigan, Gruenig, and McCracken as they received their All-American awards "brought a lump to one's throat."[94]

With this championship Leonard Cahn thought that the "golden era" had come to an end for Denver basketball. He believed the exigencies of World War II would certainly affect the quality of tournament play. Moreover, he expected that Denver's team would decline in stature. Strannigan had already joined the Navy and Jack McCracken allegedly had retired. Like all Denver basketball fans, Cahn could not see Gruenig playing without McCracken. They were, Cahn thought, "the Damon and Pythias of basketball."[95] For the same reasons Chet Nelson wondered whether the time had come to write "the obituary of Denver's entry in big-time basketball."[96] As it turned out McCracken and Gruenig continued to play basketball for six more years and to maintain their grip on Denver's affections. After having won three championships in six years no Denver team would ever again win an AAU national basketball championship. While McCracken and Gruenig had worked their magic, the next six years belonged to the Phillips 66ers.

In late August of 1942, C. L. "Poss" Parsons, who had helped to bring the tournament to Denver in 1935, died of a heart attack at fifty. Generally regarded as one of the most influential sportswriters of the Rocky Mountain Region, Parsons had used his position as sports editor of the *Denver Post* to promote the AAU basketball tournament. After seven years Denver viewed itself as the natural home of the AAU tourney, and certainly Parsons deserved his fair share of the credit for the "Dribble Derby's" success.[97]

FIVE

Phillips 66 and AAU Basketball

By the end of the 1940s, Phillips 66 justly deserved its nickname as the New York Yankees of basketball. Just as the Bronx Bombers dominated the American League, Phillips 66 was the model of excellence in AAU basketball. Between 1940 and 1950 the 66ers won eight national crowns, which included a record streak of six consecutive titles between 1943 and 1948. The driving force behind the team was Kenneth Stanley "Boots" Adams, a legend in the history of the American oil industry. In 1920 a financially strapped Adams dropped out of Kansas University and took a $125-a-month job with Phillips as a shipping clerk. Blessed with enormous energy, Adams quickly impressed his supervisors and seventeen years later Frank Phillips, the company's founder, made him the president of the company. Adams was a successful Kansas high-school athlete and played on the first basketball team ever sponsored by Phillips in 1920–21. In 1922 and 1923 Adams played with Phillips at the AAU tournament in Kansas City, but the 66ers lost both times in the first round. In the 1920s Phillips 66 was essentially a town team that played other teams sponsored by local businesses in Bartlesville, Oklahoma.[1]

One of the ironies of this early period of Phillips's basketball history was that Paul Endacott, captain of the 1923 Kansas University team and the Helms Foundation player of the year, chose Phillips because the company did not emphasize basketball. Endacott recalled that he wanted a job where he could apply his engineering skills and specifically rejected offers from firms interested in exploiting his basketball talents. While Endacott played a few games for Phillips, they were not memorable to him and paled in comparison to his patents and other contributions to the company.[2]

In 1929–30 Phillips made its first serious effort to compete at the national level in AAU basketball. Phillips hired Louis G. Wilke, who had coached two Oklahoma high school teams and Phillips University, to serve as the coach. In two seasons Phillips compiled a 98-8 record but failed to advance beyond the second round in the national AAU tournament held in Kansas City. Wilke's teams had a number of notable AAU players, including Tom Pickell, Gerald Spohn, John "Tex" Gibbons, and Floyd Burk.[3] In the 1930 tournament the 66ers picked up Bruce Drake, captain of the 1930 Oklahoma University team and subsequently its coach between 1939 and 1955. After the 1931 tournament, the Depression forced Phillips to drop basketball until the 1936–37 season, when climbing profits justified a return to basketball competition.

Phillips, like other American corporations, saw its team as part of an employee relations and advertising program. What made Phillips unique was Boots Adams's passion for his basketball team and his desire to win at the national level. To launch this new phase of 66er basketball, Adams hired Harold Schmidt to coach the team. Schmidt had played under Forrest "Phog" Allen at Kansas University in the mid 1920s and had coached teams at Hays Teachers College and the AAU. In his first year Schmidt gathered together a collection of AAU stars of the 1930s. From the McPherson Oilers, a team that disbanded after winning the 1936 AAU tournament and supplying half of the players on the first United States Olympic basketball team, Phillips plucked "College" Joe Fortenberry, a six-foot-eight center, and Jack Ragland, a six-foot-two guard. Schmidt then picked up Omar "Bud" Browning and Jay Wallenstorm, AAU Americans in 1935 and 1936, from Kansas City. The 66ers completed its list of stars by hiring Chuck Hyatt, perennial AAU All-American, and Tom Pickell, a six-foot-six center who played on two AAU championship teams while gaining All-American honors. Adams and Schmidt then used their Kansas connection to recruit Ray Ebling, a two-time Kansas All-American who set the Big Six scoring record in 1936. George Willis,

Dave Perkins, and Raymond Stephenson, all with backgrounds in Oklahoma College basketball completed the roster.[4] Leonard Cahn, a Denver sports writer, dubbed the 66ers a "dream team," and in its first year, Philips won 42 of 48 games and battled to the national AAU finals only to lose to the Denver Safeways, 43–38.[5]

After a third-place finish in the 1938 tournament, Phillips rebuilt its team when it dipped into the colleges to snag four prominent collegians. Phillips hired University of Kansas's Fred Pralle, a two-time Helms Foundation All-American. Phog Allen described Pralle as "one of the greatest guards that I have coached." Pralle stood about six feet three inches, weighed 185 pounds, and, Allen wrote, "had one of the greatest shooting eyes from long distance and the best coordination of any man I have seen, not excluding Hank Luisetti." Blessed with strength and quickness, Pralle drove around slower defenders and played tough defense. After completing his 1937–38 season with Kansas University, Pralle led the Kansas City Healeys to the 1938 national AAU championship and earned most valuable player honors. Phillips added another six-foot-three forward, Don Lockard, from the University of Arkansas. The Southwest Conference scoring champion in 1937 and all-conference in 1936 through 1938, Lockard gave Phillips another explosive player. While Phillips usually limited their recruiting to Oklahoma and adjacent states, they made an exception for Don Shields, a six-foot-four forward who co-captained Temple University in 1938, a team that the Helms Foundation selected as the best college team of the year. Shields was a three-time All–Eastern Conference selection and the most valuable player in the 1936 Olympic tournament. Finally, Phillips added Fred Troutwine, a six-foot-nine center who had won all conference honors for four years at Warrensburg Teachers College in Missouri.[6] During the course of the 1938–39 season, Adams replaced Coach Schmidt with Chuck Hyatt, who directed Phillips to a second-place finish in the 1939 tournament as the 66ers fell to Denver 25–22.

After the 1939 tournament, Phillips added two key players— Grady Lewis, a six-foot-seven-inch guard, and Bill Martin, a six-foot-one-inch guard. Lewis grew up in Mangum, Oklahoma, where he played on a high school team which compiled an astounding 74-2 record. Rankin Williams, the basketball coach at Southwestern State Teachers College in Weatherford, Oklahoma, successfully recruited Lewis by promising him that the Bulldogs would play in the national AAU tournament in Denver. After two years at Southwestern, Meyer Greenberg, the owner of Parks Clothiers in Oklahoma City, made Lewis an offer he could not refuse—one hundred dollars a month to work as a shipping clerk at his store while playing on Greenberg's AAU team and having an opportunity to complete his degree at the University of Oklahoma. At the end of the 1939 season Greenberg dropped his basketball program, and Phillips offered Lewis a job for $125 a month and a chance to continue his career. Bill Martin, who starred at the University of Oklahoma also played with Parks Clothiers, was a fierce competitor who had a deadly two-handed set shot, and gave Phillips another offensive weapon.[7]

In 1940, the 66ers captured their first AAU championship when they edged the Denver Nuggets in a hard-fought game by a score of 39–36. The two rivals had met twice before in the championship game, but the third proved a charm for the 66ers. The writers recognized the team's balance as they placed Lockard, Fortenberry, and Lewis on the first-team All-American squad and Martin on the second team.[8]

One of the interesting public relations benefits of winning the 1940 national AAU championship was that it earned Phillips an invitation to play the Ohrbach Athletic Association of New York at Madison Square Garden on November 25, 1940. Ohrbach had won the Metropolitan AAU championship in 1940 and represented New York City in Denver only to lose in the round of the final sixteen. For this exhibition Ohrbach asked Barney Sedran, a legend at City College of New York and celebrated professional, to coach the team. To highlight the occasion Frank Phillips and Boots Adams held a stag dinner at the Ambassador Hotel that served 298 guests. The menu included wild game flown in from the Frank Phillips Ranch in the Osage Hills near Bartlesville. Nine thousand fans watched the 66ers edge Ohrbach 37–35 in double-overtime, as Bill Martin scored 15 points to lead the 66ers.[9]

Competitive success strengthened the company's case for its investment in basketball. Boots Adams and other executives utilized a variety of arguments to defend the expense of a nationally competitive basketball team. Phillips argued that the team attracted outstanding applicants who would evolve into productive employees. One piece of promotional literature entitled "Team Work—For More Sales" stated that "Mr. Adams, and other Phillips executives, believe that the combination of sound mind and body is the stuff that good employees are made of."[10] Phillips quite frequently published statistics that substantiated this claim by citing the high percentage of players who remained with the company. If a player left the company, Phillips stressed that he did so to take a job with another corporation. Always sensitive to criticism that basketball players were getting a free ride, Adams emphasized that "their first job is learning the business of their department in the oil industry."[11] Phillips consistently argued that its players competed for "the pleasure of the game and the interest shown in the team by their fellow employees."[12]

Phillips's promotional literature also contended that the basketball team was good for business. In 1939 Phillips maintained that ninety million Americans either watched or played basketball, all of whom were potential customers. Moreover hundreds of sports columnists, Phillips claimed, gave the company free advertising by writing numerous columns on the team and its players. As part of its scheduling strategy, the 66ers played games in each of its sales territories. It urged employees to encourage their friends and customers "to go see the best players in the game." If they did, employees would be helping themselves, because "it takes gasoline, oil, anti-freeze and all the other products you sell to make these trips."[13] Finally Phillips pointed to the team's success as an illustration of the corporate ethic. Frank Phillips asserted that, "the teamwork of the Phillips squad symbolizes the close coordination of the entire Phillips organization."[14] After Phillips won its first AAU championship, in 1940, Chuck Hyatt stressed that the team's success rested on teamwork. He explained that no bench player sulked or hoped "to make the winning goal and have his name plastered all over the sports page as a hero." The champions, he concluded, were "a team of fighting all-stars and not a team of all-stars fighting."[15] This was an example of the corporate spirit Phillips hoped to promote.

For the players, playing basketball for Phillips enhanced their prospects for security and mobility in the company. High-ranking officers of the company traveled with the team, which meant that players had more contact with influential executives. Ed Comer, who played in the 1930s, reported that in a short time he "knew all the officers" of the company.[16] Bill Martin, a star on four championship teams in the 1940s, started his career with Phillips as a $125-per-month general clerk in the treasury department and rose through the ranks until he was named chief executive officer in 1973, a position he held for seven years. Years later Martin recalled, "I received opportunities I might not have otherwise received, because of basketball."[17]

While basketball players had more exposure to management, they did not report any animosity directed at them from their co-workers. Bill Klein, who played for three years between 1949 and 1952, said that he "never met anybody . . . that wasn't supportive of the program, they were all proud of the program."[18] Dave Perkins, who played in the late 1930s, recalled: "They all kind of looked up to us."[19] The players were heroes to the employees, and the team put Bartlesville on the map. Since Bartlesville was fairly isolated, basketball, according to Al Bunge, who played from 1960 to 1962, "was one of the main attractions of entertainment here."[20]

Phillips Petroleum Company worked diligently to develop a family atmosphere among its employees. Frank Phillips, the founder of the company, and his wife Jane were referred to as Uncle Frank and Aunt Jane.[21] Active sororities and men's clubs were organized in their names. A recreation program, which became very extensive, began by sponsoring bowling leagues and softball teams.[22] The basketball program, therefore, was just one part of an extensive effort to develop good employer-employee relations.

In Bartlesville home basketball games were social occasions. In the 1930s and 1940s the 66ers played their games in a high school gym, which accommodated approximately 1,800 fans, some of whom sat on folding chairs placed on the stage at one end of the court. Tickets for home games were sold out before the season. The demand was so great that tickets were rationed so that a season ticket entitled a fan to half the games. Tickets were color-coded and games were designated for those people holding red or yellow tickets. Visiting teams usually played two-game stands so ticket holders could see the visiting team at least once. Bob Kurland, the 66ers' Hall of Fame center, recalled that the games attracted the "high society of the community," the newly wealthy people, enriched by oil booms who were usually "fortified" by spirits imbibed at pregame cocktail parties. Women dressed in mink coats sometimes used them as cushions for the hard chairs or tucked them under the chairs. Uncle Frank and Aunt Jane frequently attended games, as did Boots Adams and the Phillips hierarchy. Whether well-heeled or not, Kurland remembered the fans as "genuine students of the game" who acknowledged great performances by players of the home or visiting teams. Given this atmosphere and the quality of 66er teams, visiting teams rarely won on the Bartlesville court. In thirty-two seasons, between 1936 and 1968, the 66ers' home record was an astounding 302-36.[23]

When the 66ers played on the road, they were a tremendous draw. For most of their history, the 66ers played a mix of league and exhibition games. Exhibition road games accounted for over half of the games played in any season, and most were played in trade territories in which wholesalers worked diligently to promote 66er games. With the exception of the war years, the 66ers usually played forty to sixty games. While Phillips normally dominated the leagues it played in, the ultimate test of any season was the AAU tournament in Denver. When the 66ers returned home victorious, they could count on a large welcoming party and a celebration, which included dancing, speech making, and free food and beer.

For some recruits Bartlesville's location, in rural Oklahoma, north of Tulsa, was a drawback. Oklahoma, Kansas, and Arkansas, however, had strong college programs, so there were plenty of players from small towns who were comfortable in Bartlesville. Some players such as Burdie Haldorson, the 66ers' career scoring leader, who played in the late 1950s, managed working arrangements outside Bartlesville in the off-season.[24]

While Boots Adams offered many good business reasons for sponsoring a basketball team, he obviously loved basketball, relished Phillips's basketball success, and enjoyed the recognition it gave him and his company. He attended games, knew the players, and often looked out for their and the team's interests. When, for example, Ev Shelton (who coached Dow Chemical in Midland, Michigan, for the 1943–44 season when Wyoming canceled its season because of the war), tried to recruit Willie Rothman, a former Wyoming star, Adams placed a call directly to Dow's president discouraging the effort.[25]

Adams was also actively involved in recruiting, and players routinely made a stop at his office on their visits to Bartlesville. Adams had a good relationship with Phog Allen who sent a number of his stars to Bartlesville. If Allen disliked the AAU, he did not let that interfere with what he considered the best interests of his players. One of Allen's favorite players was Paul Endacott, a vice president at Phillips in the late 1930s, who also helped to lubricate the Kansas-Phillips connection. When Phillips recruited Fred Pralle, Allen invited Tom Pickell, Jim Babcock, Ray Ebling, and Howard Engleman, a Kansas All-American who played with Phillips between 1941 and 1943, to his home, where they discussed the advantages of playing for the 66ers.[26]

While Phillips had a powerhouse basketball team, the AAU championship eluded the 66ers in 1941, as Twentieth Century Fox edged them in the semifinals. Since winning the AAU championship was the measure of a successful season, Phillips did not hesitate to make personnel changes in order to win the national tournament. In the off-season, Phillips recruited Hank Luisetti, the most valuable player of the 1941 tournament; John Freiberger, a six-foot-eight center from the University of Arkansas; and Jimmy Scat McNatt, a high scoring All-American at the University of Oklahoma. Chet Nelson wrote that when McNatt "starts to run you think he might get away and hide most any moment."[27] While Luisetti played only one year for Phillips, McNatt played five and the press named him an AAU All-American four times.

Unfortunately Luisetti suffered a knee injury at Madison Square

Garden in November when Phillips played in a tournament cele-
brating the fiftieth anniversary of basketball. The tournament was
the opening salvo in a campaign to raise three hundred thousand
dollars to build a museum and basketball hall of fame to honor James
Naismith. Louis Effrat of the *New York Times* reported that 16,123
attended the opening night games, "a crowd which was attributable
to the lure of Angelo (Hank) Luisetti," who was "still one of the loos-
est, most imaginative and most colorful performers in basketball."[28]
After beating the Ohrbach Athletic Association, the 66ers lost the
championship game to Twentieth Century Fox, led by Frank Lubin
and Les O'Gara. Luisetti had to leave the game in the first half with a
torn knee cartilage.[29] Although the 66ers fought their way to the title
game of the 1942 AAU tournament, with a subpar Luisetti, Phillips
lost to an inspired Denver team.

As a result of World War II, Phillips only played thirteen games
before the 1943 national tournament, far below the fifty games it
averaged between 1936 and 1942. Denver did not have a team during the regular season, and, until two weeks before the tournament,
it looked like it would not have an entry in the national tournament.
At the last moment Louis G. "Lou" Wilke, who had become an
important AAU official while serving as division manager in Denver's
Phillips office, stepped in and persuaded the American Legion to
sponsor a team built around Ace Gruenig, Bob Doll, a former star at
the University of Colorado, and several current CU players sidelined
by the war when the University dropped collegiate competition.
One of these players was Walt Clay, a freshman at CU and multisport
star at Longmont High School whom some compared to Byron
"Whizzer" White, CU football All-American and future Supreme
Court Justice.[30] The strangest look of the tournament was the presence of Jack McCracken in a Phillips 66 uniform as a playing coach.
For several years Jack McCracken had worked for Lou Wilke in
Denver as a salesman. When it became apparent that Denver would
not have a team, Phillips transferred McCracken to Bartlesville.

McCracken's most explosive new weapon was Gordon "Shorty"
Carpenter, an All–Southwest Conference forward from the University of Arkansas, who joined Phillips for the tournament and

would become one of its greatest stars. After watching him play, Chet Nelson described Carpenter as a "power type of ball player, who comes down with rebounds and fits into the 66ers' defense."[31] Another newcomer was Willie Rothman, a star on Ev Shelton's first three Wyoming teams. Rothman had played in his first tournament in 1938 when he and Curt Gowdy, who would become a famous sports announcer, came down to Denver with the Cheyenne Eagles. Phillips recruited Rothman after seeing him play for White Palace Café of Ft. Collins, Colorado, in the 1942 tournament. Because of the war Phillips called on Fred Pralle and Bud Browning to rejoin the team after Grady Lewis and Bill Martin reported for military duty.

Thirty-eight teams entered the tournament, the lowest number of entries in a decade. The presence of college and service teams, however, compensated for the decline of traditional AAU teams, and these new teams brought with them a number of talented basketball players. The pre-tourney favorite was Ev Shelton's University of Wyoming Cowboys, champions of the Mountain Five Conference, who hoped to conclude their season by winning the AAU and NCAA championships. Shelton's team featured two All-Americans, center Milo Komenich and a spectacular guard, Ken Sailors, who was one of the first players to shoot a one-handed jump shot. Although only five feet ten inches, Sailors, according to Chet Nelson, leapt "with a mighty spring," and his dribbling and passing matched his "dazzling one-handed shot."[32] Denver University entered a team of former Colorado high school stars that included Leonard "Chink" Alterman, a former all-city player at North High School; Bob Wilson, a star on Manual High School's 1939 State championship team; Loren Hays from Sterling; and Bill Weimar from Colorado Springs.[33]

The Alameda Coast Guard Sea Lions featured Jim Pollard, one of the most talented players in the nation. In 1942, as a sophomore, the former Oakland Tech High School star, was the NCAA tournament's high scorer as he led Stanford University to the championship game against Dartmouth. Although too ill to play in the title game, Pollard watched his teammates defeat Dartmouth for the 1942 NCAA crown. After his sophomore year, Pollard enlisted in the Coast Guard and

led the Alameda Sea Lions to a 26-2 record and the 1943 title in
the Pacific Association tournament played annually at San Francisco's Kezar Pavilion. At six feet five and one-half inches, Pollard
was the prototype of the modern basketball player. In addition to his
shooting, dribbling, and passing skills, he had tremendous leaping
ability, which would earn him his nickname as basketball's Kangaroo
Kid, when he played for the Minneapolis Lakers between 1947 and
1958.[34]

Another Pacific Coast Conference star, Gale Bishop, from Washington State, traveled to Denver with the Fort Lewis Reception
Center from Fort Lewis, Washington. Bishop led the Pacific Coast's
Northern Division in scoring and was an All-Conference selection
in 1943. In his first game on the Denver Auditorium floor, Bishop
scored 50 points to establish a new tournament record. A day later
Milwaukee's Allen-Bradley Corporation eliminated Fort Lewis, limiting Bishop to 16 points.[35]

In one of the biggest upsets of the tournament, the Naval Air
Station from Norman, Oklahoma, dumped Jim Pollard's Sea Lions,
38 to 35, in overtime. In defeat, Pollard scored 24 points and dazzled
the crowd with his all-around play. Six of Pollard's points came in
the last minute of play including a long one-handed shot as the gun
sounded to end regulation play.[36] Chet Nelson described Pollard's
performance as "the greatest exhibition of clutch shooting you ever
saw in your life."[37] The praise for Pollard was matched by the rave
reviews of the twenty-nine-piece Coast Guard band that accompa-
nied the basketball team to Denver. Jack Carberry wrote that "the
Coast Guard band gave out with the grandest jam, jive, and boogie
woogie session to be heard in this man's town since bands started
playing music."[38]

The basketball remained hot as well, as Denver University, the
American Legion, Wyoming, and Phillips fought their way to the
semifinals. Of all the quarterfinal games, the 66ers' narrow 34–33
win over Eckers of Salt Lake City was the most exciting. Scat McNatt
and Shorty Carpenter sparked a second-half rally against a group of
past and present collegian stars from Utah, led by Merlin Ahlquist,
Floyd Morris, and Deb Smith.[39]

The Legion went into the semifinal game against Wyoming as a definite underdog, since the Cowboys had only one loss during the season and had recorded two exhibition victories over Phillips 66. Before a standing-room-only crowd Wyoming took a 21–14 half-time lead. At the break, according to Carberry, Mayor Ben Stapleton and Denver University Chancellor Caleb Gates visited the team and "[t]he Legion boys seemed to reach up and catch a handful of greased lightening and stick it in a bottle."[40] Whether it was the pep talk or something else, the Legion held Wyoming to 12 points in the second half and won 41 to 33. For Carberry the significance of the game was more than just its outcome. The game was a showcase for reinforcing the heroic qualities of Ace Gruenig, who "delivered the clutch shots when the going was toughest" and established himself as the "greatest center in the history of the game." Carberry also had high praise for Walt Clay, who left the game to a standing ovation for battling Sailors and providing the "leadership of unconquerable youth."[41] In the other semifinal game, Phillips, led by Carpenter and McNatt, fought off a pesky Denver University team, 40–36. Leonard Alterman topped all scorers with 16 points, which helped him to win recognition on the AAU All-American second team.

Phillips simply had too much firepower and dominated the Legion 57–40 in the championship game. Jimmy "Scat" McNatt's 11 points paced a balanced Phillips attack that helped to land him a spot on the AAU All-America first team. Ace Gruenig scored 21 points and for the second year was the tournament's most valuable player. Shorty Carpenter, Bob Doll, and Kenny Sailors, who was named the most promising young player, rounded out the first team All-America. Given the exigencies of the war Chet Nelson concluded that the 1943 conclave exceeded all expectations as the teams played before more fans than any previous tournament. If the overall quality of play did not quite match past tournaments, Nelson thought this was overshadowed by "400 men playing for the fun of it all and doing a handsome job."[42] Phillips honored their 66ers at a bash at the Bartlesville Civic Center as Boots Adams reportedly strolled around the festive gathering "like a proud papa."[43]

There was an interesting footnote to the tournament. Ev Shelton's Wyoming Cowboys, following their third-place finish in Denver (the Cowboys beat Denver University), won the NCAA tournament by defeating Georgetown. To top off their season the Cowboys defeated the NIT champion, St. John's, in a game played at Madison Square Garden to benefit the Red Cross. Jack Carberry thought Wyoming's success was proof that the Denver national AAU tournament "was really the nation's World Series."[44]

When Phillips traveled to Denver in 1944 to defend its crown, Bud Browning was the 66ers' player-coach. Browning played his high school basketball in Enid, Oklahoma, and won All–Big Six honors at the University of Oklahoma for three consecutive years between 1932 and 1935. In 1935 he also won AAU All-America honors as he helped the Southern Kansas Stage Liners win the 1935 AAU championship. In 1936 Browning once again earned a spot on the AAU All-America team while playing for the Santa Fe Trailways. In 1937 and 1938 Browning played with Phillips and then retired from play until 1943. The only newcomer was guard Marty Nash, captain of the University of Missouri's 1941 team, who would earn AAU All-America honors in 1946 and 1947.

Meanwhile, Jack McCracken had returned to Denver as the player-coach of the Denver team, now called the Ambrose-Legion Jellymakers. J. L. Ambrose, the president of Ambrose and Company, which manufactured wine, jam, and jelly, collaborated with the American Legion to give the Denver club more stability. In addition to the familiar core of McCracken, Gruenig, Marsh, and Unger, the Ambrose Legion team added George Hamburg, a starter on the University of Colorado's 1942 NCAA semifinalist team, and the irrepressible Chuck Hyatt, who was stationed in Denver during the war. Ambrose-Legion prepared for the tournament by capturing the Denver Victory League, which included teams from four military bases.

Forty-seven teams from seventeen states gathered for the tenth tournament in Denver, a surprisingly large field in wartime America. Many of the players received furloughs so they could compete in the tournament, and the armed services, which used sports to build morale, sent twelve teams. Service men were given free tickets for games between Sunday and Wednesday. As new residents poured into Denver to take war-related jobs, the tournament attracted large crowds seeking entertainment.

On Sunday, March 19, the tournament began as seven thousand fans, a record number for an opening day, drifted in and out of City Auditorium. Ten games were scheduled, with the first game scheduled for 11:00 a.m. and the last at 10:30 p.m. Many diehard fans, as Jack Carberry noted, stayed the entire day, living "on peanuts and pop" supplemented by a hot dog or "a ham sandwich and a paper cup half filled with coffee."[45] At the opening ceremony, at 7:30 on Monday evening, Mayor Ben Stapleton performed his welcoming speech in eighty-three words, which, according to Jack Carberry, was "appreciated by every fan."[46]

Phillips, strengthened by the addition of veteran center John Freiberger—furloughed for the tournament—entered the "dribble derby" as the favorite. Early in the play, the Broncos of Fort Warren, Wyoming, captured the interest of writers and fans. The focal point of attention was Ermer Robinson, a clever ball handler and dangerous scorer, who would enjoy a long career with the Harlem Globetrotters after the war.

Although a few African Americans had played in the tournament in the first decade, none had stood out. Robinson was Fort Warren's leading scorer in an easy win over the University of Denver and a narrow victory over Denver's Buckley Field. When the Broncos trailed Twentieth Century Fox by four points with only thirty-five seconds left in the quarterfinal, Robinson hit two long one-handed push shots to tie the game. Jules Rivlin, the player-coach, then hit a forty-five-foot shot from midcourt with only seconds remaining to give the Broncos the victory.[47] Along with Robinson and Rivlin, the Broncos had nineteen-year-old Kenny Jastrow, and this three-some, according to Chet Nelson, ran the fast break as well as any in tournament history.[48]

The other surprise of the tournament was the Army All-Stars from Camp Carson and Peterson Field in Colorado Springs. This collection of college players was led by Ed Beisser, an All-American from Creighton University. In their second game the All-Stars earned a 49–45 upset victory over Ev Shelton's Dow Chemical Company team. Milo Komenich, Shelton's star center on the 1943 Wyoming NCAA championship team, scored 20 points in defeat.[49]

In the quarterfinals, Phillips edged Fircrest Dairy, a team from Bellingham, Washington, which included high-scoring Gale Bishop.[50] The 66ers then breezed by the Army All-Stars in the semifinals.[51] In the other semifinal game Denver's Ambrose Legion dispatched Fort Warren's Broncos by 17 points as Gruenig led all scorers with 23 points and Bob Marsh prevented Ermer Robinson from scoring a basket.[52] Phillips met Denver in the title game as the two teams renewed their fierce rivalry.

In a hard-fought duel Phillips held Gruenig to 11 points and dumped Denver, 50–43.[53] Jack Carberry reported that during the game Denver's fans blistered the 66ers with "boos, cat calls, the Bronx Cheers and the razzberries that all but ripped the roof of the auditorium."[54] While Carberry viewed the jeers as a way of cheering for Denver, they most likely reflected a sense that their aging Denver heroes faced an uphill battle against a talented and efficient rival dedicated to building a dynasty. When Boots Adams accepted the team trophy, he thanked the "Denver fans—loyal supporters of a great team." He promised "that we'll be back next year with an even better ball club, battling with all that we have to win another championship from you."[55]

The tournament drew a record forty thousand fans who paid more than thirty-four thousand dollars, or five thousand dollars more than at any previous tournament. Chet Nelson reported that "W. N. Greim, national basketball chairman and tournament maestro, announced the figures yesterday to remove all doubt that Denver, for its population, has earned the name of basketball metropolis of the nation.[56] The record bottom line was especially sweet since the Rocky Mountain AAU Association negotiated a more favorable division of the net receipts with the national AAU. The former body would receive 40 percent of the proceeds instead of the 25 percent it received in the past. Most of the money, Jack Carberry explained, was earmarked for youth sports. Carberry applauded AAU officials who worked for no compensation to make the tournament a success. He contrasted them to promoters like Ned Irish of Madison Square Garden, who "operate upon the theory that basketball is like a business and as such should turn in a profit to those who do the promotional work." Denver, Carberry continued, "believes basketball is a sport" and was rewarded by seeing its children "carry out the tradition of sportsmanship established here."[57]

When Carberry congratulated Denver on a successful tournament and its resistance to professionalism, he was responding to storm warnings that basketball could not neglect. In late March, Bob Considine, a syndicated columnist, wrote an article predicting that college basketball faced a scandal that would match baseball's infamous Black Sox Scandal. While he focused on Madison Square Garden, Considine wrote that "basketball gambling is not confined to New York. It is just as tidal in Denver, a cage-crazy town, Chicago, Philadelphia, throughout the basketball-minded middle west, and out on the coast."[58] While Denver's tournament was never to suffer the embarrassment experienced by college basketball in 1951, six years later Considine's prophetic article served notice that amateur basketball was vulnerable to external manipulation.

Another scare for Denver fans following the 1944 tourney emerged when Denver's papers reported that Ace Gruenig had lost his amateur status. Allegedly Gruenig had inserted an ad in the *Denver Post* urging fans to talk basketball at a tavern he operated in suburban Denver. Under AAU rules athletes lost their amateur status when they attempted to capitalize on their athletic fame. After an investigation, however, the AAU concluded that Gruenig had not authorized the advertisement and thus Gruenig retained his amateur status.[59] At the end of the year Jack Carberry announced that Ace had been selected as one of the twenty-one athletes or athletic administrators who were judged as the greatest in their sport or who had made significant contributions in sports administration. The sports award dinner, held in Los Angeles and hosted by the celebrated sports writer Grantland Rice, was broadcast nationally. Carberry, who was extremely fond of Gruenig, wrote that "this is the first time his greatness has been recognized nationally outside of the AAU organization itself."[60]

In March of 1945 World War II was drawing to a close as Denver held its eleventh tournament. Bud Browning's 66ers still featured Gordon "Shorty" Carpenter, Jimmy "Scat" McNatt, Marty Nash, Paul Lindemann, a six-foot-seven center from Washington State, plus Willie Rothman and Vernon Yates. The 66ers hoped to join the Wichita Henrys as the only team to win three consecutive AAU titles. A major concern was the loss of Fred Pralle, who suffered a career-ending knee injury before the tournament.

There were no major upsets in the early rounds as the four top seeds advanced to the semifinals. Fort Lewis's Gale Bishop, back for his third straight tournament, scored 62 points against a team from Hoxie, Kansas, and 32 points against the Peoria Caterpillars on successive nights. He was the center of attention until the Cessna Bobcats, led by veterans Dick Smith and Frank Grove, eliminated his team in the quarterfinals.[61] In one semifinal Phillips outlasted Twentieth Century Fox, even though Frank Lubin scored 19 points in his fifteenth AAU tournament appearance. Denver's Jellymakers romped past the Cessna Bobcats by 15 points to win the other semifinal contest.[62] This set the stage for a real barnburner as Phillips met Denver for the fourth consecutive year in the title game.

In 1945 the Ambrose Jellymakers had won the Denver's Victory League for the second consecutive year and brought a 14-5 record to the tournament. As usual Jack McCracken directed the team as player-coach and Ace Gruenig anchored the offense. Denver added Les McKeel—an All–Southern Conference selection from Murray State who led the Victory League in scoring—and Bob Hendren, a six-foot-eight forward, from the Second Air Force Base in Colorado Springs. Phillips had beaten Ambrose three times during the season, including a four-point victory before twenty thousand at the *Chicago Herald-American* All-Star Charity classic at Chicago Stadium at the beginning of the season.

Almost 7,500 squeezed into City Auditorium and watched the underdog Jellymakers jump out to a 14-point lead in the second half, which they gradually squandered. With fifty seconds left, Frank Schwarzer, a Phillips reserve, hit a lay up to give the 66ers the last points of the game and a 47–46 victory. Scat McNatt and Ace Gruenig led their respective teams in scoring with 15 points each.[63] Of all the defeats suffered by a McCracken–Gruenig-led team, this was the most heartbreaking.

A stunned Jack Carberry reported that he had been hospitalized for the game and had been frantically turning a radio dial from Bill Stern to Mark Schreiber "to understand what happened." He then turned a portion of his column over to Frank Haraway for an explanation of the defeat. While Haraway considered fate, officiating, and the failure to play a delay game as contributing to defeat, he graciously praised the "guts" and speed of the 66ers. He consoled Denver fans by reminding them that Ambrose had surprised their "most ardent followers" and that the game "was a great window for the matchless careers of McCracken and Gruenig, even in defeat."[64]

Once again the tournament set new attendance records and generated several hundred dollars more than the record-setting week of 1944. Leonard Cahn reported that standing-room-only crowds watched the games during the tournament's last three nights.[65] To ardent followers of AAU basketball, it may have seemed almost miraculous that the same team had succeeded in winning the championship three years in a row in a tournament that always attracted such a rich array of talented competitors. No one could have foreseen that during the next three years what had seemed incomprehensible would become mundane—a foregone conclusion. After three straight championships the 66ers' dynasty had only just begun.

SIX

The Rich Get Richer

In August of 1945 the United States dropped atomic bombs on Hiroshima and Nagasaki to end the Second World War. After four years of fighting, the United States stood as the world's military and economic colossus. With only 7 percent of the world's population, the United States controlled 42 percent of its wealth. Americans who reached adulthood in 1945 faced the future with confidence, intent on getting their share of the American Dream. Very quickly television, a baby boom, and economic abundance transformed American life. The only shadow on the horizon was cast by the Soviet Union, which pursued a foreign policy at odds with American interests. The resulting Cold War between the two major powers and the arms race it engendered produced an underlying current of anxiety that shaped American domestic and international politics until the Soviet Union collapsed in 1989.[1]

The population explosion, the mobility of Americans, the expansion of leisure time, the communications revolution, the Cold War, and the African American civil rights movement would all have a profound impact on American sports. In the world of basketball, the professional game had not yet dented the following of the AAU teams west of the Mississippi River. By 1945 a new brand of basketball was being played, and its potential to excite sports fans was evident. Chuck Hyatt, whose career had spanned the 1930s and 1940s as a player and coach, observed that "The trend for the past ten years has been away from ball control and defensive play, and toward shooting and fast breaks." Because of the elimination of the center jump after every basket, Hyatt believed there had been "eight minutes added to the actual playing time of a game." The combination of more game time and less structured offenses, Hyatt estimated, increased the number of shots in a game "from roughly forty-five to seventy-five." Yet it was the style of play that especially caught Hyatt's eye. He observed that "Every kind of shot imaginable has been taken and made . . . except a shot between the legs."[2] This new brand of basketball required greater athleticism, and players excited sports fans with their virtuosity.

The 1945–46 season had a new look with the creation of the American Basketball League (ABL). The companies and organizations that sponsored the teams had several goals. One was to give amateur basketball players an opportunity to continue their careers. Another was "to foster better employee relations within the sponsoring organizations." Finally, by attracting college graduates, the companies believed they would attract valuable employees. The league stressed that it was a nonprofit organization and that at least 10 percent of the profits from each league game would go to a charity in the host team's city. The teams were the Denver Ambrose Jellymakers, Salt Lake City Simplot-Deserets, Sacramento Senators, Twentieth Century Fox, J. P. Carroll Shamrocks of Los Angeles, San Diego Dons, Phillips 66ers, Kansas City M&O Smokies, and Dardie and Company of San Francisco. The league schedule called for a home-and-away series and a postseason tournament. The new league significantly raised the level of competition for teams like Phillips and Denver's Ambrose Jellymakers.[3] Although it was not openly stated, the new league had the look of a trial balloon floated by entrepreneurs eager to see if there was a market for basketball to evolve into a money-making enterprise.

Phillips won the ABL with a 12-4 mark and then captured the postseason tournament championship. The league included a collection of former college and AAU stars, including Fred Scolari, Jim Pollard, Arnie Ferrin, Paul Napolitano, Frank Lubin, Bill Strannigan, Ace Gruenig, Alex Hannum, and Jack McCracken. By the time of the AAU tournament, Bud Browning clearly had a very talented team. Bill

Martin and Grady Lewis were back from the war along with new-comers Jesse "Cab" Renick, from Oklahoma A&M, and Ed Beisser, a Creighton University All-American who earned similar honors in the 1944 AAU tournament with the Army All-Stars. They joined an experienced core of Scat McNatt, Marty Nash, Paul Lindemann, Shorty Carpenter, and Willie Rothman.

While the backgrounds of many of the basketball players of the 1930s and 1940s were unusual, few matched Jesse "Cab" Renick's. Born in rural Oklahoma in 1917, Renick's mother was one-half Chickasaw and one-half Choctaw. When no college offered Renick a scholarship upon graduating from high school in 1934, he found employment with the Civilian Conservation Corps, a New Deal jobs program. After two years with the CCC, Murray State School of Agriculture recruited Renick, whose six-foot-two-inch frame carried 186 pounds. After starring at this two-year school, Renick packed his suitcase and traveled to Stillwater where he asked Coach Henry Iba for a chance to try out for the team. Coach Iba agreed and Renick starred for the Aggies for two years until he graduated in 1940. After playing service ball in the Navy, where he served as a flight instructor, Renick joined Phillips and became a vital part of its most celebrated team.[4]

For the only time in its history, sixty-four teams entered the national AAU tournament. Because the tournament had always been bracketed for sixty-four teams, seeded teams had received byes in the first round. In 1946 no team had this luxury, and Bill Greim and his tournament committee had to schedule twelve Sunday games at the University of Denver gym in order to play the championship game by the following Saturday. Basketball teams from twenty-six states and the Hawaiian Islands converged on Denver and brought with them some of the best talent in the nation. The Pacific Fleet Marine Force featured Joe Fulks, who would lead the Basketball Association of America in scoring in 1947, and Andy Phillip, the most celebrated of the University of Illinois' "Whiz Kids." Alex Groza, the future University of Kentucky All-American, led Fort Hood. Weeks before the opening tipoff the last three nights of the tournament had been sold out.

It was not until the round of sixteen that a seeded team was knocked out of the tournament. Phillips Lee Tires, a team of ex-Phillips players, led by Joe Fortenberry's 13 points, beat the Fleet Marines in overtime. This victory set up a quarterfinal game between Lee Tires and Denver's Ambrose Jellymakers, and, for the last time, College Joe Fortenberry and Ace Gruenig faced off in an AAU tournament. In that game Denver's Ambrose Jellymakers made all of its twenty free-throw opportunities and outlasted Lee Tires 56–49. Gruenig and George Hamburg each scored 15 points for Denver and Fortenberry scored 14 points for Lee Tires. In another quarterfinal game Milo Komenich and Dale Sears each scored 12 points and Twentieth Century Fox beat the Salt Lake Simplot-Deserets. Arnie Ferrin, a star on the University of Utah's 1944 NCAA championship team and future Minneapolis Laker, led his team with 7 points. Tee Connelley's San Diego Dons, with Jim Pollard and Kenny Sailors, beat a strong American Basketball League team, the San Francisco Dardis. Phillips 66 was the fourth team to survive the quarterfinals as it trounced the Miramar Pendleton Marines, despite 19 points by Bobby Wanzer, a future National Basketball Association (NBA) star with the Rochester Royals. Jimmy "Scat" McNatt had 20 points for Phillips to neutralize Wanzer.[5]

In the semifinals the San Diego Dons, behind Jim Pollard's 20 points, topped Denver in an exciting game before 7,500 fans. Gruenig scored 18 points against Pollard in "one of the most brilliant duels in tournament history," according to Leonard Cahn.[6] After watching Pollard play, Chet Nelson wrote: "Pollard is listed as a center but he is really a center, guard, and forward bundled into one sleek, greyhound type of frame."[7] The Dons won without Kenny Sailors, who joined the team with the understanding that he would leave the tournament to play in the East-West College All-Star game. Tom McCarty, a five-foot-nine guard, pumped in 13 points to compensate for the loss of Sailors. In the other semifinal game the speed and depth of Phillips 66 were too much for Twentieth Century Fox, and the 66ers triumphed 43–36.[8]

In its bid for a record-setting fourth consecutive championship, the powerful 66ers faced a team that was the product of a San Diego

basketball junkie, Dr. William T. Rice. An all-city center at Manual
Arts High School in Los Angeles who played junior college ball,
Rice graduated from the University of Southern California Dental
School and moved to San Diego, where he practiced dentistry and
organized basketball teams. Rice's Dons lost in the first round of the
1945 national AAU tournament, but after that season he recruited
Tee Connelley, a former Denver Nugget to serve as player-coach.
Mom-and-Pop teams such as the Dons supplied much of the charm
of the AAU tournament.[9] In the championship game Phillips simply
wore down the Dons in the second half and captured its fourth
straight title. The 66ers' Shorty Carpenter led all scorers with 15
points and Phillips limited Pollard to 10 points. After the Jellymakers
stopped Twentieth Century Fox in the consolation game, Ace Gruenig accepted the third-place trophy for Denver and announced his
retirement, while his fans gave him a "tumultuous ovation."[10] Two
days after the tournament Jack Carberry reported that Gruenig had
played against the advice of his doctor, who told Ace that he had a
serious heart problem.[11]

     At the gate the tournament was a resounding success. Almost
forty-five thousand people spent a record thirty-nine thousand dollars to see the games, and many others were turned away. Leonard
Cahn, however, argued that the tournament field was too large and
needed to be reduced in size in order to avoid 9:00 a.m. and 10:30
p.m. games and that a new facility was needed to accommodate eager
fans.[12] Jack Carberry called the "facility situation in our town . . . a
sorry mess." When he pressed Mayor Ben Stapleton about plans for
a new arena, Carberry ran into a smoke screen.[13] The Denver sports
editor feared that Denver risked losing the tournament by failing to
build a new arena. In addition to inadequate seating, which meant
that thousands of angry fans were turned away from the tournament,
Carberry explained that the costs of promoting a sporting event at
City Auditorium made it difficult to earn a profit. While it only cost
two hundred dollars to rent "the town barn," promoters faced other
costs. The loudspeaker system did not work, which meant that a
loudspeaker had to be leased at a cost of $22.50 to $50 a night. In
order to keep the required number of doors open for safety rea-

sons, the promoter had to hire twenty-six Pinkertons at six dollars each a game. Finally the promoters had to pay the custodian's bill. Carberry estimated that it cost as much as a thousand dollars to stage a basketball game. What really stuck in Carberry's craw was that a promoter had to provide "twenty-four of the best seats in the house for Hizzoner Ben Stapleton, members of the city council, and others in the official family." Since City Auditorium belonged to the "tax-paying citizens," Carberry boiled over at the "twenty-four passes which cheated Joe Doakes." The only exception to Carberry's hostility to free riders were "small boys, whose inherent right, we think, gives them the privilege of sneaking in if they can."[14]

The domination of the tournament by Phillips 66 also presented a dilemma. During the 1946 tournament Boots Adams floated a trial balloon in which he stated that perhaps the Phillips-Denver rivalry had become so vicious that it would be best if it "was allowed to subside."[15] Chet Nelson believed that while Phillips had been "stung pretty badly by Denver crowds," the crowd's jeers merely expressed "the normal attitude toward a champion." He argued that "the gambling element" was "largely responsible for the disgraceful demonstration against teams meeting the local favorites."[16] Just as in the case of the New York Yankees, Phillips was the Goliath that nobody loved, especially in its rival's home town. After winning the championship, Boots Adams announced that Phillips would remain in the ABL, which was another issue. His statement emphasized "We are interested in promoting amateur basketball and definitely will have no part of professional basketball."[17] His statement suggested that there was sympathy for converting the ABL into a professional league, which he opposed.

Jack Carberry also addressed the issue of the Phillips dynasty. He argued that for the Ambrose Jellymakers and Twentieth Century Fox, "Patience is the answer. Patience and smart building for the future." Both teams, Carberry continued, were going to have to forget about their former stars, the Ace Gruenigs, Jack McCrackens, Frank Lubins, and Art Mollners. While he admired all these players, Carberry thought they were "through as big-time competitors simply because their legs won't carry them around fast enough to stay with the Pollards, the McNatts, the Carpenters . . . now dominating the hardwoods." In Denver's case, Carberry thought the Jellymakers needed another Ace Gruenig, "for great teams in this big league of basketball are built around the big guy in the middle."[18]

While Denver tried to figure out how to compete with Phillips, Boots Adams did not stand still. In the spring of 1946 Bob Kurland, a three-time All-America center from Oklahoma A&M, decided to join Phillips and forego a professional basketball career. Although a native of St. Louis, Missouri, where he played at Jennings High School, the gangly Kurland chose to accept a scholarship from Henry Iba at Oklahoma A&M in the fall of 1942. Iba gave Kurland a room in the gym and, as he promised, worked with him to improve his skills and coordination. Iba also added an inch and a half to Kurland's six-foot-ten-and-one-half-inch frame so that A&M could claim to have a seven footer. Because of the war Kurland was immediately eligible for varsity competition but played sparingly as a freshman. In his sophomore year Kurland scored 444 points and won his first All-America recognition. In his junior and senior years, Kurland led the Aggies to back-to-back NCAA championships, the first college team to enjoy that distinction. In both years he was selected the tournament MVP and in his senior year led the nation in scoring. Kurland was also responsible for the college rule prohibiting goaltending in 1944. Although choosing amateur over professional basketball was not an easy decision for Kurland, the unavailability of guaranteed contracts and his notoriety in Oklahoma persuaded him to reject fifteen thousand dollars to play in the fledgling professional league for two hundred dollars a month with Phillips, a chance to play on the 1948 Olympic team, and an opportunity to advance in the company.[19]

Another important addition to the Phillips roster in 1946 was R. C. Pitts, a football and basketball star at the University of Arkansas, who had joined Phillips briefly in 1942 before entering the Army Air Forces. At six feet four inches and 185 pounds, the hard-nosed Pitts gave Phillips one of the toughest defensive players in the amateur game. Kurland and Pitts joined veterans Marty Nash, Ed Beisser, Shorty Carpenter, and Cab Renick. Jim "Scat" McNatt, Willie Rothman, and Grady Lewis did not return for the 1947 season. McNatt and Lewis had been AAU All-Americans, while Rothman had been a solid performer as a starter or reserve. McNatt worked with Phillips until he retired, Rothman was a successful businessman in Greeley, Colorado, and Lewis played and coached professionally for four years before enjoying a successful career with the Converse Shoe Company.

In Kurland's first season the ABL increased from nine to eleven teams. While the San Francisco Dardis dropped out, new entries were the Pocatello Simplots, Oakland Bittners, and Continental Airlines, which played its home games in Oklahoma City. Of the three new teams, the Oakland Bittners were the most formidable. They were the brainchild of Lou Bittner, who had opened a tax consulting and insurance business in Oakland in 1941. A Notre Dame graduate, Bittner was a sports enthusiast who would sponsor a variety of amateur teams and athletes in the Oakland area during his lifetime.[20] In the summer of 1946, the team's credibility shot up when Bittner announced that he had persuaded Jim Pollard to join the Bittners. After the war, Pollard was the most sought-after basketball player on the West Coast. Following the 1946 AAU tournament Les Harrison of the Rochester Royals, Eddie Gottlieb of the Philadelphia Warriors, and others attempted to persuade Pollard to play professionally. Instead the Oakland native chose to return to his hometown and play with the Bittners.[21]

Bittner surrounded Pollard with some of the best talent in the Bay Area. Paul Napolitano was a sharp-shooting forward from Oakland's McClymonds High School who had played with the University of San Francisco and the Alameda Sea Lions. Don Burness was a product of San Francisco's Lowell High School and a very smooth guard who started on Stanford's 1942 NCAA championship team with Pollard. Oakland Tech's Bob Alameida, the other guard, played for Clarence "Nibs" Price at Cal-Berkeley. Don Williams, who played at Oakland High and co-captained Stanford's 1940 and 1941 teams, was an excellent shooter. Warren "Slats" Taulbee, another Oakland product, was a rugged center who played at Marin Junior College and in the service. Bill Calhoun, a Lowell High School star with some AAU experience, did not play college basketball but was a good guard and a defensive specialist, playing in the National Basketball League and National Basketball Association after the 1946–47 season. Bill Wheatley, a member of the 1936 Olympic team, coached the Bittners.[22]

The dominance of Phillips and the emergence of Oakland forced Denver to rebuild. The team, now called the Nuggets, started out very slowly. While Jack McCracken was back for his last year as player-coach, the team played uninspired basketball, and as Frank Haraway wrote, "to say that the Nuggets missed the 'Acer' is putting it mildly."[23] One new look for the Nuggets was that Jay Ambrose appointed Hal Davis to serve as the team's general manager. A native of Cheyenne, Wyoming, Davis had a background in the newspaper business and sports information.[24] After suffering several defeats, Davis began to make some personnel changes. He brought Gruenig out of retirement and then released two popular veterans, Bob Marsh and Art Unger, but kept Ralph Bishop, a star before the war. Davis also decided that Coach McCracken would have to give more playing time to younger players and emphasize the fast break rather than the deliberate post play utilized by past Denver teams. Denver's goal, Davis stressed, was to mold "a team as perfect and as powerful in this type of play as was the Denver predecessor in another year of the then-prevailing trend." Davis assured Denver's fans that McCracken and Gruenig were "playing their roles letter-perfect" as they gave the team stability during this period of transition.[25]

In January of 1947 Davis secured the missing ingredient in his rebuilding program when the Nuggets added Notre Dame All-American, Vince Boryla. Colorado Senator Edwin C. "Big Ed" Johnson, a rabid sports fan, arranged to have Boryla, who was in the service, transferred from Fort Sheridan in Illinois to Lowry Air Force Base, where he would be available to play for the Nuggets.[26] Along with Boryla, Denver's other newcomers were Jim Darden, a quick guard from Wyoming; Ralph Langer, an All-America forward from Creighton University; and Ed Sholine, a center from Colorado A&M.

While Denver searched for a winning formula, Phillips and Oakland dominated the league. They met for the first time in league play on February 10 in Oakland Auditorium. The 66ers were undefeated in league play and had a forty-three game-winning streak, while the Bittners had only lost one league game. Almost eight thousand fans squeezed into Oakland Auditorium, and a couple thousand reportedly were milling about outside without a ticket. According to Don Williams, who scored 13 points that night for the Bittners, it was the biggest game in Oakland's basketball history.[27] Trailing by ten to begin the second half, Phillips crept to within one point, 35–34, when Coach Bud Browning placed Bob Kurland under the basket to intercept Bittner shots as they approached the basket, a tactic that was still legal in the AAU. The Bittners managed to maneuver around Kurland's goal-tending and held on to win 59–47. Pollard bagged 19 points, while the Bittners limited Kurland to 5 points.[28]

Neither team lost another game until their much-awaited rematch in Bartlesville on February 26. As anticipated, "Every inch of space was taken up," a reporter wrote, "with spectators sitting in the aisles and chairs placed in two unused entrances." By this game the Bittners had added Ron Livingstone, a six-foot-seven center, who gave Oakland much-needed size and depth. With the ABL championship at issue, Phillips won a hard-fought game 36–32. Kurland led the 66ers with 18, and R. C. Pitts limited Pollard to 4 points.[29]

After the completion of the league season the ABL held its postseason tournament in Denver. This provided the setting for the highlight of Denver's season. In the semifinals the Nuggets upset the powerful 66ers 48–44 before a capacity crowd of very partisan and hysterical fans, who gave Vince Boryla—who led all scorers with 19 points—a deafening ovation when he left the floor. Jack Carberry and Chet Nelson also praised the play of Denver's veterans, Ralph Bishop and Ace Gruenig, and the leadership of player-coach Jack McCracken. The notion that Gruenig had heart problems, Carberry argued, had been dispelled by his performance. The 66ers, wrote Carberry, "beat the old man something awful," but "they didn't stop him—his great heart carried on."[30] Chet Nelson thought the victory "diminished any threats of drowsiness among Denver basketball fans. It was one of the best things that ever happened."[31] In the championship game the Oakland Bittners, led by Jim Pollard, pulled away from the Nuggets before an overflow crowd for a 52–38 victory.[32]

On March 16, a week after the ABL tournament, fifty-four teams congregated in Denver for the fortieth AAU tournament. The 1947 tournament followed form until Wednesday when three American Basketball League teams fell to underdogs. Coors Brewery of Golden, which had won the *Rocky Mountain News* YMCA tournament and an automatic bid to the AAU national, clobbered the San Diego Tecate Dons. Les Major and Bobby Wilson each scored 20 points, leading the attack for the Brewers over Tee Connelley's Californians. In the second upset of the day, Alpine Dairy surprised Continental Air Lines as big Bob Graf scored 15 points. Finally Southern Methodist University, playing as the Dallas Majors, stunned the Idaho Simplots.[33]

In the quarterfinals Phillips crushed Coors Brewery, and the Oakland Bittners overwhelmed Dallas. The Denver Nuggets entered the semifinal round by subduing Twentieth Century Fox in the last tournament meeting between Ace Gruenig and Frank Lubin. Vince Boryla topped all scorers with 14 points. The last semifinalist was the Alpine Dairy, which squeaked by another ABL team, the Los Angeles Carroll Shamrocks.[34]

In the semifinals the Bittners polished off the Nuggets, 55–40, before a disappointed standing-room-only crowd. Jim Pollard scored 27 points, played superb defense, and generally dominated the game for Oakland. The 66ers overwhelmed Alpine Dairy to set up an Oakland-Phillips championship game.[35] In the title game R. C. Pitts once again shackled Pollard, who was held to 5 points, and the 66ers prevailed over the Bittners 62–41. Ron Livingstone kept the Bittners in the game with 25 points. Bob Kurland scored 17 points for the champs and was joined on the All-America team by teammates Gordon "Shorty" Carpenter, Cab Renick, and Marty Nash. Two first-year Denver Nuggets, Vince Boryla and Jim Darden, won spots on the All-America team along with four Oakland Bittners, Paul Napolitano, Ron Livingstone, Bill Calhoun, and Jim Pollard.[36]

After winning its fifth straight title, sportswriters hailed Phillips as basketball's New York Yankees. Each year Phillips produced a better basketball team, and many, including Leonard Cahn, wondered when the 66ers would be dethroned.[37] Jack Carberry was the most troubled by the shape of the tournament and its domination by Phillips. Carberry took his annual swipe at Denver's inadequate facility and the limited seating that denied so many fans an opportunity to see the tournament. In response to angry letters claiming that the restrooms had not been cleaned in thirteen years of tournament play, the cynical Carberry replied that the Champa Street facilities "have not been cleaned since the afternoon before William Jennings Bryan was nominated for the presidency in July 1908." Warming to his topic, Carberry felt sure that "the Curtis Street rooms were cleaned sometime late in the administration of the late great Robert W. Speer."[38]

When he turned to the tournament, one of Carberry's major complaints was that the AAU allowed competition in which there was a wide disparity in the ability levels of the teams. After Phillips embarrassed Old Dominion of Roanoke, 103–27, Carberry stressed that the outcome was meaningless since the two teams were so unevenly matched. For the Denver columnist any definition of sport had to include meaningful competition. The tournament had evolved into an event that matched "the kids who play for fun" against "men who make the game of basketball their business."[39] Bob Brachman of the *San Francisco Examiner* suggested that one solution to this problem was to have the "strictly amateur kids" play a qualifying tournament with the top eight teams winning the right to enter a sixteen-team tournament with the ABL teams.[40] While Brachman's proposal was never fully implemented, as he outlined it, in a few years the AAU adopted a policy of inviting fewer teams to reduce the mismatches in the early rounds of the tourney.

Carberry also took the national AAU to task for demanding 60 percent of the profits from the tournament. Since the Rocky Mountain Association promoted and managed the tournament, he thought it should have the 60 percent share. Carberry continued to praise the Rocky Mountain AAU's generosity in using tournament money

to support youth sports. Carberry's concerns over the facility, amateurism, and revenue sharing were legitimate subjects of debate. The
success of the Phillips 66ers, however, did not sit well with Carberry
and caused him to make some far-fetched claims. The worst was that
the bracketing favored Phillips and that the 66ers, had been given
"a very sweet ride" by the tournament committee.[41] Carberry was
also outraged by AAU rules that permitted goaltending. His attack
on this "abomination" was clearly prompted by the ease with which
Bob Kurland batted balls away from the basket.[42]

Several days after the 1947 tournament the AAU and NCAA met
in New York City and the AAU agreed to ban goaltending, to allow
players five rather than four fouls during a game, and to move to
two twenty-minute halves rather than four ten-minute quarters.[43]
Despite all of his concerns, Carberry did not want Denver to lose the
tournament and knew that Boots Adams coveted the tournament for
Oklahoma City. He thought the tournament's chances of success in
Oklahoma City were slim. While Oklahomans would follow their
college teams, Carberry argued that they did not have the same
enthusiasm for AAU basketball. Nonetheless Phillips enthusiasts were
"swimming in oil money" and were "definitely set upon making the
bid to the AAU to take the tourney away from Denver."[44]

Phillips was not impressed with Carberry's fusillade. On the goaltending issue Bud Browning observed: "We don't make the rules—
we just play under them and we'll continue to do so until they're
changed." A writer for the *Bartlesville Examiner* asserted that Carberry "would be the first to squawk if an AAU tourney rolled around
and there was no Phillips entry. An AAU tourney without the Sixty-
Sixers would be almost like a wedding without the bride." If Carberry
wanted to do something useful, the writer continued, "he might devote some of his space . . . to crusading for a more adequate home
for the tournament." The auditorium was too small, its sight lines
were "atrocious," and there were no dressing facilities, so the players
had to dress in their hotels and take a bus to the game. Finally, the
writer concluded, the floor was sagging, which gave it "the appearance of a slight ocean ground swell."[45] To be fair to Carberry, he had
been blasting the city on the facility issue. While he had previously

counseled patience in the face of Phillips's dominance, by 1947 he had become too frustrated to exercise much objectivity.

In May of 1947 Denver amateur basketball took a jolt when Jay Ambrose dropped his sponsorship of Nugget basketball. New sponsorship was provided by two Denver businessmen, Emil P. Berkowitz and Harry Roberts, who retained Hal Davis as general manager.[46] Chet Nelson observed that the new arrangement did not offer the promise of stability. He believed that Denver needed "a big corporation tie-up, with solid secure jobs for athletes, before our AAU basketball setup can take on a long range perspective and offer any assurance of permanency.[47] The departure of Jay Ambrose from amateur basketball also had ramifications for the American Basketball League. According to Jack Carberry, Ambrose had organized the ABL and invested some of his money in maintaining the league. While Ambrose incurred only a small loss in operating the Nuggets in 1946–47, Kansas City, Hollywood, Los Angeles, Salt Lake, and San Diego, Jack Carberry reported, were swimming in red ink.[48]

When the 1947–48 ABL season opened, only five teams were in the league: Phillips, Denver, Oakland, Sacramento, and Phoenix, which had not played in the previous two campaigns and did not finish the 1947–48 schedule. While the ABL teams fought red ink, they also had to cope with raids upon their talent from professional teams. After the 1947 tournament, for example, the Oakland Bittners lost Jim Pollard, Bill Calhoun, and Paul Napolitano to the pros. Leonard Cahn was particularly pessimistic as he predicted "the era of high powered AAU teams has ended." Professional basketball, he thought, had "knocked the props out from under the 'simon pure' variety." More critical of the AAU than ever before, Cahn argued that "the framework of AAU basketball was built on a weak, hypocritical foundation." Cahn predicted that professional basketball would replace AAU ball "within a few years."[49]

Jack Carberry was in partial agreement with Cahn. He wrote: "The entire AAU basketball setup is just another word for hypocrisy. It is a phony and a sham, and it has been such over a great many years." Only a very gullible person, he continued, believed "that the great names which have filled AAU rosters, both through the season and at tournament time, have got there because the players just love the game of basketball." At the heart of the problem, he contended, was the relationship between the ABL and AAU. The major problem was "the latter's often amazing and always confusing views and actions relative to the rules of eligibility and amateurism."[50] Specifically Carberry was critical of the AAU's rule that prohibited basketball players from competing in amateur games because they had been professionals in the past, Thus, rather than jumping on the professional basketball bandwagon like Leonard Cahn, Carberry wanted to reform amateur basketball.

Carberry's criticism of AAU rules was persuasive. If a player had played professionally and was cut, why should he have been prohibited from subsequent amateur competition? Paul Napolitano, for example, played one year with the Minneapolis Lakers, which meant he would never play amateur basketball again.

But Carberry did not have much else to offer in the way of reform, because the options were limited. Only large corporations with substantial work forces like Phillips could succeed over the long haul. The ABL failed because most of the sponsors did not have the resources or the commitment to amateur basketball as played by Phillips.

When the AAU awarded Denver its fourteenth tournament, it was against this background of controversy. While Carberry expected Denver fans to support the tournament with their same enthusiasm, he thought "The general over-all caliber of ball which will be offered in the March tournament will be inferior to that presented in many AAU tournaments of the past." The domination of AAU basketball by Phillips, the decline of the ABL, and the challenge from professional basketball convinced Carberry "that AAU basketball must be revamped entirely if it is to retain the place it once held in the world of athletics."[51]

Despite the difficulties that plagued AAU basketball, one of its great attractions for gifted players in 1948 was that it offered an opportunity to compete for a place on the Olympic basketball team. Because of World War II the athletes of the world had not congregated under the Olympic flag since Berlin in 1936. In 1948, as in 1936, the Olympic basketball team would be selected by a tournament played in Madison Square Garden. Three of the eight teams invited to New York would be the top three teams in the 1948 national AAU tournament. Naturally the prospect of playing in the Olympics was a tremendous recruiting device for amateur teams and added luster to the Denver tournament.

In Denver, Hal Davis completed the rebuilding program begun in 1946–47 in an effort to make a run at the Olympics. The only returnees from the previous season on the 1947–48 Nuggets roster were Jim Darden, Vince Boryla, Jack Gray, and Ralph Bishop as the coach. New additions included Roy Lipscomb from St. Mary's of Winona, Minnesota, Ron Livingstone from the Oakland Bittners, Bob Salen and Ward Gibson from Creighton University, Ed Little from Marshall College, and Winston "Hank" Balke from Southwestern College in Winfield, Kansas. While Davis publicly acknowledged the contributions of Jack McCracken and Ace Gruenig, he wrote that it was time "to make room for other McCrackens and Gruenigs whose contributions may someday be as important."[52]

Gruenig and McCracken, despite many retirement announcements, returned to play for Murphy-Mahoney Chevrolet, a dealership run by Russ Lyons. Affectionately calling his team the Graybeards, Lyons surrounded Gruenig and McCracken with former Denver stars Bob Marsh, Bill Strannigan, Larry Varnell, and former Phillips 66er Willie Rothman. While the Nuggets played in the American Basketball League, the Graybeards played an exhibition schedule.

Early in the season Jack Carberry reported that the Nuggets had obviously failed "to catch the fancy of Denver's public" as they struggled on the court and at the gate.[53] Chet Nelson wondered whether the Nuggets had priced themselves out of the market by asking $2.80 for a ticket.[54] Lurking in the background was the perception that Denver fans simply refused to adjust to the passing of the "old order" of McCracken and Gruenig. In February, however, the Nuggets got hot and Vince Boryla jumped into second place in ABL scoring. After edging Phillips the Nuggets won two close games over the Oakland Bittners, which helped to generate fan support.[55]

In the meantime the sports press succeeded in promoting a match-up between the Nuggets and the Murphy-Mahoney Graybeards, billed as the game of the year. Before a standing-room-only crowd of 6,500, the Nuggets turned back the idols of the past 59–47. Once again Ace Gruenig demonstrated his ability to get up for a big game and led all scorers with 20 points. When he left the floor with thirty seconds remaining, Chet Nelson observed that "the big partisan crowd all but lifted the roof with applause."[56] The venerable Jack Carberry wrote that Gruenig's performance "warms the cockles of a guy's heart." Carberry never thought the Graybeards could win but he didn't want to see the Acer or Jumpin' Jack embarrassed. Now was the appropriate time, Carberry thought, for Ace Gruenig, the greatest center in the history of the game, to hang them up—to keep that memory ever green among the 6,500 who saw him Monday night "wheeling and dealing . . . as he has . . . for the thirteen years Denver has come to know and love him."[57] The Nuggets completed the ABL season with an impressive 16-8 mark to finish in second place, five games behind Phillips. Vince Boryla was the second leading scorer in the league and Jim Darden captured the fifth spot.

While Hal Davis successfully rebuilt the Nuggets, the Phillips 66ers and Oakland Bittners had not stood still. Phillips coach Bud Browning made two significant additions to his already powerful squad. One was Gerald Tucker, a two-time college All-American from the University of Oklahoma, who gave Phillips a high-scoring forward. In March of 1947 Tucker led Oklahoma to the NCAA championship game, which the Sooners dropped to Holy Cross. The other addition was Lew Beck, a clever All-American guard from Oregon State, which lost to Oklahoma in the first round of the 1947 NCAA tournament. Going into the tournament, Phillips brought with it a 60-3 mark and its third straight American Basketball League title.

Two of Phillips's losses were to the Oakland Bittners, a team that had undergone a significant rebuilding process. To run the team from the guard position, Oakland added five-foot-six-inch Morris "Mushy" Silver, who was Lew Beck's running mate on Oregon State's

1947 NCAA tournament team. As a high school senior Silver was the captain of San Francisco's George Washington High School's 1940 undefeated city championship team coached by Lloyd Leith, a prominent basketball official of the period. Voted the most popular high school player in 1940 by the students, Silver won a free trip to Denver to watch the AAU tournament. After three varsity seasons at the University of San Francisco and three years of service ball in Europe, Silver finished his college career at Oregon State. Fast and quick, Silver was a pesky defender, had great court vision, and was a creative passer. To replace Jim Pollard the Bittners recruited Don Barksdale, a native of Oakland, who led the UCLA Bruins in scoring in 1946–47, which earned him All-American basketball honors. During the 1947–48 season with the Bittners, the six-foot-six-inch, two-hundred-pound Barksdale led the ABL in scoring with a 16.7 average to finish ahead of Vince Boryla and Bob Kurland. While African Americans had played in the AAU tournament before Barksdale, none had played in the Missouri Valley League or the ABL.[58]

One of the most interesting issues raised during the ABL season was whether Barksdale would play in games scheduled in Bartlesville and Oklahoma City. At the time Oklahoma was fighting efforts to desegregate its public schools. Also no African Americans had played in an integrated athletic contest in the state's history. The Big Seven, according to Jack Carberry, deferred to Oklahoma state law, so that black athletes did not accompany their teams when they played in Oklahoma. Carberry saw Barksdale's case as the equivalent of Jackie Robinson's historic entry into major league basketball.[59] The Bittners' schedule called for two games against the 66ers in Bartlesville and two games in Oklahoma City. The two games in Bartlesville were sold out before the season and the hometown fans waited in anticipation to see Barksdale, whom Bud Browning called "the greatest Negro basketball player today."[60] Spectators with red tickets got to see the first game, while those with yellow tickets had to wait a day to see the African American star.

On the evening of January 7, before a standing-room-only crowd in the College High gym, Don Barksdale turned in a remarkable performance under extreme pressure as he led the Bittners to a 45–41 victory. The 66ers had not lost in their previous thirty-six games and had not suffered a defeat on their home floor since 1944. Sportswriters who covered the game showered Barksdale with superlatives as he scored 17 points and held Bob Kurland to one basket and three free throws. Bob Graham wrote of Barksdale: "He handles a basketball with the sure touch of a virtuoso; he fakes 'em out of position with a nod of his head; he glides over the court like a brown panther, and boy can he shoot."[61] The other star of the game for Oakland was Morris "Mushy" Silver, who scored 8 points and set up his teammates with an array of no-look passes. Laymond Crump wrote that as the shortest player on the court, Silver "looked more than a little out of place among the big boys until he got the ball in his hands. Then he was the biggest guy on the court."[62] When Bartlesville's fans cheered Barksdale, George Durham, sports editor of the *Bartlesville Enterprise*, wrote: "Never, since we moved to Bartlesville last spring, have we been so proud to be listed as citizens of the city."[63] In three subsequent games, two of them exhibitions, Phillips beat Oakland handily, but Barksdale played without incident. The teams split two games in Oakland at the end of the season.

By March all the AAU teams had geared up for the national AAU tournament in Denver. The goal of every team in 1948 was to finish in one of the top three spots in order to compete in the Olympic tournament. Denver writers immediately noticed that Murphy-Mahoney and the Nuggets were the top seeds in the lower bracket, which set up a possible semifinal match-up. Oakland and Phillips were the top seeds in the other bracket. The 1948 tournament was also the first to use City Auditorium's annex, which prompted one writer to call the tournament a "two-ring cage circus."

In the early rounds none of the top four seeds were seriously challenged except for the Oakland Bittners. In the second round, the Bittners turned back Denver University, which was led by two AAU veterans, Kenny Jastrow and Leonard Alterman.[64] Denver's Murphy-Mahoney Graybeards delighted Denver fans when they trounced the U.S. Naval Academy in the quarterfinals. After Ace Gruenig left the floor with 42 points, he received, "an ovation that had not been equaled in the history of the tournament."[65] The Murphy-Mahoney victory set up a dream game, a rematch between the Nuggets and the Graybeards. The Nuggets had not been tested until the quarterfinals, when they met a tough Twentieth Century Fox team. The Californians still had Frank Lubin and in a bid for an Olympic birth had recruited Dave Minor and John Stanich—two UCLA stars—and big Alex Hannum, from the University of Southern California. The Nuggets prevailed as Jimmy Darden scored 19 points and played a great floor game, while Vince Boryla added 17 points. Bob Kurland's 21 points paced Phillips as it topped Salt Lake City's Eckers, while Oakland defeated a college all-star team from Kokomo, Indiana, to advance to the semifinals.[66]

In a game that kept Denver fans on the edges of their seats, the Nuggets had to go into overtime before subduing the Graybeards, 60–56. In the first half the Nuggets were cold and, at one point, fell behind by 11 points as Ace Gruenig, Willie Rothman, and Bill Weimar (picked up from Denver University for the tournament) led the Graybeards to a 4-point halftime lead. In the second half the Nuggets took a 7-point lead, which the Graybeards whittled down to one point with 15 seconds left in the game, when Murphy-Mahoney's Larry Varnell stole the ball from the stalling Nuggets and Winston Balke cleanly blocked his attempted lay-up, which would have given the Graybeards the lead and perhaps the upset. With twelve seconds left in the game Boryla fouled Gruenig before he shot and Ace calmly sank the one free throw awarded to him and sent the game into overtime at 51–51. By the end of the regulation time, the Graybeards had lost Bob Marsh, Bill Strannigan, Willie Rothman, and Jack McCracken to fouls. In overtime, the Nuggets outscored the Beards, 9–5, and walked away with a hard-fought victory. Once again, Ace Gruenig played a big game in the twilight of his career as he led all scorers with 24 points. Vince Boryla led the Nuggets with 22 points.[67]

Along with the all-Denver donnybrook, Phillips and Oakland also played a tense semifinal game, which was tied eight times before the 66ers won. In the first half Kurland and Barksdale committed four fouls apiece, which altered the tempo and strategy of the game, and

Oakland led by a point at the half. After Phillips grabbed an 8-point lead in the second half, the Bittners cut it to 2 with a minute left but could not break the 66ers' delay game.[68]

The championship game marked the eighth time that Denver and Bartlesville had met for the national AAU since 1937. For thirty-two minutes the Nuggets and the 66ers battled to a standoff at 48–48. In the last eight minutes, Phillips held Denver scoreless and claimed its sixth consecutive championship, 62–48. Gerald Tucker, Bob Kurland, and Cab Renick led a balanced scoring attack for the 66ers. Vince Boryla's 14 points led Denver's scorers. In the third-place game the Oakland Bittners trounced the Graybeards and earned a berth in the Olympic tournament. Barksdale scored 21 points and Les O'Gara canned 19 for the winners. Ace Gruenig tallied 17 points for Denver but 15 were in the first half. When the Acer left the game with 6:42 left to play he received "a tumultuous ovation from the 7,000 fans." In his last AAU tournament Gruenig led all scorers with 104 points and made the AAU All-America team for his tenth time.[69] Roy Lipscomb, Jim Darden, and Vince Boryla from the Nuggets, Cab Renick, R. C. Pitts, and Bob Kurland from the 66ers, Les O'Gara, Warren "Slats" Taulbee, and Don Barksdale from Oakland filled out the All-America team.

A week after the AAU tournament Denver, Oakland, and Phillips joined four college teams and the Brooklyn YMCA in New York to determine who would represent the United States in the 1948 Olympic Games in London, England. The Olympic Basketball Committee placed the three AAU teams in the upper bracket with Brooklyn YMCA (champions of the YMCA tournament). The lower bracket paired four college teams: the University of Kentucky (1948 NCAA champion), Baylor University (NCAA runner-up), the University of Louisville (NAIB champion), and New York University (NIT runner-up). The St. Louis Billikens, the NIT champion, turned down the opportunity to play in the Olympic tournament when their athletic board decided that the academic responsibilities of the players could not justify more absences from school. The winner and second-place team in the tournament would win the right to place five players each on the Olympic team, while the tournament committee would select four at-large players from the competition.

In the opening round of play the Nuggets held off the Oakland Bittners to advance to the semifinal round. Boryla led all scorers with 21 points but sprained his knee near the game's end. In another close game Baylor edged New York University and Dolph Schayes. In the other two games, Kentucky easily defeated Louisville, and Phillips humbled the Brooklyn YMCA.[70] In the semifinals, Phillips dominated the underdog Nuggets, who played without the injured Boryla. Kurland's 21 points and Carpenter's 15 points led the 66ers. In the other semifinal game, Kentucky walloped Baylor, as Alex Groza's 33 points topped all scorers.[71] This set up a championship game between the two dominant teams of amateur basketball, Phillips and Kentucky. The Wildcats, dubbed the Fabulous Five, were coached by Adolph Rupp, the "Baron of the Bluegrass." A native of Halstead, Kansas, who had played under Phog Allen at Kansas, Rupp had turned Kentucky into a basketball power, where he coached from 1930 through 1972. Fiercely competitive, a strict disciplinarian, and imperious, Rupp, who had a vast collection of amusing anecdotes, was a master at cultivating the press and had few peers as a promoter of college basketball.[72]

In a game that needed little hype, eighteen thousand screaming fans packed Madison Square Garden and watched Phillips edge Kentucky, 53–49. Kurland led Phillips with 20 points and held Kentucky's Groza to 4. Another Kentucky All-American, Ralph Beard, kept the Wildcats in the game with 23 points.[73] The Olympic Basketball Committee selected Bob Kurland, R. C. Pitts, Lew Beck, Jesse "Cab" Renick, and Gordon "Shorty" Carpenter from Phillips, and Alex Groza, Wallace "Wah Wah" Jones, Cliff Barker, Ken Rollins, and Ralph Beard from Kentucky to play on the Olympic team. They were joined by Vince Boryla of Denver, Jackie Robinson of Baylor, Ray Lumpp of New York University, and Don Barksdale of Oakland, the first African American to play on a U.S. Olympic basketball team. In *They Cleared the Lane: The NBA's Black Pioneers*, Ron Thomas writes that Barksdale's selection involved vigorous debate. Fred Maggiora, an Oakland politician and member of the Olympic Basketball Committee, told Barksdale that some committee members opposed his selection because he was black. With Maggiora as his advocate, the opposition to Barksdale's selection relented, and the black Californian made history.[74]

For Bud Browning the outcome of the 1948 season was "a dream come true." Ever since the McPherson Globe Refiners defeated his Kansas City Santa Fe Trailways in 1936, Browning had hoped he would have another chance to represent the United States in the Olympic Games. By defeating Kentucky, Browning earned the distinction of serving as the second person to coach an American Olympic basketball team.[75] Adolph Rupp was his assistant.

The world had changed considerably since 1936, when basketball had made its first appearance as an Olympic sport. By 1948 the war had reoriented international politics and left the United States and the Soviet Union as the world's dominant powers. Since the International Olympic Committee had not yet recognized the Soviet Olympic Committee, the Soviets did not send a team to London, so that athletic competition between the two superpowers was postponed until 1952.[76]

Unlike in 1936, the 1948 U.S. Olympic basketball team carefully prepared for the competition it would face in London. The five 66ers, along with Don Barksdale and Jackie Robinson, practiced for four weeks in Bartlesville, while the five Kentucky Wildcats, joined by Vince Boryla and Ray Lumpp, trained in Lexington. While the Olympic tournament had generated thirty-five thousand dollars for the U.S. Olympic Committee (usoc), three exhibition games were scheduled between Phillips and the University of Kentucky to raise additional funds. As a promotional venture, the exhibitions were a natural, since they matched the two top amateur teams in the United States.

On June 30, 6,500 fans packed the Tulsa Pavilion and watched Phillips top Kentucky. On July 2, in Kansas City, seven thousand watched Kentucky square the series in double overtime as Don Barksdale led all scorers with 22 points. The rubber game was played in Lexington, Kentucky, on July 10, at night, on a portable floor assembled in Stoll Football Stadium. Fourteen thousand fans, the largest crowd ever to see a basketball game in Kentucky, saw Bob Kurland and Don Barksdale pace a second-half comeback to earn the 66ers a victory.[77] No African American had played on an integrated team in Kentucky before 1948, and Guy Tiller, of the *Atlanta Journal*, reported that every time Barksdale scored a basket, "the crowd gave him a thunderous ovation."[78] While Barksdale earned the crowd's cheers, his experiences in Lexington were more complicated than an easy triumph of merit over racism. Since Lexington was a segregated city, Phillips and Barksdale had to agree that the black star would stay with a black family rather than with the team at a Lexington hotel. A day before the game Barksdale received a death threat that caused him to think twice about competing. Once the game began Barksdale forgot the threat and his teammates fed him the ball, shared a water bottle with him (no separate bottle for him), and provided support he never forgot.[79] Four days later the Olympic team sailed for the United Kingdom, where they played four games in Scotland to warm up for the Olympic competition.

While the heavily favored Americans won the gold medal, they had one scare in the qualifying rounds. In its third game the United States met Argentina and with three minutes left in the game the score was knotted 55–55 before the Americans prevailed at 59–57.[80] The close contest was influenced by an Olympic rule that allowed teams to suit up only ten of their fourteen players. In this game, Coach Browning kept Bob Kurland on the sidelines, a decision the Phillips mentor clearly regretted. After this narrow victory, no team came within 25 points of the Americans, who won the gold medal game over France by 40 points. Les H. Peterson of the United Press reported that the Americans were the object of abuse the moment they took the court for their first game because of their superior height.[81] Kurland, a special target of the boobirds, shrugged off the abuse and commented: "I guess they just aren't used to tall people."[82] Foreign critics also thought the Americans were too tough and rude. More realistically, the basketball competition simply demonstrated that there was a wide gap in basketball skills between the United States and the other nations of the world.

After the 1948 Olympics, the Phillips 66ers and the University of Kentucky Wildcats returned as the standards of excellence in AAU and college basketball. In 1948–49 Kentucky returned four of its five starters and won its second straight NCAA title. Phillips, by contrast, lost Shorty Carpenter, R. C. Pitts, and Cab Renick, who replaced Bud Browning as the 66ers' coach. After its remarkable six consecutive AAU championships, Phillips still looked invincible. Coach Renick, who was the first Native American to win an Olympic gold medal since Jim Thorpe in 1912, had Bob Kurland, Lew Beck, Gerald Tucker, and Dick Reich as well as a program that was very attractive to college stars. While Phillips, with its great tradition, would always be formidable, in the 1950s AAU championships were surprisingly more elusive. The significance of the 66ers' accomplishments between 1943 and 1948 would become clearer with the passage of time.

PART 3

The National Industrial Basketball League

The economic and geopolitical context of the AAU tournament between 1936 and 1948 was the Great Depression and World War Two. In the next twelve years the United States enjoyed an economic boom and Americans had more disposable income to devote to leisure activities. During this period AAU basketball enjoyed its greatest stability and tapped deeply into the burgeoning pool of basketball talent. At the core of AAU basketball was the National Industrial Basketball League (NIBL). Several corporations adopted the Phillips model and provided basketball and employment opportunities to collegians eager to extend ballplaying careers. The most successful was the Peoria Caterpillar Company, which collected five national championship trophies in nine years.

While the AAU tournament continued to draw capacity crowds and generate great excitement, this period was bittersweet for Denver fans. In 1949 a combination of poor facilities and Phillips's success led to an AAU decision to move the tournament to Oklahoma City for one year. While Denver's fans embraced the tournament when it returned in 1950, the inability of Denver teams to win the national championship began to disappoint them. After 1948 only one Denver team would advance to the championship game.

The 1950s were also a watershed for college and professional basketball. Although the basketball scandals of 1951 rocked the sports world and reminded the observant of the ability of gamblers to corrupt athletic contests, the college game nonetheless continued to blossom. One of the reasons was the appearance of a new pool of talent from the African American community. A new civil rights environment and the prospect of increasing revenues were opening doors, and in marched Bill Russell, Wilt Chamberlain, Oscar Robertson, Elgin Baylor, and others who eventually integrated collegiate basketball across the nation.

In 1949–50 the National Basketball League and the Basketball Association of America merged to form the National Basketball Association (NBA). In the 1950s the Minneapolis Lakers and then the Boston Celtics put the NBA on the map. By 1960 the growing popularity of the NBA was beginning to generate salaries that would make it virtually impossible for NIBL teams to compete for talent. Until 1960 NIBL teams could offer the prospect of lifetime employment or job training leading to transferable skills. As long as professional basketball salaries were in the five-thousand- to fifteen-thousand-dollar range, a player was wise to choose long-term earning power over the risks of the pro game. In the 1950s the other attraction of playing AAU ball was a chance to play on the Olympic team, a goal which NIBL teams used as a recruiting device. While the AAU, college, and professional games flourished in the 1950s, the dynamics of basketball as a business were working against the AAU.

SEVEN

Bartlesville versus the Bay

The biggest news of the 1948–49 season was the decision made by the AAU to hold the 1949 national tournament in Oklahoma City. On the surface Denver was the victim of its own success. The 1948 tournament had drawn its usual sellout crowds, but critics argued that Denver's facilities were inadequate to meet the demand for tickets. Moreover, Boots Adams wanted the tournament at a location where 66er fans could see his team. He responded to fears that there were financial risks in departing from tradition by reportedly guaranteeing the AAU ten thousand dollars regardless of ticket sales.[1]

In another important and expected development the American Basketball League, which had limped through the 1947–48 season, finally collapsed. Sportswriters believed that there was a direct relationship between a viable amateur basketball league and a successful national amateur tournament. By 1948 it was clear that major American corporations had the best chance of providing a program capable of attracting quality players. In 1947–48 companies in the Midwest had formed the National Industrial Basketball League (NIBL). The 1948–49 season included three of those teams, the Peoria Caterpillars, the Akron Goodyear Wingfoots, and the Milwaukee Allen-Bradleys, along with the Phillips 66ers and the Denver Chevrolets. The league committed itself to amateurism, which meant that the companies had to employ the players on their rosters.

The debate over the definition of amateurism had become more intense in 1948 because of the success of Phillips. For the corporations who organized the NIBL, the issue of employment represented the crucial distinction between an amateur and professional. The critics of Phillips Petroleum argued that the basketball players were employed for their basketball skills rather than their business or technical skills and scoffed at claims that the basketball players were legitimate employees. Phillips responded vigorously to the scoffers by demonstrating that 80 percent of its basketball players remained with the company, many in positions of responsibility. Phillips made no effort to explore the meaning of amateurism beyond the simple assertion that athletes were paid to work and not to play. After the Madison Square Garden tournament Joe Williams, a syndicated sports columnist, argued that it was simplistic to argue that Phillips recruited Bob Kurland solely for his potential in management. Williams, however, found it difficult to distinguish Phillips from the University of Kentucky or any university that recruited young men to its campus primarily for their athletic skills, if faithfulness to the principles of amateurism was the scale of measurement.[2] Three years later, in 1951, Kentucky suffered by comparison when it was revealed that two of its Olympians, Alex Groza and Ralph Beard, cooperated with gamblers to control the outcome of college games in exchange for cash.[3]

The extent to which Phillips attempted to defend its amateur status occasionally led to some embarrassing inconsistencies. In February of 1948 Bud Browning suggested that Phillips was so committed to its principles that some key players would be unable to compete in London, if the 66ers won that right, because "[t]hey couldn't be spared that long from work . . . and we would take only those who the company feels could conscientiously be allowed to make the trip without pushing their load at the plant on somebody else."[4] After Phillips had won the Madison Square Garden tournament, Boots Adams announced that not only would the five players named to the Olympic team attend the games, but the remaining seven players of the 1948 team would be sent to London as guests of the company.[5] John Lardner, who wrote for *Newsweek*, was not convinced by those who tried to squeeze collegiate, AAU, and Olympic sports under the umbrella of amateurism. In the United States some "openly" made

Jack McCracken, as a player and player-coach, was generally acknowledged as the leader of Denver's three AAU championship teams. He is a member of the Naismith Hall of Fame. (Photo courtesy of the Naismith Hall of Fame)

Robert "Ace" Gruenig (*center*) was a ten-time AAU All-American whose trademark was a sweeping hook shot with either hand from the center position. He is a member of the Naismith Hall of Fame. (Photo courtesy of Julie Davis Bell and family)

Vince Boryla was a two-time AAU All-American and member of the gold-medal 1948 United States Olympic team. He spent twelve years with the New York Knickerbockers as a player, coach, and general manager and served as the president and general manager of the ABA Utah Stars (1970–74) and the NBA Denver Nuggets (1984–87). He is seen shooting over Jesse "Cab" Renick of the Phillips 66ers. (Photo courtesy of Julie Davis Bell and family)

Johnny Dee was the fiery coach of the Denver–Chicago Truckers between 1957 and 1961. Before coaching the Truckers, Dee led the University of Alabama to the Southeastern Conference Championship in 1956. He coached Notre Dame between 1964 and 1971. (Photo courtesy of John Dee Jr.)

The 1948 U.S. Olympic team won the gold medal in London, the first Olympic Games since the 1936 Olympics in Berlin. (Photo courtesy of the Naismith Hall of Fame)

Bob Kurland was a three-time college All-American for Henry Iba at Oklahoma A&M (Oklahoma State University). He was a six-time AAU All-American and a member of the gold-medal Olympic basketball teams of 1948 and 1952. He is a member of the Naismith Hall of Fame. (Photo courtesy of Conoco-Phillips)

Chuck Hyatt, a three-time college All-American at the University of Pittsburgh, led the Tulsa Diamond DX Oilers to AAU championships in 1934 and 1935. He coached the Phillips 66ers for three seasons and an AAU championship in 1940. He is a member of the Naismith Hall of Fame. (Photo courtesy of Conoco-Phillips)

Burdie Haldorson was a four-time AAU All-American and a member of the gold-medal 1956 and 1960 Olympic teams. He holds all of Phillips's scoring records. (Photo courtesy of Conoco-Phillips)

Omar "Bud" Browning was an AAU All-American who won greater recognition as the coach of the Phillips 66ers. He led Phillips to five consecutive AAU championships between 1944 and 1948. He coached the 1948 Olympic team to a gold medal in London. Browning became the winningest coach in AAU tournament history when his teams won championships in 1962 and 1963. (Photo courtesy of Conoco-Phillips)

Angelo "Hank" Luisetti, a three-time college All-American at Stanford University, is credited with perfecting a running one-handed shot. In 1938 he was the first collegian to score 50 points. He won AAU All-American honors twice and captivated fans with his dribbling, passing, and defensive skills. Luisetti coached the San Francisco Stewart Chevrolets to an AAU championship in 1951. He is a member of the Naismith Hall of Fame. (Photo courtesy of the Naismith Hall of Fame)

Jim Pollard was the leading scorer on Stanford's 1942 NCAA championship team. Nicknamed "Jumping Jim," Pollard won AAU All-American honors twice before starring for the NBA's Minneapolis Lakers. He is a member of the Naismith Hall of Fame. (Photo courtesy of Arilee Pollard)

Left to right: Coach Alvin Kyte, Les O'Gara, Don Barksdale, Morris "Mushy" Silver, Bob Alameida, and Jack Abel of the Oakland Bittners. Don Barksdale was the first African American basketball player to represent the United States in Olympic basketball competition as a member of the 1948 Olympic team. A four-time AAU All-American, Barksdale led the Oakland Bittners to the 1949 AAU championship. Barksdale played in the NBA for four years and was the first African American to play in an NBA All-Star game. (Photo courtesy of the Naismith Hall of Fame)

Top row, left to right: Les O'Gara, Frank Lubin, and Dale Sears; *bottom row, left to right*: Carl Knowles, Art Mollner, and Fon Johnson. Frank Lubin was one of the legends of AAU basketball whose playing career spanned three decades. A two-time AAU All-American, Lubin represented the United States in the first Olympic basketball tournament, won by the U.S. team, in 1936. He is pictured with five of his teammates at Twentieth Century Fox, winners of the 1941 AAU tournament. (Photo courtesy of Fon Johnson)

Warren Womble (*center*) coached the Peoria Cats to five AAU championships between 1952 and 1960. He coached the 1952 Olympic team to a gold medal in Helsinki and served as an assistant to Pete Newell on the 1960 Olympic gold-medal team in Rome. He is pictured here with players Frank McCabe (*left*) and Ron Bontemps (*right*). (Photo courtesy of Warren Womble)

The Peoria Cats won their fourth championship in 1958 when they
defeated the Denver–Chicago Truckers in four overtimes. (Photo
courtesy of Warren Womble)

Alex Hannum (*right*) coached the Wichita Vickers to the 1959 AAU
championship. He coached the St. Louis Hawks (1958) and Philadelphia
76ers (1967) to NBA championships and the Oakland Oaks to an ABA
championship in 1969. He is a member of the Naismith Hall of Fame.
(Photo courtesy of the Naismith Hall of Fame)

Dick Boushka (*with the ball*) was a member of the 1956 Olympic team and a two-time AAU All-American. He led the Air Force All-Stars (1957) and Wichita Vickers (1959) to AAU championships. (Photo courtesy of the Naismith Hall of Fame)

"a living from their talent" and were called professionals. "The rest," Lardner continued, "are called amateurs, but almost without exception their purpose is to profit from the thing they do best." The Olympics were becoming too big to be left to amateurs, and Lardner believed that Phillips proved that point. The oil company stretched credibility beyond its breaking point, he concluded, when it asked people to believe its basketball team advertised "the oil company as a hobby."[6]

In 1948–49 basketball in Denver became more complicated. Shortly after the 1948 AAU tournament, nine Denver Chevrolet dealerships announced that they would sponsor a basketball program patterned after Phillips 66. They named Russ Lyons, sales manager for Murphy-Mahoney Chevrolet and the coach of the Graybeards, to coach the team. A spokesman for the Chevrolet dealers explained that civic welfare or community service was their goal, not profit. Russ Lyons added that basketball recruits would be offered "substantial jobs" and they would be "workers first and basketball players second."[7] As the Denver Chevrolets made plans to enter independent amateur basketball, Hal Davis, general manager of the Nuggets, moved in a different direction. Jack Carberry reported that the Nuggets had lost about eighteen thousand dollars and that it was highly unlikely they would continue their sponsorship.[8] By summer most of the Nuggets were headed in different directions. Vince Boryla, Bob Salen, and Ed Little enrolled at Denver University; Roy Lipscomb joined Phillips; and Ron Livingstone headed for Wyoming.

In late July, Davis used Carberry's column to make his case for professional basketball. Essentially Davis argued that professional basketball was more honest since it openly paid people for their skills. He believed that it was impossible for colleges and the AAU to regulate amateur sports, especially with regard to the financial incentives offered to athletes. In 1948–49 Davis secured a franchise in the nine-team National Basketball League (NBL).[9] A major flaw in Davis's plan was that it lacked financial investors. When Davis tried to sell stock, there were no buyers. The team played its games in a reassembled hangar transported from the Farrugut Training Base in

Idaho to the University of Denver campus. With no investors, Davis had to rely on gate receipts to pay the bills, but the team failed to draw fans.

A losing record and competition from the AAU Denver Chevrolets doomed the professional Nuggets. While Syracuse and Detroit entered teams in the league, most of the NBL clubs were from middle-sized midwestern cities such as Hammond, Anderson, Oshkosh, Sheboygan, and the Tri-Cities. As Denver struggled through its first season, Davis signed Ace Gruenig to a contract to generate some interest. The thirty-five-year-old Gruenig played forty-nine games and averaged 11.4 points, which gave him the ninth best average in the NBL. Coach Ralph Bishop and players Leonard Alterman, Ward Gibson, and Jim Darden were former Nuggets on Denver's first professional team, while Morris Udall, from the University of Arizona, and Al Guokas, from St. Joseph's College, were two of Davis's more notable recruits. The Nuggets finished last in the NBL's Western Division with an 18-44 mark.[10]

In 1949 the NBL merged with the Basketball Association of America to form the National Basketball Association (NBA). In 1949–50 the Nuggets once again finished in last place, with a record of 11 wins and 51 losses. Jimmy Darden, Al Guokas, and Jack Cotton were the only returning players form the previous year. The team's high scorer was Kenny Sailors, former AAU and University of Wyoming All-American. After two seasons, the financially strapped Denver professional franchise folded and the Mile High City was, once again, exclusively an AAU town."[11]

In their first season, the Denver Chevrolets compiled a respectable 11-5 record in the NBL, second to Phillips, which lost only one of its sixteen league games. Coach Russ Lyons succeeded in recruiting Jimmy Reese and Jimmy Collins (two former University of Wyoming stars), Thornton Jenkins (an All–Big Six selection from the University of Missouri), Harold Howey (an All-Conference guard from Kansas State), Gordon "Shorty" Carpenter (the great Phillips star), Harry Stokes (a three-time All–Rocky Mountain Conference selection from Colorado State College in Greeley), Blake Williams (from Oklahoma A&M), Les Majors (an AAU veteran who was a multisport star at Longmont High School in Colorado), and Johnny Langden (from the University of Texas).[12]

Going into the AAU tournament at Oklahoma City, Denver's Chevrolets were a very solid 26-8. Four of Denver's losses were to Phillips, but Denver did own a victory over the 66ers in Bartlesville. Before the tournament, Carberry gave the Chevs his stamp of approval and noted that the players were "chosen with an eye to their future in the organization as much as for their ability to play ball."[13] In the quarterfinals, however, Alpine Dairy of Seattle stunned the Chevs, as Bill Vandenburgh, University of Washington captain, led all scorers with 18 points. It was the first time a Denver team had failed to make the semifinals since 1940. In the semifinals Phillips crushed Alpine Dairy to set up a championship game between the 66ers and the Oakland Bittners.[14]

The mixture of race, resentment, and sports intensified the normal drama of a national championship game. After having won six consecutive AAU titles, the competitive Boots Adams obviously wanted to display his team and accept the championship trophy before the friendly fans of Oklahoma City. After the 1948 season Phillips had added Roy Lipscomb (who started for the Denver Nuggets in 1947–48), A. L. Bennett (an All–Missouri Conference guard from Oklahoma A&M), Kenny Jastrow (an All–Conference guard at the University of Denver), Johnny Stanich (an All–Pacific Coast Conference guard from UCLA), and Alvin Williams (an All–Southwest Conference forward from the University of Arkansas). Going into the title game Cab Renick's 66ers had dropped only three games in fifty-three contests and had won the NIBL championship.

In 1949 Lou Bittner made Bob Alameida, who played on the first two Bittner teams, his coach. To his nucleus of Don Barksdale, Les O'Gara, and Morris "Mushy" Silver, Lou Bittner added Chuck Hanger (a great leaper and good scorer who was picked by Nibs Price as one of the five greatest players he coached in his thirty years at the University of California), Ed Voss (a starter on Stanford's 1942 NCAA championship team), and Dave Minor (an outstanding African American guard who had played with Barksdale at UCLA). Minor played his high school basketball at Froebel High School in Gary, Indiana, and John Christgau, who has written a history of the jump shot, credits him as one of the first players to have this shot in his repertoire. At six feet two inches and 190 pounds, Minor possessed a chiseled body and tremendous leaping ability. As a junior at Froebel (1939–40) he set the Indiana high-jump record at six feet four inches and won the long jump. As a senior (1940–41), Minor led Froebel to the final four of the Indiana state tournament. After a year at Toledo University Minor entered the service, toured Europe as a heavyweight boxer for the Western Base All-Star Boxing Team, and made the All-Service Basketball team in 1945–46. After the service, Minor played two seasons at UCLA before rejoining his Bruin teammate, Don Barksdale, with the Bittners. In describing his style of play, Leonard Cahn wrote, "Where Barksdale is poetry in motion, Minor plays with all the intensity of a charge of the light brigade." In describing Minor's jump shot, developed as a freshman at Froebel, Cahn described it as hard and flat as if it was "coming out of a cannon."[15]

Going into the championship game, the Bittners had compiled a 60-1 record. Leonard Cahn of the *Rocky Mountain News* reported that the Bittners had more than the usual incentives going into the championship game. During the season Phillips refused to play the Bittners because the 66ers believed Oakland violated the amateur code. The 66ers also used their influence with the NIBL to expand the boycott of the Bittners. When Peoria and Denver made a swing to the Pacific Coast, they did not schedule the Bittners. More galling to the Bittners was the decision of the San Francisco Stewart Chevrolets, a new AAU team coached by Hank Luisetti, to join the boycott. As a result the Bittners played a host of exhibition games, which included contests against college and university teams.[16]

Because the Bittners had finished third in the 1948 AAU tournament, they automatically received a bid to play in the 1949 tourney. Since low attendance had generated little revenue during the season, the Bittners entered the Pacific Association basketball tournament in hopes of winning the round-trip airline tickets to Oklahoma City, as well as bragging rights in Northern California. Ray Haywood, who covered the Bittners for the *Oakland Tribune*, made it clear that the dollar-starved Bittners wanted those free tickets, but they also wanted a chance to play Stewart Chevrolet of San Francisco. Since the tournament went according to form, the top two Bay Area teams met in the finals, and before five thousand screaming fans, mostly for the Stewarts, Oakland managed to win a narrow 53–50 victory. Although Haywood did not want to look too far ahead, he wrote that the Bittners "would dearly love to bring the national title back to Oakland . . . by meeting and beating the team (Phillips) in the (AAU) final, where you have to play because you can't say 'no.'"[17]

Another part of the drama was that Don Barksdale and Dave Minor, because they were African Americans, were not allowed to room with their teammates. Oklahoma still segregated blacks and no exception was made for the AAU tournament. For Barksdale in particular, it must have been ironic to meet some of his former Olympic teammates, including coach Cab Renick, a Native American, in a Jim Crow state.

In the early rounds of the tournament the Bittners squeezed by Dallas's Hooker-Vandegriff Motors and the Peoria Caterpillars while no Phillips opponent came closer than 17 points to the champions. In the championship game five thousand fans squeezed into Municipal Auditorium and watched the Bittners win a hard-fought contest, 55–51. Don Barksdale led all scorers with 17 points, Chuck Hanger and Ed Voss held Bob Kurland to 9, and Mushy Silver limited John Stanich to 6. After the Bittners had ended "the longest monopoly in major basketball history," Bob Brachman of the *San Francisco Examiner* observed: "If there was a mistake in their play, we couldn't see it."[18]

Lou Bittner was ecstatic. Harry Farrar reported that upon accepting congratulations from a Phillips representative, Bittner replied: "We won't dodge Phillips any time."[19] Although Bob Kurland was not replying directly to Bittner, he observed, "We got beat because the Bittners were a better team. That backboard power murdered us." Kurland was not accustomed to losing big games and added, "I don't like it one bit." He vowed that his preparation for 1950 would start "right now" and in a year "you Bittners better be wound tight."[20] The seemingly inexplicable loss left Oklahoma fans, according to reporters, "stunned," "bitter" and "unhappy." While spectators and writers searched for explanations, Lou Wilke only half-jokingly observed: "They (Phillips) were waiting for those boos they always got in Denver. When they didn't get a 'riding,' maybe they didn't know what to do."[21] Wilke may have been half right. Perhaps the Bittners had entered the lion's den and used the boycott directed against the team and racial segregation as the foundation for a championship effort. Fifty years later Morris "Mushy" Silver remembered the game as the most memorable of his career.[22]

Except for the *Oakland Tribune* none of the major papers commented on the racial implications of the game. As other athletic pioneers against racism, Barksdale and Minor demonstrated the character and talent to prevail in the most difficult of competitive environments. Ray Haywood of the *Oakland Tribune* reported that they were booed during the games. However, Haywood also wrote that Barksdale, who was the high-point man of the tournament, received the biggest response when the all-star team was presented.[23] As in the case of Jackie Robinson, white fans had the capacity to acknowledge great performances regardless of an athlete's skin color.

A week after the Bittners won the championship three hundred people gathered at the Athens Athletic Club to honor them. Ray Haywood noted that "if as many people had paid money to see the Bittners play basketball during their home games, the team and its sponsor might have considered the season more of a success." For Haywood there was something bittersweet about the whole affair. He obviously found it amusing that "civic dignitaries, politicians, and sporting figures, very few of whom had seen the Big B's play, spent two hours praising them." The Bittners were "the orphans of Oakland Auditorium" who graciously acknowledged the praises heaped upon them. Haywood believed that something very special had happened. For one year "the Nation's finest basketball had been played in the Oakland Auditorium." Men, under the direction of Bob Alameida, had subordinated their individual goals to form "a single-spirited unit" to win a national championship.[24] The writer's respect arose from the team's commitment to excellence in the face of disinterest.

After all of the cheering and backslapping, Lou Bittner had to face the reality that he was losing money and dropped his sponsorship of Oakland basketball. Grace Brothers Brewery became the new sponsor of Oakland's AAU team, which was called the Oakland Blue 'n Gold. When Lou Bittner died in 1980 Don Barksdale remembered him as "a great guy" who "went broke trying to promote basketball in Oakland." Barksdale was especially appreciative because Bittner gave him a chance to prolong his career until 1951, when it was easier for a black player to move on to the NBA. Long before the A's, Raiders, and Warriors, Barksdale reflected, Lou Bittner "did something for the city" by putting it "on the map as a national champion."[25]

Despite the drama of the championship, the tournament had attracted slim crowds. More telling, Oklahoma City grossed only forty-one thousand dollars, which was thirty-two thousand dollars less than the 1948 Denver tournament.[26] Near the end of the week it was clear that Denver could, once again, host the tournament. Not only were the dollars below expectations, but, as San Francisco's Bob Brachman added, "that crazy tournament atmosphere was missing. People went to sleep early in this tournament show. Nobody ever did in Denver."[27] While Jack Carberry was prepared to welcome the tournament back to Denver, he was more than a little sore with the AAU. When J. Lyman Bingham, assistant to the president of the AAU, declared that Denver lost the tournament because of the apathy of the Denver press, he enraged Carberry, who called the charge "hogwash." Over the years Carberry had vented his displeasure with Bingham, his ten-thousand-dollar salary, and his crimped reading of the amateur code. Carberry reminded Bingham and his readers that the "Denver newspapers 'made' the tourney." In some of his harshest prose, Carberry fumed that what bothered Bingham was that "the Denver newspapers failed to glorify Mr. J. Lyman Bingham—or to bow in reverence before the name of Phillips 66, even as Mr. J. Lyman Bingham bows." The outraged sports editor added that "the Oklahoma City tourney was not an Oklahoma City promotion, it was a Phillips promotion."[28]

Leonard Cahn was more skeptical about the tournament's return. He acknowledged that "the tournament was a vital factor in developing basketball to its present peak" in Denver. But he thought the tournament "had degenerated into a third-rate hodge-podge event and stripped of its few top teams, the event could be played in a telephone booth so far as national interest is concerned." Given the competition from the college and professional game, Cahn thought, "The high power AAU type of basketball appears definitely over the hill."[29] While sportswriters offered mixed opinions about the national AAU tournament, in 1950 it returned to Denver, where it would remain through 1968.

The 1950 AAU tournament kicked off a decade of memorable games and performances. As Leonard Cahn observed, the 1950 tournament was Denver's first without its two most celebrated players, Ace Gruenig and Jack McCracken. He urged tournament officials to acknowledge "the debt we all owe to them."[30] Before looking forward Jack Carberry also recalled the tournament's history, in which Denver's "sports-minded citizens saw to it that the five hundred to eight hundred players, coaches, and team sponsors from out of town were royally entertained." Although Carberry had resented the AAU's decision to award the 1949 tourney to Oklahoma City, he believed that in the later years of the tournament Denver "just sort of took the AAU for granted." Carberry reported happily that Denver was ready "to show the AAU visitors that Denver appreciates them, and is truly glad to have them back at home in the city where they and the tournament belong."[31] Two days before the tournament Mayor Quigg Newton issued a proclamation that declared March 20–27 National Basketball Week and directed "the attention of the people to its observance."[32]

Despite all the criticism of Denver's City Auditorium, the 1950 tournament returned to its familiar venue. The players still dressed in their hotel rooms and took taxis to the Denver auditorium, which, according to Ray Haywood of the *Oakland Tribune*, "You would have to see to appreciate." The 1950 tournament was "thick" with professional scouts, who, Haywood wrote, aggressively pursued amateur stars. Die-hard fans still brought their lunches in the early rounds, "so they wouldn't miss any of the twelve games played." Finally Haywood reported that the "Dawn Patrol," a collection of sports writers, publicists, coaches, and hangers on, were still visiting their favorite haunts, talking basketball, and stepping up "when it was your turn to buy a round." In short, the tournament provided something for everybody.[33]

As usual the hometown team, in this year, the Denver Chevrolets, was the center of attention, but Carberry thought they were in "for a rough time" and did not expect them to advance beyond the quarterfinals.[34] In the 1949–50 season the Chevs were 21-13 but a modest 5-5 in the NIBL. The team added Oklahoma A&M's Tom Jaquet and J. L. Parks plus the University of Colorado's Les Metzger to the nucleus of Shorty Carpenter, Thornton Jenkins, Blake Williams, Jimmy Reese, and Johnny Langdon. Before the tournament the Chevs picked up John Pilch, a Wyoming star. The favorite was Phillips, which entered tournament play with a 47-1 record (9-1 in the NIBL) and another deep and talented team that featured Roy Lipscomb, Bob Kurland, Gerald Tucker, and Lew Beck.

In 1950 Stewart Chevrolet of San Francisco sent an impressive team to Denver. Sponsored by Murt Stewart, a businessman with a Chevrolet dealership in the Mission District, the team was coached by Hank Luisetti and in its second year of play. In early March before five thousand fans, the Stewarts won a free trip to Denver by edging the Oakland Blue 'n Gold in the Pacific Association tournament, a victory that Harry Hayward of the *San Francisco Examiner* described as the "sweetest one in the two-year history of the Stewarts."[35] Leading the San Franciscans was George "the Bird" Yardley, a six-foot-six jumping jack, who broke Luisetti's conference scoring record at Stanford. While Yardley played brilliantly in three AAU tournaments, he is best remembered as the first NBA player to score two thousand points in a season.[36]

Another forward was George Walker, a star at the University of California whose long arms and slender build earned him the nickname the Spider. Half Native American, half African American, Walker played his first competitive basketball in the service during World War Two, when he flew in a B 26 squadron. After the war, Walker went to Cal-Berkeley on the GI Bill and played on some of Cal's most successful teams.[37] Luisetti's guards were Andy Wolfe, an

All-American at Cal, and Cliff Crandall, an All-American on Oregon State's 1949 final four team.[38] Billy Burke from St. Mary's; Don Henrickson, a center from Cal; Bob Walker, George's brother and captain of Cal's 1949–50 team; and Stu Inman, San Jose State's all-time leading scorer, completed the team.

While Luisetti had not played in the AAU tournament since 1942, his impact on San Francisco basketball had been immeasurable. The Bay Area's love affair with Luisetti rested on an appreciation of his formidable skills, well-documented accomplishments, and unfailing graciousness. In 1943 and 1944 Luisetti played for St. Mary's Pre-Flight team and made the All-Service team each year. For the Bay Area, however, the basketball highlights of these two years were the epic contests between St. Mary's Pre-Flight Air Devils and the Alameda Coast Guard Sea Lions that pitted Luisetti against Jim Pollard. Bob Stevens of the *San Francisco Chronicle* considered Luisetti "the most incredible athlete" he had ever seen and, at twenty-seven, "still the same imperturbable, effortless magician of the hardwoods."[39] Pollard, Stevens thought, was "the only man ever developed in this area to consistently challenge" Luisetti.[40] Six years younger than Luisetti, Pollard won All-Service honors three times during the war. Fifty years later, he recalled that Luisetti had helped to recruit him to Stanford and readily acknowledged that when he was a high school kid, Hank was his hero.[41]

The two players competed against each other once in 1943 and three times in 1944. By narrow margins, St. Mary's won all four games, played before capacity crowds in San Francisco's Civic Auditorium. While directing his team to four victories, Luisetti also outscored Pollard for the series, which only added to his stature in the Bay Area.[42]

After the 1944 season, Luisetti and Pollard never competed against each other again, but at the end of the twentieth century Bay Area fans still remembered their duels. In 1944–45 Pollard was stationed in Hawaii and led the Coast Guard Cutters to the Central Pacific Area championship. In 1945 Luisetti survived a bout with spinal meningitis, which ended his career as a basketball player. In

1950, when Luisetti returned to Denver as the coach of the Stewart Chevrolets, his name was still magical to basketball fans.

For Denver fans the tournament got off to a bad start when Cliff Nelson Fuels from Toledo, Ohio, shut down the Regis Rangers in a first-round game. With Bob Fisher, Bobby Wallace, Bryce Heffley and Dick Petry, Larry Varnell had briefly turned Regis College of Denver into a small-college power.[43] Featuring a balanced scoring attack, the Denver Chevrolets won three consecutive games, which earned them a spot in the semifinals against the 1949 champions now playing as the Oakland Blue 'n Gold.[44]

Despite having won the 1949 championship, Ray Haywood reported that the Oaklanders failed to attract fans to their home games in the 1949–50 season. Barksdale, Hanger, Silver, and Minor were back and reinforced by more Bay Area talent, which included John Bennington and Don Lofgren (who led the University of San Francisco to the 1949 National Invitational Tournament Title), Ken Leslie (a star at Lowell High School in San Francisco), Mike O'Neill from Cal-Berkeley, and Dick Faszholz, a former Oakland high schooler. While Oakland's disinterest in the Blue 'n Gold troubled Hayward, he wrote that it was different in Denver, "where the champion is cherished. One day in this atmosphere is sufficient to inspire even the most blasé with the old collegiate daring-do."[45]

In a hard-fought game that was not decided until the final ten minutes, Oakland, riding Don Barksdale's 22 points, downed the Denver Chevs. In the other semifinal game, Phillips 66 dominated the second half and overwhelmed San Francisco Stewart Chevrolet.[46] For the twelfth time in its fourteen years of tournament play, the 66ers were in the finals. In a rematch of the 1949 championship, Phillips crushed Oakland 65–42 in one of the tournament's most one-sided championship games as Gerald Tucker led all scorers with 14 points. In the third-place game Johnny Pilch scored 19 points as the Denver Chevs outlasted the San Francisco Stewarts.[47] Whatever the pre-tournament anxiety of promoters, there was no backlash in Denver against the AAU. According to an unnamed writer "the AAU virus took over in the later stages and the old time AAU fever raged in packed houses during the last three nights."[48] The tourney netted five thousand dollars more than the Oklahoma City tournament of the previous year.

For the 1950–51 season the NIBL increased in size to eight teams and for the third straight year the Phillips 66ers won the league title with a 22-3 record. Before the season the Denver Chevs, now coached by Shorty Carpenter, added Bob Fisher and Bryce Heffley from Regis College, Dan Kahler from Southwestern College, and John Stanich from UCLA and Phillips. The Chevs kicked off their season by representing the United States in the first basketball World Championships held in Buenos Aires, Argentina. Playing before enthusiastic crowds, Denver survived close games with Chile, Egypt, and Brazil and took a 5-0 mark into the championship game against host Argentina. In front of twenty-five thousand screaming fans the Argentineans prevailed as seven Chevs fouled out, giving Argentina 32 points from the free throw line to 14 for the Americans.[49] After its South American adventure, Denver suffered through a 5-14 league season and failed to receive one of the coveted top tournament seeds. Dale Toft, from Denver University, and Wayne Tucker of the University of Colorado were recruited for the tournament. Toft was only a junior and had to receive permission from the Skyline Conference, because this conference had generally barred undergraduates from AAU competition on the grounds that independent amateurs were semiprofessionals. One writer annoyed by this policy was Leonard Cahn, who argued that "[i]n reality, both the colleges and the high-powered AAU teams brew their subsidy programs out of the same kettle." Cahn thought that the Skyline Conference's policy had hurt the AAU tournament and was extremely hypocritical since this conference permitted members to play in "the commercial temple of the Madison Square Garden."[50]

During the 1940s stories about gambling at Madison Square Garden were frequently found in Denver papers, and just before the 1951 AAU tournament Frank Hogan, the district attorney for New York, arrested thirty college players for taking money from gamblers in a point-shaving scheme that shocked sports fans. The revelation of payoffs to control the scores of games alarmed Lou Wilke and

Willard Greim enough to seek the assistance of District Attorney Bert M. Keating and Morals Bureau Chief Verne McCoy. While Greim and Wilke insisted there was no evidence of past or present efforts to control the outcomes of AAU tourney games, they wanted to reassure Denver fans that everything was "on the up and up."[51]

On the opening day of the tournament Jack Carberry's concern was with the competition and he hoped "Phillips gets whipped—and good. And if that is a hell of a way for a sportswriter who is supposed to be neutral . . . let anyone make the most of it." Carberry conceded that Phillips "played fairly and squarely" and deserved credit for the success of AAU basketball. The problem was that Phillips had "won too consistently, like Notre Dame . . . and the New York Yankees." Carberry hoped that some team would come along and "just wallop the daylights out of the champions."[52]

The 1951 tournament blended the old and the new in AAU basketball and proved a real barnburner. Frank Lubin returned with Kelbo's Hawaiian Barbeque from Los Angeles. At the age of forty-one Lubin pleased his many fans by pouring in 37 points to lead his team to a first-round victory over Barksdale's Air Force Base of Shreveport, Louisiana. While Phillips defeated Lubin's team in the second round, he returned for two more tournaments in a memorable career that included an Olympic gold medal (1936) and an AAU championship (1941). John and Marian Jordan, better known as Fibber McGee and Molly, a popular radio comedy team, brought in one of the new amateur teams. The Jordans found little to laugh at as their McGees fell to the Kable Kolts of Mount Morris, Illinois.[53] A dark-horse team that knocked off a couple of seeded teams was the Jamcos of Sioux City, Iowa. After crushing the Renton Sportsmen from Renton, Washington, the Jamcos upset Allen-Bradley, an NIBL team from Milwaukee, and then surprised Houston's Ada Oilers. Led by Bob Pierce, a University of Nebraska star, and Don Bartlett from South Dakota State, the Jamcos finally ran into Hank Luisetti's Stewart Chevrolets, who prevailed by a lopsided score of 88–42.[54]

The Denver Chevs, who won their first two games rather handily, stumbled in the quarterfinal game against the Peoria Caterpillars, who were led by big Frank McCabe of Marquette University and sharp-shooting Howie Williams of Purdue University.[55] For the disappointed Denver fans the darlings of the tournament quickly became the players of the Poudre Valley Creamery of Fort Collins, Colorado. This team was a collection of several players from Colorado A&M including Glendon Anderson, Bill Gossett, George Janzen, and Johnny O'Boyle. They earned a berth in the AAU tourney by winning the *Rocky Mountain News*–YMCA regional AAU tournament a week before the national. After a hard-earned win over the Geyser Independents, a team described as a "bunch of ranch hands" from Montana, the Aggies cruised by the VFW of Natchitoches, Louisiana. In the quarterfinals Poudre Valley met Vandergriff Motors of Dallas, Texas, which had pulled off the biggest upset of the tournament up to that time when it outscored the second-seeded Oakland Blue 'n Gold.[56] The Oaklanders, with Don Barksdale, Dave Minor, and Chuck Hanger, had represented the United States team, which had won the Pan-American Games in early March in Buenos Aires, Argentina. The Dallas team, however, had Paul Mitchell and Jack Brown (Southern Methodist stars), Marcus Freiberger (a six-foot-eleven center from the University of Oklahoma), and Paul Nolan, a six-foot-ten post player from Texas Tech. In a battle between Cinderella teams, Poudre Valley scored 21 unanswered points midway in the first half and turned back a Dallas rally in the second half, when the Texans came within 8 points of the lead. Glen Anderson with 20 points and Bill Gossett with 19 led the Aggie scorers. With their victory Poudre Valley became the first unseeded team to make the semifinals since 1941.[57]

The 1951 semifinal games matched those of any previous AAU tournament for sheer excitement. In the first game of the evening Poudre Valley's Blitz Kids, so-named by Leonard Cahn, grabbed a 37–30 lead over the tough Peoria Caterpillars at the end of the first half. In the second half the bigger Cats wore down the Aggies and near the end of the game Howie Williams gave the Diesels their first lead since early in the contest, 57–55. At the three-and-one-half-minute mark Bill Gossett tied the game with a pretty hook shot and Peoria responded by choosing to stall for the last shot. With less than ten seconds left Howie Williams missed a shot from the top of the free-throw circle that bounced to Poudre's Johnny O'Boyle, who pivoted, dribbled twice, and threw in a desperation two-hander from sixty-five feet to win the game. Leonard Cahn, who had seen every Denver tournament, called it "the most sensational clutch shot in tournament history . . . the answer to a scenario writer's dream." O'Boyle's heroics, one of the most remembered plays in tournament history, shoved into the background a remarkable shooting performance by Glen Anderson, who scored 21 of his 25 game-high points in the first half.[58]

Following Poudre Valley's victory Denver fans watched another dramatic semifinal game between the Stewart Chevrolets of San Francisco and the Phillips 66ers, the defending champions. The Stewarts were essentially the same team that had finished fourth in 1950. For the third consecutive year the San Franciscans had met Oakland in the finals of the *Examiner*–Pacific Association tournament and fell to their Bay rivals, 59–58, in three overtimes. Don Barksdale, just back from the Pan American games in Buenos Aires, scored 23 points, and Bob Brachman of the *San Francisco Examiner* wrote that the Oakland star had convinced everyone "he belongs among the greatest basketballers of all time, whoever they may be."[59]

While Andy Wolfe and Billy Burke were no longer with the Stewarts, the nucleus of Yardley, Crandall, Henrickson, and George Walker returned. A key addition during the regular season was guard Frank Kuzara, a starter on the University of San Francisco's 1949 NIT championship team, who possessed a deadly two-handed set shot. To strengthen his team, Luisetti added Bob Payne, Oregon State's leading scorer, Augie Bullwinkle from St. Mary's College, and Joe Greenbach from Santa Clara. A week before the tournament, Luisetti took his team to nearby Boulder, where his players practiced at the University of Colorado, coached by Bebe Lee, Luisetti's teammate on St. Mary's Pre-Flight team during the war.

Bob Kurland led a Phillips team that included veterans Paul Courty, A. L. Bennett, Al Williams, Ken Pryor and Bill Kleine. Among its rookies were George King—two-time small-college scoring champion at Morris Harvey, who later played seven years in the NBA before coaching successfully at West Virginia and Purdue—

Claude Houchin, a high-scoring guard from Kansas; Bus White-head, a two-time All–Big Seven selection from the University of Nebraska; and Wayne Glasgow, who earned the same honors at the University of Oklahoma. The defending champions were big, deep, and versatile. During the season the 66ers had defeated the Stewarts in Bartlesville, but Luisetti's team ended the 66ers' fifty-eight-game winning streak in San Francisco when George Yardley and Frank Kuzara combined for 35 points to lead the Californians.[60] While the 66ers bounced back to edge the Stewarts, they lost twice to Oakland Blue 'n Gold on this road trip, the first time a team had beaten Phillips in consecutive games in fifteen years.[61]

In the semifinal contest Phillips fought back from an 8-point deficit to tie the game at the end of regulation time. In the first overtime period the two teams traded baskets. Stewart Chevrolet held the ball for all but five seconds of the second period, but the strategy failed when Kuzara missed a set shot with five seconds left in the game. In the third overtime, the Stewarts jumped into a lead when Al Williams fouled Yardley on an attempted lay-up after the Bird had intercepted a pass. After Yardley made his first free throw, Luisetti chose to take the ball out of bounds rather than shoot the second free throw. Although Phillips got the ball back following a jump ball, Crandall made a crucial steal to give the ball back to the Californians. After King fouled Yardley purposely, and the latter made the first free throw, Luisetti again passed on the second free throw for possession of the ball. Kuzara iced the game with a free throw that gave the Stewarts a 66–63 victory. Yardley led all players with 25 points and Crandall added 21 points, while Kurland tallied 24 points before fouling out.[62] The loss was the first for the 66ers after thirty-eight consecutive wins in the Denver tournament, a streak that began in 1943. Phillips had failed to make it to the championship round for the first time since 1941.

The championship game was anticlimactic. When Poudre Valley stepped on the floor, it was the first unseeded team to play in the AAU championship game since Henry Iba's Maryville Teachers lost in the 1932 finals. Although the Cinderella team was only 10 points down at the half, George Yardley and the Stewarts were too tough for Poudre Valley Creamery, which fell 76–55. Yardley's 32 points established a new scoring record for a championship game.[63]

Despite the theatrics surrounding the 1951 tournament, the Dribble Derby came under strict scrutiny from Leonard Cahn when he committed the heresy of suggesting that the AAU brass send the tournament as far away from Denver as possible.[64] His major problem with the tournament was the unevenness of competition in the early rounds of play. Because Cahn thought there were not enough good independent teams, he argued that the answer to this problem rested with the colleges, some of whom he would invite to the tournament. If conferences allowed their teams to play under their colors, Cahn recommended paying the expenses of several schools from revenue gained by reducing the field. If reforms were not made, Cahn thought, the tournament would die a "natural death."[65]

Chet Nelson was one of those who loved the tournament and hoped that Cahn was wrong about its future in Denver. Nonetheless, Nelson agreed with Cahn that the NIBL was a shambles and did not generate enough quality teams. In the 1950–51 season three teams did not make their trips to the Pacific Coast and a couple more joined them in playing less than the twenty-five games scheduled. Since none of the major press services recognized the NIBL, the results of its games were not reported nationally. To save the tournament Nelson implied that the NIBL had to establish its credibility as a legitimate league.[66] Denver offered an excellent example of the difficulties of maintaining a quality independent basketball team. After the 1951 season the Denver Chevrolet dealers announced their decision to pull out of amateur basketball. The 1950–51 team had not competed well, and its biggest crowd of the season, 3,200, was an exhibition against Fibber McGee and Molly, which was supplemented by a fifteen-minute skit by the team's sponsor, comedians Jim and Marian Jordan.

Russ Lyons, who had mobilized the Chevrolet dealers in 1949, attempted to keep the team the team alive by developing a civic sponsored team subsidized by Denver businessmen.[67] In the late 1930s the first Denver Nuggets team offered a precedent for such an approach. When Lyons failed to win the required support, the Central

Bank of Denver adopted the team at the eleventh hour and Denver remained in the amateur basketball business. Max G. Brooks, Central's vice president, recalled that he and several colleagues thought that by sponsoring a basketball team, the bank, which was rather small in 1952, would benefit from the exposure in the community.[68]

EIGHT

Here Come the Cats

Tournament stakes were much higher than usual in 1952, an Olympic year, as teams and players congregated in Denver. As usual, Phillips 66 entered the tournament as a favorite. For the fourth consecutive year, the 66ers had won the NIBL with a 17-5 record as each team played twenty-two games.

Because of the uncertainty of the Denver operation, only six players returned to the Central Bankers from the previous year: Bob Fisher, Tom Jaquet, J. L. Parks, Don Slocum, John Stanich, and Blake Williams. Lyons successfully recruited three Colorado Aggies—Glen Anderson, Bill Gossett, and George Janzen—who had led the Poudre Valley Creamery to the 1951 tournament finals. In the NIBL the Bankers struggled through an 8-14 season but managed victories over Peoria, Stewart Chevrolet of San Francisco, and Phillips in Bartlesville. Less than two weeks before the tournament, in a surprise move, Lyons resigned as the coach of the Central Bankers, and Max Brooks, vice president of Central Bank, named Larry Varnell to replace him. Varnell had played with several Denver AAU teams and had a successful run as coach of the Regis College Rangers for five seasons between 1946 and 1951.[1] While Eddie Kohl and Tom Kavanaugh, two Regis stars, were added to the team for the 1952 tournament, the unsettled state of the Bankers meant that they were not to be a factor in the tournament. After trouncing Adams State, the Bankers bowed to the Fibber McGees.[2]

There were other teams in the 1952 tournament that Denver fans could support. The U.S. Air Force All-Stars from Tinker Air Force Base had five players who had played their college ball in Colorado: Bobby Wallace, Dick Petry, and Bryce Heffley from Regis, Sid Ryan from Denver University, and Wayne Tucker from the University of Colorado. Denver's Jussell Electric won the *Rocky Mountain News–YMCA* tournament with Denver University players like Freddie Howell, Dick Gray, and Dale Toft. Before the tournament Jussell picked up Ronnie Shavlik, a six-foot-eight center, who on the Saturday night before the kickoff of the AAU tournament had led Denver East High School to its second straight state high school championship. Shavlik played his college basketball at North Carolina State and won All-American honors in 1955 and 1956. After an easy opening round victory, Jussell topped the Santa Maria Golden Dukes, an NIBL team, before it fell to a powerful Peoria Caterpillar team.[3] The Air Force All-Stars, with former Colorado collegians leading the way, beat the Graham Plowboys (Hardin Simmons University) and Milwaukee's Allen-Bradley, setting up a quarterfinal match with a powerful NIBL team, the Oakland Atlas-Pacific Engineers.

While Oakland was minus Don Barksdale and Dave Minor, who had moved into the NBA, it still had a very strong team. Bob Matheny, a star at Cal-Berkeley, teamed up with Ken Leslie at the guard position. Jim Ramstead from Stanford, Jim Loscutoff and Bob Peterson from Oregon, and Ben Gibson from St. Mary's College joined Chuck Hanger and Mike O'Neill in the front line. For the third time in four years, Oakland had topped the San Francisco Stewarts in the final of the *Examiner–*PA tournament and garnered the all-expenses-paid trip to Denver.[4] The Stewarts, the defending AAU champions, entered the tournament without two 1951 stars, George Yardley and Frank Kuzara, who were playing on service teams. Both Bay Area teams had finished the NIBL with 16-6 records, one game behind Phillips. In the quarterfinals the Bay Area's Olympic dreams were snuffed out in two close games. In a low-scoring contest, which was tied at 34 after regulation time, Ladell Anderson from Utah State and Bobby Wallace led the Air Force All-Stars to a 40–34 victory in overtime. In another quarterfinal upset, little Billy Donovan of Loyola Marymount, Jack Stone of Kansas State, and veteran Les O'Gara led

Fibber McGee and Molly over Stewart Chevrolet of San Francisco, 43–41. The victory pleased many old-timers because Art Mollner, who played on the 1936 Olympic team and on so many Hollywood teams, coached the McGees.[5]

The 1952 quarterfinals were particularly important because the four winners won the right to play in the Olympic tournament. Joining the Air Force and Fibber McGee and Molly in the semifinals were NIBL powers Peoria and Phillips. Anchored by Bob Kurland, the 66ers had great size with Bus Whitehead and Bob Pierce, two University of Nebraska stars, in the front line, while Wayne Glasgow, Ken Pryor, Paul Courty, and Loy Doty gave the 66ers ball handling and outside shooting. The 66ers had won the NIBL title and had beaten Peoria in two of their three regular season meetings. Peoria had played in the tournament on six previous occasions, but this was to be its first trip to the finals. Warren Womble, the Caterpillar coach, had carefully built a team along the Phillips model. In the 1951–52 season Womble added forward Ron Bontemps from Beloit College and Marcus Freiberger from the University of Oklahoma to a team with such veterans as Dan Pippin from the University of Missouri, Frank McCabe from Marquette University, and Howie Williams from Purdue University.

In the semifinals Peoria dominated Fibber McGee and Molly and the 66ers smothered the Air Force All-Stars, as Kurland scored 19 and controlled the boards.[6] Although the experts favored Phillips in the finals, the Caterpillars bulldozed the 66ers 66–53. Howie Williams, Peoria's sharp-shooting guard, hit nine of eleven shots from the field and led all scorers with 20 points, while Dan Pippin followed with 17 points. McCabe and Freiberger limited Kurland to 14 points. There was a certain irony in the final score, since Phillips liked to stamp its victories with 66 points, but in this game the 66 belonged to the Caterpillars. In the third-place game the Air Force All-Stars nipped the Fibber McGees 48–47 in overtime.[7]

The tournament grossed forty-five thousand dollars, a five-thousand-dollar improvement over 1951, but netted only four thousand dollars because higher rental fees increased expenditure by seven thousand and a spring snowstorm hurt attendance on the last two nights. Since the national AAU took home a mere $4,325, rumors spread again that Denver was about to lose the tournament. Jack Carberry sympathized with the AAU and thought the city unfair as it imposed "staggering costs . . . for the use of our decaying forty-four-year-old city auditorium."[8] The city reported that it had lost money on the tournament and argued that the auditorium, according to the commissioner of supplies Waldo Cochrell, had to "operate at cost."[9] While the costs to the tournament directors was going up, Lou Wilke, chairman of the national AAU basketball committee, stressed that the AAU expected to make five thousand dollars from the event. One solution, Wilke thought, was to have "the Chamber of Commerce or other business groups" subsidize the tournament. Since the tournament brought Denver revenue and recognition, Wilke concluded, "If the tournament isn't worth something to the city, we should just forget it."[10]

The AAU championship did not end the debate over the quality of the AAU tournament. Leonard Cahn thought the Olympic tournament would prove a good yardstick for measuring AAU basketball, although he thought that neither the NCAA nor the AAU had teams equal to Kentucky and Phillips in 1948.[11]

Obviously bragging rights in amateur basketball were at stake in the 1952 Olympic tournament. Adding even more drama to the event, one of the teams fighting for the honor of representing the United States was Forrest "Phog" Allen's Kansas Jayhawks. Ever since 1936, when Allen had unsuccessfully lobbied to coach the first Olympic team, the Jayhawks' coach had been a constant critic of the AAU. At the age of sixty-six, with his first NCAA title under his belt, Allen hoped to cap an already successful season by leading the American Olympic team to Helsinki and winning the Olympic tournament. There was some irony in Allen's success in 1952. In the 1930s and 1940s Allen, the first president of the National Association of Basketball Coaches, was an aggressive advocate of raising the baskets from ten to twelve feet in college basketball. While Allen once listed thirty-two reasons for such a change, the most important was that the ten-foot basket gave big men too great an advantage that "reduced basketball to a freakish demonstration and has put an almost unbearable handicap on the finer athletes of a normal six-foot height."[12] Because Allen loved Kansas and its rural values, he also prided himself on recruiting in-state athletes. In 1948 Allen suffered through a 9-15 season, the second losing campaign of his career, and revised his priorities. During the 1947–48 season Allen recruited Clyde Lovellette, a six-foot-nine center from Terre Haute, Indiana. Heavily recruited by Indiana, Purdue, and Notre Dame, Lovellette said he chose Kansas because Allen persuaded him that he was putting together a team that could win the NCAA championship and go to the Olympics. In 1952 Lovellette averaged 28.6 points per game and led Kansas to its first NCAA championship. Phog Allen had achieved the first half of his dream.[13]

Although his basketball résumé paled in comparison to Phog Allen's, Warren Womble, the coach of the Peoria Caterpillars, was also on a mission in the spring of 1952. Womble was only thirty-two years old but basketball was in his blood. Born in Aylsworth, Oklahoma, Womble grew up in Durant, Oklahoma, where he came under the spell of Southeastern State College's basketball coach, Bloomer Sullivan. Womble's father had a grocery store on the edge of the college campus, which made it easy for him to grow up in the gym and soak up everything Sullivan knew about basketball. Sullivan had worked for Henry Iba for several seasons and, like Iba, stressed fundamentals. Womble rated Sullivan's knowledge of basketball with the best college coaches of that generation. When he entered South-eastern, in the fall of 1938, Womble knew every play that Sullivan ran and their multiple options. By his own admission, Womble was not a particularly gifted athlete but a good leader and ferocious defender. The war interrupted his college career, but Womble returned to Southeastern, where he played from 1946 to 1948, before Peoria recruited him in the 1948–49 season.

As an Oklahoma native, Womble played against, watched, and ad-mired the Phillips 66ers. While Womble hoped to play for Phillips, the 66ers were not interested in him. In retrospect Womble doubted that he was good enough for Phillips, but he left Oklahoma with a fierce desire to make Bartlesville pay for its disinterest. Although the Peoria Caterpillar Company did not have a rich basketball tradition when Womble arrived, it had the resources to build a first-class program. Because the Caterpillar Company employed almost twenty-thousand people in Peoria, it had the capacity to absorb a few basketball players. The driving force behind the basketball program was Jim Monroe, the plant manager, who had worked his way to that position without the benefit of a high school education. Louis Niemuller, the chairman of the board, enjoyed the team's success and welcomed its public relations value but was fairly far removed from its operation.

After Womble's first months in Peoria, he wondered if he had made the correct decision. Since he did not have any machine-shop experience, Womble worried that his future with Caterpillar was limited. Moreover, at twenty-nine and playing on bad ankles, Womble considered himself over the hill as a player. Womble informed Jim Monroe that he planned to leave Caterpillar, return to Oklahoma, and pursue a coaching career. After thinking about it for a day, Monroe offered Womble the head coaching job at Peoria. Although Marv Hamilton coached the team, Monroe wanted to promote him to a different position in the plant, which would open up the coaching job. Womble finished the 1948–49 season as a player, assisted Hamilton in 1949–50, and assumed head coaching responsibilities for the 1950–51 season. Since Womble had served as the mascot of Bloomer Sullivan's Southeastern State basketball teams, he had dreamed of coaching a basketball team.[14] In only his second year as a head coach, Womble found himself with an opportunity that had eluded coaches who had devoted their lives to the game.

As in 1948 the Olympic Basketball Committee established college and independent amateur brackets. The winners of each bracket would play each other for the mythical amateur championship and, if it chose, could name seven of its players to the Olympic team. The coach of the tournament champion would direct the Olympic team, while the mentor of the runner-up would serve as an assistant.

In one departure from the 1948 model, the opening round of the Olympic tournament was divided between Kansas City's Convention Hall and New York's Madison Square Garden. On March 29, before a sellout crowd of 10,500 in Kansas City, Phillips squeaked by Fibber McGee and Molly in double overtime. Wayne Glasgow, a 66er guard, led all scorers with 24 points, including a long push shot with two seconds left to play to win the game. The McGees had strengthened their squad prior to the tournament when they added John Arndt of Loyola of Los Angeles and Al Roges of Long Island University, who scored 17 points to lead the McGee scorers. Arndt and Roges had played well in the AAU tournament for the U.S. Naval Air Station from Los Alamitos, California, which had lost to Phillips by 10 in the third round. The McGees would have picked one of their teammates, George Yardley, but he broke his right wrist before the AAU tournament, which robbed him of his dream to play on the Olympic team. In the second game Lovellette scored 29 as Kansas swamped Southwest Missouri State, the National Association of Intercollegiate Basketball (NAIB) champion, by 27 points.[15]

In the first round at Madison Square Garden the Peoria Caterpillars barely got by the U.S Air Force. The Cats were behind by 4 at the end of the third quarter, but Howie Williams led them to victory by scoring 8 points in the fourth quarter. Ron Bontemps and Frank McCabe paced the Cats with 17 and 16 points respectively, while Bobby Wallace with 17 points and Bryce Heffley with 13 led the Air Force. In the other game at the Garden, LaSalle, the NIT champs with All-American Tom Gola, downed the Redmen of St. John's, the NCAA runner-up.[16]

The winners in Kansas City flew to New York knowing that they were playing for the right to go to the Olympics. In the opener at the Garden, ten thousand fans watched Peoria surprise the experts, for the second time in ten days, as the Caterpillars defeated Phillips. Ron Bontemps with 16 and Howie Williams with 15 led a balanced scoring attack for the Caterpillars. In the second game the celebrated Lovellette lived up to all expectations, scoring 40 points as Kansas eliminated Tom Gola's LaSalle Explorers.[17] At six feet nine inches and 240 pounds, Lovellette possessed a soft hook that had sports writers comparing him to George Mikan and Bob Kurland. After the game Forrest Phog Allen, Kansas's celebrated coach, selected Lovellette, Bill Lienhard, Bob Kenney, John Keller,

Bill Hougland, Dean Kelley, and Charley Hoag for the Olympic team. Warren Womble took his starting five, Ron Bontemps, Frank McCabe, Marcus Freiberger, Dan Pippin, and Howie Williams and then added Bob Kurland and Wayne Glasgow from Phillips.[18] By insisting on taking seven of his players, (Kentucky took five in 1948), Allen denied Tom Gola, who had an outstanding tournament, a place on the Olympic team.

The following night Kansas and Peoria squared off to decide the Olympic team's head coach and to determine the mythical amateur champion of the United States. Since Kansas had won the NCAA and defeated the NIT and NAIB champions, a victory over Peoria would give the Jayhawks a clear claim to amateur superiority. In a wild finish, Kansas, which had trailed throughout the game, caught Peoria with less than fifty seconds left and tied the game at 60 each. With fifteen seconds left Lovellette, who had connected for 22 points, stole the ball from Marcus Freiberger, drove in for a potential winning lay-up, but unbelievably missed the shot. The ball was batted out to Ron Bontemps, who fired the outlet pass to Howie Williams, who hit a long one-handed shot after taking two quick dribbles to win the game at the buzzer. In the consolation game Phillips walloped LaSalle so that the AAU teams answered those critics who doubted their ability to compete with the best college teams.[19]

Because the Soviet Union was participating in its first Olympics, the political ramifications of the Helsinki Olympics were immense. The United States was a heavy favorite to win the gold medal in basketball and cruised through its first five games, including an easy win over the Soviets in the first meeting of the Cold War superpowers.[20] In its sixth game the United States squeaked by Brazil 57–53. On the same day the Soviets predicted that they would win the overall Olympics. Although the Olympic Committee did not endorse a scoring system, the media had developed one early in the twentieth century in order to increase interest in the games. The Soviets erected a scoreboard where the Soviet athletes were housed and on it they posted updated point totals and the names of all Soviet medalists. The Olympic games, a Soviet spokesman said, were a test of "the sporting virtues of each competing nation," and the Soviets expected their system to prevail.[21]

The United States met Argentina in the seventh game, which it had to win to play for the championship. Because Argentina had almost upset the United States in 1948 and had won the South American championship, it was not taken lightly. In a hard-fought game, the United States, paced by Lovellette's 25 points, prevailed, as seven Americans left the game on fouls. The championship game was a rematch with the Soviet Union, who had edged pesky Uruguay. As Warren Womble looked forward to the championship game, he predicted that the United States, if it played well, would win by 30 points.[22] The Soviets, however, decided to play a very deliberate game so that the United States led by a mere 2 points, 17–15, at halftime. With five minutes left, 4 points separated the teams, but the game ended with the Americans on top 36 to 25.[23] After the game Bob Kurland observed: "Don't kid yourself; in four years' time they will be tough to beat."[24] The U.S. basketball victory coincided with the gold medal performances by Americans in boxing and swimming, which allowed the United States to pass the Soviets in the unofficial standings and prompted the Russians to erase the point totals from their scoreboard.

Despite some minor problems, Denver's Willard "Bill" Greim, president of the International Basketball Federation, was pleased with the Olympic games. A standing-room-only crowd watched the championship game, and other games drew capacity crowds. Basketball was on its way to becoming a truly international game.

After the Olympics, Bob Kurland announced his retirement as a player. In six years he had played on three AAU championship teams and won two Olympic gold medals. At twenty-seven Kurland said: "Athletics, my old coach, Hank Iba, used to tell me, were just a phase, a step to something better. I'm ready to move on to something else."[25] As one of basketball's first talented big men, Kurland was often the target of anti-Phillips hecklers. Yet he accepted this philosophically and earned the respect of writers and players. Forty-five years after Kurland retired, George Walker, who guarded him for the San Francisco Stewarts, remembered Kurland as an outstanding player who always hustled and "seemed to drive that team."[26]

In 1952–53 the Central Bank and Trust Company put into action a more coherent plan for its basketball team. Central Bank hired Larry Varnell as its coach and eleven players, stressing that its basketball operation was a nonprofit activity designed to promote "good will, effective advertising, and the addition of willing workers to the list of personnel at the Bank." While the assets of Central Bank exceeded seventy million dollars, it stressed that it was much different from the large industrial corporations in the NIBL like Phillips 66, the Peoria Caterpillars, or Akron Goodyear. Central Bank described itself "as a tight-knit, family-like institution employing about 250 men and women." But like the other companies, the bank stressed that AAU basketball offered "something to athletes unchallenged by any other sports attraction—security and a useful life in the years to come with an established, recognized firm."[27]

In preparation for the 1952–53 season some of the Bankers' new recruits were Dick Eicher, a six-foot-five forward from Eastern Washington College who had played the previous season with the NIBL's REA Travelers from Artesia, New Mexico; Ben Gibson, a six-foot-eight-and-one-half center from St. Mary's of California; Freddie Howell, a six-foot guard from Denver University; Roger Stokes, a six-foot-four forward from the University of Colorado who had played with Dick Eicher on the REA Travelers; and Glen Smith, a six-foot-four forward who had starred in the Skyline Conference for the University of Utah. Although the Bankers struggled to a seventh place finish in the NIBL with a 6-10 record, Glen Smith was the league's second leading scorer, an NIBL All-Star, and the NIBL's most valuable player.

In 1953, after years of controversy, the AAU tournament finally left the Denver City Auditorium for the Denver Auditorium Arena. This facility, adjacent to the Auditorium, was built for basketball and sat 7,500 fans. With excellent sight lines, Denver now had a fine arena in which to play and watch basketball. In another break with the past, the tournament committee limited entries to thirty-two teams.

Going into the 1953 AAU tournament, the experts thought Los Alamitos Naval Air Station of Long Beach, California, the Peoria Caterpillars, and Phillips 66 were the favorites. Although Phillips had lost Bob Kurland, it added two college All-Americans, Chuck Darling and Clyde Lovellette. A six-foot-eight center, Chuck Darling had moved to Denver from Helena, Montana, after his sophomore year of high school. Darling led Denver's South High School to a state title in 1947. The following year, Darling had not fully recovered from measles when South lost to Manual High School in the state title game. Like most Denver high school players Darling spent many hours at the AAU tournament and patterned his sweeping hook shot after Ace Gruenig's. Darling's high school success caught the eye of Lou Wilke who learned of Darling's interest in geology, which he had developed in Montana. When Darling went off to the University of Iowa, it was with the idea of graduating with a geology degree and working and playing for Phillips Petroleum Company. As a senior Darling was the Big Ten Player of the Year, won All-American honors, and earned a Phi Beta Kappa key.[28] Lovellette was the all-everything center from Kansas who bypassed a professional contract and played for one year with Phillips. After the 1952 season Phillips chose to replace Jesse "Cab" Renick with Tom Scott, who had coached for five years at the University of North Carolina. Scott had played basketball at Pittsburg State College in Kansas, so he had roots in the Great Plains. During the regular season Phillips won its fifth straight NIBL title with a 13-3 mark and entered the AAU tournament with a 49-4 record.

Despite their regular-season success, the 1953 tournament was a disaster for the 66ers. In its second game, on a Wednesday afternoon, before a mere one thousand spectators, Everybody's Drug Store of Eugene, Oregon, pulled off one of the great upsets in AAU history when it soundly whipped the Phillips 66ers 70–52. Everybody's team was typical of so many amateur teams that were put together for a run at the national tournament. Chet Noe, whose 28 points not only made him the game's high scorer but exceeded the combined total of Lovellette and Darling, starred at the University of Oregon and was added to the team a week before the tournament. After winning the Oregon AAU tournament, the team members and their coach, Bob Hamilton, had to solicit funds from the citizens of Eugene in order to pay for their air transportation to Denver. For Denver fans the excitement generated by Everybody's triumph eased some of the disappointment when Denver's tournament hopefuls also fell in the Wednesday round of sixteen. San Diego's Grihalva Buick, paced by Hugh Faulkner and Jim Hoverder, knocked a cold-shooting Central Bank team out of the tournament.[29]

In the quarterfinals Jim Hoverder maintained his hot hand and scored 22 points as Grihalva Buick surprised the Quantico Marines. In the most exciting quarterfinal game, Los Alamitos Naval Air Station edged out Sampson Air Force Base from Geneva, New York, when Al Roges hit a jump shot with five seconds left in the game. The Peoria Cats fought off the Ada Oilers, and entered the semifinals with Everybody's Drugs, which downed another dark horse, the Ritz Café of Carbondale, Illinois.[30]

In the semifinals Everybody's Drug Store ran into bad luck when Chet Noe was sidelined with the flu and his team fell to Los Alamitos, which became the first service team to reach the finals in tournament history. The Flyers were led by a healthy George Yardley; Al Roges and Hal Uplinger, both from Long Island University; and John Arndt from Loyola of California. In the other semifinal Peoria broke open a close game when Dan Pippin scored 12 points in the fourth quarter and the Cats eliminated Grihalva Buick.[31] By making it to the semifinals, Grihalva Buick and Los Alamitos Naval Air Station had maintained the tradition of a strong California presence in the Denver tournament. The twist was that in 1953 Southern California teams rather than teams from the Bay Area captured the tournament's attention. Although Grihalva Buick lost, Dick Grihalva, a General Motors dealer in San Diego, declared his intention to recruit the quality players by offering them "good jobs" with opportunities for "profit-sharing."[32] Grihalva's coach was Fon Johnson, a member of the 1941 championship team from Twentieth Century Fox. In addition to Faulkner and Hoverder, Johnson had recruited the ageless Les O'Gara, a teammate on the 1941 team, and Glendon Anderson, former Colorado Aggie star who was stationed in San Diego with the Marines.

The championship game was a match-up of two extremely talented teams. The Peoria Cats, the defending champions, returned its starting line-up of Howie Williams, Dan Pippin, Frank McCabe, Ron Bontemps, and Marc Freiberger, all Olympic gold medalists. Peoria, had greater depth and size than Los Alamitos and, despite George Yardley's 29 points, won its second consecutive championship. Howie Williams with 17 points led a balanced scoring attack, which included 15 points each from Dan Pippin and Ron Bontemps.[33] Leonard Cahn had high praise for these three Cats, whom he classed with "illustrious All-America standouts of old. They can play in any league for my money."[34]

While the tournament grossed only one thousand dollars more than the previous year, the net increased by two thousand dollars because of declining expenditures. Jack Carberry relished Everybody's Drug Store's upset victory over Phillips, not just because Everybody's was the underdog, but because "Phillips had been so cocksure" about winning the championship. For Carberry, however, the larger issue was the nature of the event itself. While he believed the tournament had been and could remain a major sporting event, he thought Denver and the national AAU had failed to promote it properly. The general attitude, he wrote, was "let Greim do it." While Carberry had nothing but praise for Willard Greim, he recognized that Greim's hands were full with running the tournament. In addition, Carberry believed that tournament invitations had to be limited to quality teams.[35]

In the 1953–54 season the Denver Central Bankers made two key additions to their team. One was Ladell Anderson, an excellent six-foot guard from Utah State, who had played for the U.S. Air Force All-Stars, who took third place in the 1952 national AAU tournament. The other was Frank Kuzara, a five-foot-nine guard with a deadly two-handed set shot who had starred at the University of San Francisco and made the 1951 AAU All-America team as a member of Stewart Chevrolets, the 1951 champs. During the NIBL season

Denver tied for second place with the Akron Goodyears with a 9-5 record, the Bank's first winning season in the NIBL. For the first time in NIBL history, Phillips shared the league championship with Peoria, both with 10-4 records.

In 1954 the tournament was streamlined to twenty-four teams in an effort to upgrade the quality of the games in the early rounds of play. In still another departure from tradition, going back to 1935, the opening round of play was Monday rather than Sunday.

In their opener, behind Dick Eicher's 21 points, the improved Bankers topped Fort Leonard Wood and then advanced to the semifinals when they outlasted Kirby Shoes of Los Angeles as Frank Kuzara bagged 21 points. The Bankers' opponent in the semifinals was the Peoria Caterpillars. Warren Womble still had Ron Bontemps and Frank McCabe as the Cats sought their third consecutive title. To reach the semifinal game, the Cats had to beat San Francisco's Young Men's Institute (YMI), which had easily defeated its first two opponents. With rugged Jim Loscutoff and springy George Walker at the forwards, YMI possessed a tough inside game. Jim Walsh of Stanford and Raymond "Rip" Gish of Western Kentucky were excellent shooters and Al "Cappy" Lavin, formerly of San Francisco, was a clever ball handler and passer who directed the offense. After YMI took the lead in the third quarter, Peoria fought back to jump on top with 2:40 remaining and held on to win 66–65. Ron Bontemps scored 20 points to lead all scorers and converted four free throws at the end of the game to preserve the victory.

In the other semifinal bracket Grihalva Buick faced Fort Sill, Oklahoma, the tournament's dark horse. In the quarterfinals Grihalva had stunned Phillips 63–58 behind Jim Hoverder's 20 points and Glendon Anderson's 18 points. Their performances neutralized a 23-point effort by Chuck Darling who kept the 66ers in the game with his shooting and rebounding.[36] Stung by their early exit in 1953, Phillips had asked Omar "Bud" Browning to come out of retirement to coach for one year and prepare Gerald Tucker, former Phillips star, to replace him in 1954–55. Uncharacteristically, for the second consecutive year the 66ers were not a major factor in the tournament.

Going into the semifinal game with Peoria, Denver had a string of fifteen consecutive victories on the Auditorium Arena floor. Down by one point at the half, Denver took the lead 54–50 with just under seven minutes to play and slowed the game down to take time off the clock. The strategy did not work as planned but two clutch free throws by Ben Gibson and one by Freddie Howell knotted up the score at 59–59, with thirty-five seconds to play. At this point, Ron Bontemps called time to determine how Womble wanted to finish the game. An AAU All-American as a forward in 1953, Bontemps, in three years, had never tasted defeat in a national tournament game. While Bontemps was a dangerous offensive player from the forward position, Womble had moved him to guard following the retirement of Howie Williams. Womble knew that Bontemps would score less but he needed a player who understood the offense to run the team on the floor. During the time-out a fatigued Bontemps uncharacteristically sat down on the floor. Womble, who never allowed his players to sit during time-outs, asked his star, "What's wrong?" Bontemps looked up and said, "What do you want to run?" Although Bontemps had not scored a field goal for the entire game, Womble instructed his team to take the clock down to six seconds and then clear out for Ron.[37] As 6,800 roaring fans implored the Bankers to take the game into overtime, Bontemps knifed through the Denver defense to score the winning basket on a driving lay-up. Peoria's victory spoiled a 20-point performance by Denver's Glen Smith and snuffed out the Mile High City's best chance at a title since the Denver Chevrolets lost in the 1950 semifinal round. In the other semifinal game, Jim Hoverder, Ken Leslie, and Joe Stratton scored in double figures as Grihalva Buick defeated Fort Sill, 63–55. The championship game consequently was a rematch of the 1953 semifinal contest.[38]

In coaching Grihalva into the championship game Fon Johnson brought with him almost two decades of AAU experience. As was true of so many athletes, AAU basketball had presented Johnson with unexpected opportunities and experiences. Born in 1916, Johnson grew up in tiny Cowley, Wyoming, near the Montana border. He ran track, played football and won all-state basketball honors at a high school with less than a hundred students. In 1937 and 1938, the six-foot-two, 195-pound Johnson played on two Wyoming AAU championship teams that competed in the Denver tournament. After a year at the University of Utah, Johnson headed for California where he played for Clifton's Cafeteria before Bud Fischer recruited him to Twentieth Century Fox. In 1941 Johnson and Twentieth Century Fox had a banner year. In January and February Johnson barnstormed with the team as it played in Tokyo, Japan, and the Philippines. In March, Johnson returned to Denver with the Hollywood team that defeated the Olympic Club for the national AAU title. Finally, in November of 1941, Twentieth Century ended a remarkable year by defeating Phillips 66 to win the Naismith Plaque at Madison Square Garden in honor of the fiftieth anniversary of basketball. During the train ride back to California, Japan bombed Pearl Harbor and Johnson enlisted in the U.S. Navy where he continued to play basketball. After the service Johnson played two seasons for the San Diego Dons and then played and coached several local San Diego AAU teams before joining Grihalva Buick.[39]

Although hard fought, the championship game had none of the pyrotechnics of Peoria's narrow victories over San Francisco and Denver as the Cats captured their third consecutive title. Dick Retherford with 19 points, Kirby Minter with 14, and Ron Bontemps with 11 led Peoria, while Glendon Anderson had 19 for Grihalva. In the third-place game Glen Smith scored 28 points for Central Bank as Denver dominated Fort Sill.[40]

The 1954 tournament was a great success. Even Leonard Cahn, the tournament's greatest critic, admitted that the AAU "is back in business in Denver."[41] Although there were fewer teams, the tournament grossed $48,000, about $3,000 more than the previous year. The tactic of inviting only twenty-four teams had reduced expenses by $4,000 so that the net of $17,780 was the largest of any tournament except that of 1948. The success of Central Bank and the overall quality of play were important in reviving interest among local fans.[42]

In four short years the AAU had answered its critics. Reducing the number of tourney participants and building a new basketball arena provided tougher competition in a great atmosphere. And the dynamics of the tournament had changed in an important way. Phillips, which had won seven AAU tournaments in the 1940s, no longer looked invincible. After winning in 1950, the 66ers had failed to win a crown in the next four years, its longest drought since it revived its basketball program in 1936–37. While Peoria threatened to become a new dynasty, Coach Womble would have to rebuild his team after 1954, which gave his competition a reason to be optimistic. The evidence that the 66ers' dynasty had ended and that Peoria's streak was in jeopardy suggested that Denver's fans could look forward to an unpredictable tournament featuring more evenly balanced competition with many close, exciting games.

NINE

From Bartlesville to Seattle

In the 1954–55 season Central Bank named Vince Boryla to replace Larry Varnell as the Bankers' coach. Between 1949 and 1954 Boryla played with the New York Knickerbockers and averaged 11.2 points in 285 games. Because of his success in AAU basketball with the Nuggets and college basketball with Denver University, where he was an All-America selection in 1949, Boryla was closely identified with Denver basketball. Central Bank strengthened its roster when it added Glendon Anderson, who had played with Grihalva Buick while in the Marines, and George Janzen, another ex-Marine, who had played at Colorado A&M and for Poudre Valley Creamery in 1951. In the NIBL season the Bankers won twelve and lost twelve and tied for third place behind Phillips and Peoria.[1]

Spicing up the 1955 tournament field was the presence of North Carolina State—the Atlantic Coast Conference champion—with Ronnie Shavlik, former Denver East High School star. The Wolfpack, coached by Everett Case, boasted a 28-4 record and sportswriters rated the team fourth in the national basketball polls. Although N. C. State won the Atlantic Coast Conference championship in 1955, the Wolfpack did not play in the 1955 NCAA tournament because of a rules violation. Between 1954 and 1956 Shavlik led the Wolfpack to three consecutive ACC titles and still holds the school's rebounding record with 1,595. Another college team in the tournament was the University of Colorado Buffaloes playing under the flag of the Luckett-Nix Clippers. Harvey "Hap" Luckett, a Phillips jobber in Boulder, and Ed Nix, a barber on the campus, had sponsored amateur teams for years. Their team was composed of seven seniors who had played on one of the most successful basketball teams in Buffalo basketball history. In 1954 CU, coached by Bebe Lee, tied Kansas for the Big Seven Conference title and won the right to represent the conference in the NCAA tourney after it won the tiebreaker. In the first game of the regional, Bradley University knocked CU out of the tournament. In 1955 CU was the undisputed Big Seven champion and won the midwest regional by defeating Tulsa and Bradley, becoming the only CU team ever to play in the final four. In the semifinal round played at Kansas City the Buffs drew Bill Russell and the San Francisco Dons, who prevailed 62–50. After defeating Iowa in the consolation game, CU returned to Boulder and their seniors prepared for the national AAU tournament.[2]

Leading the Boulder entry into the AAU tournament were Burdette "Burdie" Haldorson, a six-foot-eight center who relied on a deadly hook shot to lead the Big Seven in scoring during his junior and senior years, and forward Bob Jeangerard, a tough defender with a good shot. The other forward was Bob Yardley, George Yardley's brother, who had played a reserve role during the season. The guards were Charley Mock and Tom Harrold, CU regulars who played together at Muncie High School in Indiana. Because Harrold had sprained his ankle in pregame warm-ups before the San Francisco game, Jamie Grant, another reserve, started at guard, but Harrold played significant minutes after the first game. Wil Walter was the seventh senior on the team. Since Bebe Lee did not coach the team during the AAU tournament, the players coached themselves.

San Francisco's Olympic Club, absent from Denver since 1941, sent a powerful team. Three of its stars were six-foot-nine Ken Sears, Santa Clara's all-time scoring leader; Jim Loscutoff, a future Boston Celtic from the University of Oregon; and Ron Tomsic, Stanford's great scorer.

After several years of tournament frustration, Phillips had completely rebuilt its team and Gerald Tucker directed the 66ers to their seventh straight NIBL title. Chuck Darling was the only returning player from the previous year as Phillips surrounded him with a good blend of size and speed. Some of the key additions were Arnold Short, a sharpshooter from Oklahoma City University; Jim Walsh, a former Stanford star with AAU experience; Gib Ford, a star at the University of Texas; and Bill Hougland, a forward on Kansas's 1952 NCAA championship team.

Defending champion Peoria lost Ron Bontemps and Frank McCabe, who had played on all three of its AAU championship teams, but Warren Womble added two University of Kansas stars, B. H. Born and Allen Kelley, plus Joe Stratton from Colgate and Grihalva Buick. They joined veterans Dick Retherford, Kirby Minter and Eddie Soloman. The Quantico Marines with Ritchie Guerin, a future NBA star, and Seattle's Buchan Bakers also sent strong teams.[3]

After drawing a bye in the first round, Denver's Central Bankers lost in round two to the Quantico Marines, sparked by Ritchie Guerin. The disappointed local fans quickly got behind the Luckett-Nix Clippers from nearby Boulder. In the first round the Clippers trounced Alaska's Panhandle Flyers behind the hot-shooting Haldorson and Jeangerard. The Flyers were a throwback to the earlier days of the tournament. They were a group of players from various occupations who funded part of their travel costs by holding a spaghetti-dinner dance in Anchorage. The following night six thousand fans waited until 10:00 p.m. to watch the Clippers blow out Houston's Ada Oilers, as Jeangerard and Halderson maintained their torrid shooting by scoring 28 and 27 points, respectively. CU's victory set up a quarterfinal game with Warren Womble's Peoria Caterpillars, who were seeking their fourth consecutive title. When Peoria defeated Seattle's Buchan Bakers in overtime, it was the fifteenth consecutive tournament victory for the Caterpillars but a costly one since they lost B. H. Born with a badly sprained ankle.[4]

Before six thousand screaming fans who braved a March snowstorm to watch the quarterfinals, the Luckett-Nix Clippers stunned the Peoria Caterpillars, 70–67. After Burdie Haldorson scored 33 points, Ben Calloway of the *Denver Post* described him as "a high flying Eagle, soaring all alone above the rest of the flock."[5] Bob Yardley added 13 and Bob Jeangerard tossed in 11. In other quarterfinal games Ritchie Guerin popped in 22 and led the Quantico

Marines past Kirby Shoes of Los Angeles. Although Ronnie Shavlik scored 20 points for North Carolina State, the Wolfpack fell to Olympic Club as Jim Loscutoff scored 19, followed by Ron Tomsic's 16, Ken Sears's 12, and Bob Matheny's 12. The only NIBL team left in the tournament was the Phillips 66ers, who skated by Gregory Clothiers of Greeley.[6]

The semifinal games were as tough and exciting as any in AAU history. In the opener the Olympic Club's Ken Sears, who led all scorers with 28 points, hit two free throws with nine seconds left to play to tie Phillips at 51–51. As the buzzer sounded, Jim Walsh, who had played on San Francisco's Young Mens's Institute in 1954, hit a thirty-foot desperation shot for Phillips and gave the 66ers the win in regulation time. In the nightcap of the semifinals Charley Mock hit four key free throws and the Clippers prevailed over the Quantico Marines. Bob Yardley's 13 points led a balanced scoring attack for Luckett-Nix as Haldorson left the game on two different occasions with a sprained ankle. Leonard Cahn was ecstatic as he marveled at the "wonder kids" and referred to them as the "seven blocks of granite."[7]

The battered Clippers were decided underdogs going into the championship game. Counting the two NCAA games the CU Buffs/Clippers were about to play in their seventh game in nine days. Despite their fatigue they battled the 66ers for forty minutes, before 7,500 fans packed into the Denver Auditorium Arena, and lost at the buzzer when Jim Walsh, for the second straight night, made a thirty-five-foot shot to give Phillips a 66–64 win and their ninth national AAU championship. Haldorson's 24 points and Jeangerard's 19 points led the Buffs, while Walsh, Chuck Darling, and Bill Hougland each scored 14 points for the victorious 66ers. Leonard Cahn, who had seen every Denver tournament, called the contest "the most dramatic title game finish in tournament history."[8] Cahn also thought 1955 "was the greatest tournament ever" due to the presence of so many college stars.[9] Certainly the gate substantiated his claim as the gross of $59,653 exceeded the old record of 1948 by a couple hundred dollars.

Although Denver and Boulder fans were disappointed with the

results, the run by the cu seniors was so captivating that any gloom was short-lived. One person who was probably happy to see the weekend was Harvey "Hap" Luckett, one of the team's sponsors, who admitted that, for good luck, he had not changed his clothes all week.[10] Almost thirty-five years later Fred Leo, one of the pioneers of Denver sports broadcasting, recalled that the 1955 championship game was one of the most listened to up to that time in Colorado basketball history.[11] By the end of the twentieth century no other major Colorado University basketball team could claim to have generated as much excitement and enthusiasm for college basketball as the 1955 Colorado team.

The performances of Haldorson and Jeangerard had an interesting impact on Denver's amateur basketball. Max Brooks, vice president of Central Bank, believed it was imperative that the Bankers acquire Haldorson and Jeangerard. If Central Bank was unsuccessful, Brooks thought that it should get out of the NIBL. When Haldorson announced that he would accept a position with Phillips, Brooks made good on his threat and withdrew Denver from the NIBL. Brooks did not disguise his annoyance with Phillips, whose resources, he said, were "just too much for us."[12] While Central Bank continued to sponsor a basketball team, it played an independent schedule in 1955–56. Although Burdie Haldorson was drafted by the St. Louis Hawks in the fourth round of the NBA draft, he chose Phillips because he thought this offered him the best chance to play in the 1956 Olympics.[13] Bob Jeangerard also joined Phillips for the 1955–56 season.

Although an encore seemed impossible, the 1956 tournament matched the 1955 Dribble Derby for surprises and excitement. To begin with, the tournament introduced Johnny Dee to Denver and his starting five from the University of Alabama, playing under the banner of Alabama's Mobile Ada Oilers. Dee's Crimson Tide had just completed the most successful basketball season in Alabama's history. In 1956 Alabama won the Southeastern Conference with a perfect 14-0 record, including a 101 to 77 triumph over Adolph Rupp's Kentucky Wildcats, the first time a team had scored 100 points against Rupp. As the conference champion, Alabama had an automatic bid to the NCAA tournament but refused to accept it when the NCAA ruled that Alabama's seniors were ineligible because the Southeastern Conference had allowed them to play as freshmen. Since 1956 was an Olympic year, the Denver tournament offered Dee's seniors a shot at the Olympic tournament and a chance to play on the Olympic basketball team. Bud Adams, the son of Boots Adams, had sponsored the Houston Ada Oilers in past tournaments and had a branch office in Mobile, Alabama. When Adams offered to sponsor the Crimson Tide in the national AAU tournament, Dee accepted and took his starting five, all from the Midwest, to Denver: Jerry Harper, George Linn, Leon Marlaire, Dennis O'Shea, and Dick Gunder.[14]

The Wichita Vickers was another new team in the AAU tournament. In the 1950s the Vickers Petroleum Company described itself as "the last of the independents" in the oil business. The company had a refinery in nearby Potwin, three hundred employees, and three hundred service stations between Iowa and Colorado. Although considerably smaller than its major corporate competition, the company's president, Jack Vickers, and vice president, Jim Vickers, were self-proclaimed basketball junkies, determined to assemble a competitive team. Their decision to sponsor a basketball team, Jim Vickers recalled, was the result of the convergence of a number of developments. Wichita was a good basketball town and Jack and Jim knew Henry Levitt, the sponsor of the legendary Wichita Henrys. When Gene Johnson, another link to Wichita's basketball past, walked into the Vickers office to sell them on the idea of reviving AAU basketball, he found a receptive audience. Jack and Jim Vickers also saw the advertising potential of the basketball team. Because the Missouri Valley Conference was very strong in the 1950s, they also believed that it would be possible to recruit regional basketball talent. Finally, Wichita State University had just built a field house that sat ten thousand fans, so the Vickers had access to a good facility.[15]

The Vickers succeeded immediately in recruiting an outstanding collection of players. Jim Vickers, an outstanding golfer at the

University of Oklahoma, used this connection to sign Les Lane, an All-American guard for the Sooners. To complement Lane in the backcourt, Wichita added Nick Revon, a speedy playmaker from Southern Mississippi who had a year of AAU experience with Houston's Ada Oilers. Jim Vickers used a different connection to recruit the highly sought-after Dick Boushka, an All-American at St. Louis University. At six feet five inches and 210 pounds, Boushka was a deadly shooter who could play defense and learned the transition game from Eddie Hickey, a future Naismith Hall of Famer. Boushka had been a Wisconsin All-State football and basketball player at Champion Jesuit High School in Prairie du Chien. Four years earlier Jim Vickers had graduated from the same school. In addition to the old school tie, Boushka had a college degree in engineering with an emphasis on techniques for discovering oil. Boushka chose Vickers over Phillips because the company was smaller and he saw a better opportunity for advancement. Twenty years after making that decision, Boushka was president of the company.[16]

Cleo Littleton was another Missouri Valley Conference star on the Vickers' first squad. An African American, Littleton was one of the most celebrated high school players in Wichita's history. Named to the Kansas High School All-State team in 1950 and 1951, Littleton led East High to the state championship in 1951. Littleton's high school coach was Ralph Miller, a football and basketball star at the University of Kansas, who was just beginning an extremely successful coaching career that would take him to Wichita University (today Wichita State University), Iowa, and Oregon State, and see him earn 657 collegiate victories and induction into the Naismith Hall of Fame. After he had won the state championship in 1951, Wichita University hired Miller, who successfully recruited Littleton. At Wichita University Littleton scored 2,164 points in four seasons, which garnered him All–Missouri Valley Conference four times and All-America honors as a senior.

There was a less pleasant side to the experience of being an African American player at Wichita. At a time when few African Americans played college basketball at predominantly white universities, and before the civil rights movement had made an impact, Littleton often had to stay with African American families when the Shockers played road games. As the team's star, he took a great deal of abuse. When Littleton considered quitting, Lynwood Sexton, a football, basketball, and track athlete at Wichita University in the late 1940s, was there to mentor him. A graduate of Wichita East High School, Sexton also had to fight the stings of racism in the Missouri Valley Conference and Littleton remembered Sexton as his idol and as a man who befriended many of Wichita's African American athletes.[17] In 2001 Sexton entered the Kansas Sports Hall of Fame for his athletic accomplishments and service to the Wichita community.

While Littleton was an excellent shooter, at six feet four inches and 185 pounds, he was not big enough to play inside in the NBA and had not developed the ball-handling skills to play outside. Although drafted in the fifth round by the Detroit Pistons, Littleton, who was interested in a business career, elected to stay home and play for the Vickers. During Littleton's three years in the NIBL he was the only African American in the league. When the team traveled in Oklahoma and Texas he was still excluded from hotels and could not eat with his teammates, who brought his meals to him in the bus. Reflecting upon his career, Littleton believed that playing for Vickers was a good decision. It prolonged his basketball career and gave him important business experience.[18]

While Ralph Miller and Cleo Littleton are both in Wichita State's Hall of Fame, their relationship did not extend beyond the basketball court. Miller admitted that he was demanding and critical of mistakes and that "I really never got over that." While Littleton respected Miller's knowledge of the game, he did not enjoy playing for him and thought Miller's domineering style reflected a view that "with black athletes you really have to pound them to get them to work." Their cool relationship was completely severed in 1958 when Miller offered unsolicited advice against Littleton's plan to build a home in a white neighborhood in Wichita. For the next thirty-five years, two of the most prominent names in Wichita basketball history never spoke to each other.[19]

Two other fixtures on the Vickers team who made their first tournament appearances for Wichita in 1956 were Wade "Swede" Halbrook and Jerry Mullen. Halbrook was a seven-foot-three center from Oregon State, while Mullen was a six-foot-four swingman who had started on San Francisco's 1955 NCAA championship team.

The 1956 tournament get off to an auspicious start when Pasadena Mirror Glaze registered the first upset of the week as it KO'd the second-seeded Peoria Caterpillars, in the latter's first game of the tournament. Ben Callaway of the *Denver Post* said it was one of "the biggest upsets in the forty-nine-year history of the event."[20] Mirror Glaze was a real Cinderella team with three of its players—John Davis, Jim Bond, and Bob Hopkins—from tiny Pasadena Nazarene College. Clyde Cook, who scored 18 points, attended Los Angeles Bible Institute. The Akron Goodyear Wingfoots was the second NIBL team to get knocked out of the tournament when they fell to the Alabama team, the Ada Oilers, 85–77. Alabama's Jerry Harper scored 30 points, three more than his teammate George Linn.[21]

Thursday's quarterfinals produced a collection of barnburners. Allen-Bradley of Milwaukee, historic tournament underachiever, slipped by Denver Central Bank in overtime. Although Allen-Bradley had finished last in the NIBL, coach Wally Sprangers picked up two college stars, Terry Rand of Marquette and Dick Miller of Wisconsin, to strengthen his team and support Grant and Russ Wittberger, along with Rube Schulz, who were all seasoned NIBL veterans. Larry Varnell had returned to the Bankers' bench and Denver added Jim Hoverder, who had starred in several AAU tournaments for San Diego's Grihalva Buick. Just before the tournament Varnell picked up Ron Shavlik, former Denver East and North Carolina State star, to back up Ben Gibson, but a broken left wrist limited his playing time. Dick Eicher was the team's leading scorer and Frank Kuzara and Ladell Anderson gave the team strong guard play. While the Bankers had trailed throughout the game, near the end they caught and passed their opponents, who rallied to take the game into overtime at 75–75. The teams traded baskets in the overtime, and then Allen-Bradley stalled for the last two minutes. With three seconds left Russ Wittberger hit a shot from the corner and sent the Bankers to the showers. Terry Rand with 20 led Milwaukee, while Dick Eicher hit 24 and Ladell Anderson 20 for the Bankers.[22] Leonard Cahn, for one, praised the effort and was the first to declare that in the second half Denver left everything on the floor. He thought the loss proved that Denver's decision to leave the NIBL over the loss of Burdie Haldorson and Bob Jeangerard had hurt the team competitively.[23]

Mobile's Ada Oilers surfaced as another tournament spoiler when they hung on to beat the Wichita Vickers. All of the Alabama seniors scored in double figures, while Dick Boushka topped Wichita with 18. The tournament's other dark horse, Pasadena Mirror Glaze, battled Seattle's Buchan Bakers for the entire game before falling 68–64. George Swyers led the Bakers with 22 points. The only team to win a quarterfinal game by double figures was Phillips 66, which outscored the Chicago Ranier Comets 106–90 in a game that featured great individual performances and plenty of physical contact. The Comets were comprised entirely of African Americans, led by University of Indiana star Wally Choice and Chicagoans "Sweet" Charley Brown, who would star at Seattle University, and Willie "the Bird" Jones, who played at Northwestern University and then the Detroit Pistons. While Choice hit for 28, Haldorson and Darling answered with 22 each and three other 66ers scored in double figures.[24]

In the semifinals, which would determine the two AAU representatives to the Olympic tournament, Alabama's bubble finally burst. Before seven thousand fans, most of whom rooted for the underdog collegians, Johnny Dee's team fell to Phillips by two points, 71–69. Dee chose to play his seniors for the entire game and they climbed within 2 points of a tie with thirty-five seconds left before Phillips successfully froze the ball. Burdie Haldorson with 19 points and Bob Jeangerard with 12, who had led the University of Colorado to the 1955 AAU finals, played important roles in defeating the Alabama collegians. In the other semifinal game Seattle's Buchan Bakers became the first Seattle team to reach the finals in the national AAU tourney by beating a stubborn Allen-Bradley five. While George Swyers remained hot with 21 points, the difference in the game was Bruno Boin, a six-foot-eight sophomore from the University of Washington, who relied on a deadly hook shot to score 17 points in his best game of the tournament.[25]

With their victories Phillips and Seattle brought to the championship game divergent basketball traditions. In 1955 Phillips had won its ninth title and entered the 1956 tournament strengthened by the addition of Haldorson and Jeangerard as well Joe Dean, an All–Southeast Conference guard from Louisiana State University. The Pacific Northwest had sent teams to Denver since the 1930s, with their best performances coming in 1947 and 1949 when Alpine Dairy lost in the semifinals. Businesses in the Seattle area sponsored teams in the Northwest League where they played for the right to compete in a state postseason tournament, sponsored by the *Seattle Post-Intelligencer* for twenty-six years. The winner of the state tournament then had to play the winner of the Oregon–Inland Empire tournament for the right to represent the Northwest in Denver.

The inspiration for the Buchan Bakers came from Warren "Bud" Howard, who had grown up in Seattle and played basketball for Jack Friel at Washington State between 1938 and 1940. After World War II Howard approached Colin Buchan, the oldest son of the owner of the Buchan Bakery, George Buchan, about sponsoring an AAU team in the Northwest League. Colin convinced his father that the advertising generated by a basketball team would pay off in sales. While the Buchan Bakers entered the Northwest League in 1947–48, it did not win the right to represent the Northwest until 1952. After suffering a humiliating loss to Allen-Bradley, Howard recognized that the Bakers needed a tougher schedule and more talent if they expected to be competitive in Denver. After 1953 Howard, who had coached the team since 1947, focused his efforts on scheduling, recruiting, and public relations, and turned over the coaching to others.[26]

In 1955 Frank Fidler, a successful coach at Seattle's Garfield High School, agreed to coach the Bakers. Born in Cornelius, North Carolina, just a mile from Davidson College, Fidler played baseball and basketball at Appalachian State. After he graduated from college Fidler entered the service, and the Air Force sent him to Seattle in

1944. Following the war Fidler started teaching at Garfield High School, where he established his reputation as a basketball coach. In five years he won a city championship and helped establish Garfield's rich basketball tradition. Fidler continued to teach during the five years he coached the Bakers. Calm and analytical, Fidler tried to figure out what his players did best and then gave them an opportunity to do that on the floor. In 1959 he left coaching to move into public school administration, a path that would lead him back to Garfield High School as its vice principal and principal.

When Fidler became Buchan's coach, the core of his team was already in place. Two of Fidler's guards, Charlie Koon and Joe Cipriano, both at five feet eleven inches, were outstanding ball handlers who had led the University of Washington to a third-place finish in the 1953 NCAA tournament. Stan Glowaski, a six-foot-three guard from Seattle University, was a strong defender who could score. In the frontline were Ed Halberg, an athletic forward from the University of Oregon, and Dean Parsons, a six-foot-eight center with a good shot from the University of Washington. After losing in double overtime to Peoria in 1955, Howard recruited four players who made significant contributions in 1956. While the Seattle team had normally relied on players from the Northwest, it successfully recruited George Swyers, a six-foot-four guard who had averaged almost 33 points a game as a senior at West Virginia Tech. In the front line the Bakers picked up Phil Jordan, an extremely talented six-foot-ten center, who drifted into the Northwest League after two years at Whitworth College. Filling out the front line were two University of Washington stars, Frank Guisness, an agile forward, and Bruno Boin, a six-foot-eight center with a sweeping hook shot.[27]

In 1955–56 the Buchan Bakers had not participated in the National Industrial Basketball League but they had played a sixty-game schedule that included a tour of Japan and the Philippines. Moreover, prior to the tournament, the Bakers split a four-game series with the Wichita Vickers. Consequently, when the Bakers entered the tournament, though an underdog, they were ready to compete.

In the championship game the Bakers fell behind early, and Boyd Smith, who covered the game for the *Seattle Post-Intelligencer*, reported that "the packed crowd settled back to see a romp."[28] By halftime the Bakers regrouped and trailed 31–30. The two teams traded the lead in the second half until the 2:25 mark, when Burdie Haldorson tied the game for Phillips. At this point Fidler elected to hold the ball until he took a time-out with twenty seconds left to play, when he designed a play for George Swyers to take the game's last shot. As the final seconds ticked off, Swyers's jump shot fell through the basket and gave his team a 59–57 upset victory.[29] The Buchan Bakers were the toast of Seattle as they brought back the AAU trophy and two AAU All-Americans, George Swyers and Charlie Koon.

By every standard the 1956 tournament was a great success. Exciting games, large crowds, and great upsets marked the week-long event. Jack Carberry, for one, praised the quality of the event and fan support, but wondered why there was no "visual sign of our town's appreciation." He observed "no welcoming banners flying in our streets. Not a sign as a window display, as far as we have been able to discover, is in a store window or a hotel lobby." Carberry saw Denver as a "tourist town" and believed the city's growth depended on converting visitors into new residents. Denver had not done enough to woo its visitors.[30] The veteran sports editor also worried about the tournament's future because, Carberry thought, it was too dependent on NIBL teams. He thought the future of the AAU tournament depended on reviving the AAU in districts of the United States that failed to produce quality teams.[31] While Carberry understood that the fiftieth national AAU tournament was a given for 1957, he worried about 1958, which was Denver's centennial year. Wichita had just built a ten-thousand-seat arena, and it planned to make a bid for the tournament. Carberry reminded his readers that the bottom line of athletic events was money. He approved of efforts to prepare the Denver Coliseum, with 12,000 seats, for future tournaments, 4,500 more than the Auditorium Arena held.[32]

A week after the Denver shootout, basketball fans turned their attention to Kansas City for the Olympic Trials. Unlike the previous three Olympic tournaments, which included eight teams from college and AAU ball, the 1956 Olympic Basketball Committee devised a four-team round robin tournament, with each team playing each other once. The selection of Melbourne, Australia, as the location of the 1956 Olympic Games influenced the choice of this format. Because Australia is in the Southern Hemisphere, its summer corresponds to the winter months in North America. Since the games were planned for November, the competition would take place during the heart of the academic year and the beginning of the collegiate basketball season in the United States. Consequently, the College All-Star team would consist solely of players who had just completed their eligibility and, at most, would miss the beginning of the NBA or NIBL season.

In previous Olympic years, the Olympic Basketball Committee had made its job simpler by allowing the two teams that made the finals of the Olympic Trials to name anywhere from five to seven players. This limited the at-large selections and reduced the role of politics in selecting the team. While the method of selecting the previous four Olympic teams automatically excluded some great players, it did reward team excellence and was a powerful incentive for collegians to play AAU basketball. As late as the 1950s, when NBA salaries were not extraordinarily high, many outstanding players still chose to play AAU ball for a chance at job security and to represent their country and participate in the Olympic experience. In 1956, the U.S. Olympic Basketball Committee had to select twelve players, allocating the winning team five players and choosing the remaining players at large.

The tension between selecting the best players for the Olympics and institutional politics was illustrated in the cases of Wilt Chamberlain and Elgin Baylor, two of the most gifted players of their or any basketball era. Jack Carberry reported that AAU officials unsuccessfully approached the Big Seven months before the AAU tournament and asked it to waive its rule prohibiting freshmen from playing in the AAU tournament. The reason was that Chamberlain was a freshman at the University of Kansas and the AAU wanted him on a team in the Denver tournament so that he would be eligible for the Olympic tournament. The refusal of the Big Seven to budge infuriated Carberry, who believed that it was "the inherent right of every American boy of amateur status to earn for himself through his skills, a place on the United States Olympic team."[33]

In Elgin Baylor's case Seattle University twice denied him a chance to compete for a spot on the Olympic team. In the summer of 1955, Baylor decided to leave the College of Idaho and transfer to Seattle University. Because of his transfer Baylor was ineligible to play collegiately for one year, but stayed active by playing AAU basketball with Westside Ford in Seattle's Northwest League. Frank Fidler tried to add Baylor to the Bakers for the AAU tournament in Denver and then again for the Olympic tournament in Kansas, but Seattle University rejected both requests. The United States could have had an Olympic team with Bill Russell, Wilt Chamberlain, and Elgin Baylor, three players who defined their positions in the 1950s and 1960s.

The Olympic Basketball Committee allowed each of the AAU teams to add four players to their rosters. The Buchan Bakers picked up Dick Eicher from Central Bank, Dick Boushka from the Wichita Vickers, S. L. Shofner from Akron Goodyear, and Terry Rand from Milwaukee's Allen-Bradley. Phillips selected Jerry Harper and George Linn from the Mobile Ada Oilers, Jim Bond from the Pasadena Mirror Glaze, and Dick Miller of Allen-Bradley. The College All-Stars, coached by Bucky O'Connor of Iowa, featured Bill Russell and K. C. Jones of the two-time NCAA championship San Francisco Dons, Hal Lear of Temple, Carl Cain of Iowa, and Willie Naulls of UCLA. Bruce Drake, former coach of the University of Oklahoma, directed the Armed Force's All-Stars, which included Ron Tomsic of Stanford, Gib Ford of Texas, Al Bianchi of Bowling Green, and Ritchie Guerin of Iona.

In the first night of the three-day event, the Armed Forces All-Stars, paced by Ron Tomsic's 28 points, upset Phillips in overtime. Burdie Haldorson, with 22 points, led the 66ers. In the second game, Bill Russell with 24 points joined by K. C. Jones with 18, Hal Lear with 15, and Willie Naulls with 14, led the College All-Stars by the Seattle Buchan Bakers. Dick Boushka hit 20 points to lead Buchan's scorers.[34] In the second night of the tournament Phillips bounced back from a 5-point halftime deficit to defeat the Buchan Bakers, 72–64. Haldorson, Chuck Darling, Jim Walsh, and Joe Dean scored in double figures to pace Phillips. George Swyers with 14 and Dick Boushka with 14 were the only Bakers in double figures. In the second game Bill Russell scored 29 to lead the College All-Stars past the Armed Forces All-Stars, 72–64. Tomsic, for the second night, led the servicemen with 17 points.[35] This set up a championship game in which Phillips, according to a formula devised by the Olympic Basketball Committee, had to beat the College All-Stars by at least 5 points to win the tournament. If it won by less than 5 points, Phillips needed the Buchan Bakers to defeat the Armed Forces All-Stars to claim the championship. Because of the sheer brilliance of the six-foot-ten Bill Russell, the experts gave the College All-Stars the edge in this match-up, but Phillips prevailed 79–75. One of the keys for the 66ers was Chuck Darling, who scored 19 of his game-high 21 points in the first half to give Phillips a 12-point lead. Jim Walsh had 18 and Joe Dean 16 to help fight off the All-Stars in the second half. Hal Lear scored 23 for the All-Stars followed by Bill Russell with 19 and Willie Naulls with 16. While the All-Stars scored six more baskets, they shot only 32.6 percent from the floor, and the 66ers, with sixteen more free throws, had enough to win the game.

The 4-point margin of victory was not enough to assure Phillips the tournament championship without a Seattle victory. With Phillips cheering on the sideline, the Buchan Bakers defeated the Armed Forces All-Stars, 82–79, as Dick Boushka scored 25 points for the Bakers. As a result the Olympic Committee named Gerald Tucker the Olympic head basketball coach and five 66ers—Chuck Darling, Burdie Haldorson, Bill Hougland, Bob Jeangerard, and Jim Walsh—to the Olympic team. The Olympic Committee selected Bill Russell, K.C. Jones, and Carl Cain from the College All-Stars, Ron Tomsic, Gib Ford, and Bill Evans from the Armed Forces, and Dick Boushka from Seattle to complete the squad.[36] The Olympic Committee named Bruce Drake, Tucker's coach at the University of Oklahoma, to assist him.

After the Olympic Committee announced the Olympic team, the

first to cry foul were the Buchan Bakers. Not one of the players on the AAU championship team that won in Denver was on the Olympic squad. The Seattle team was particularly bitter because Charlie Koon, who averaged 15 points in the tournament, was overlooked. While Wichita's Dick Boushka played brilliantly for the Buchans during the tournament and earned a place on the team, Frank Fidler believed that at least one of his players deserved a spot on the Olympic squad. The Bakers also believed that Willie Naulls, a UCLA All-American, and Hal Lear, from Temple University, the most valuable player in the 1956 NCAA tournament, had also been overlooked.[37] A strong case could also have been made for Texas Christian University's Ray Warren, who put up impressive numbers for the Armed Forces. The selection committee answered charges made by sportswriters that politics rather than performance determined a number of choices by claiming that fears of zone defenses and the need for familiarity with offenses were important in choosing the team.[38] Ten years after the tourney Bill Russell, in *Go Up For Glory*, agreed with Frank Fidler that, in some cases, politics prevailed over performance.[39] By giving the winning team five players, reducing the squad from fourteen to twelve, and not giving the same number of roster positions to the champion and runner-up, as had been done in the past, the selection committee had made its task more difficult.

The controversy did not dampen the excitement in Bartlesville as the champion 66ers returned home. A huge crowd met the players at the airport, and they were driven through the streets in downtown Bartlesville as their admiring fans cheered their victory. An obviously excited Boots Adams promised that the company would send all the 66er players who did not make the Olympic tournament team to Melbourne along with their wives. Adams saw the team's performance and employer support as qualities that had "powered our company's great success in every phase of business."[40]

In the fall of 1956 the Olympic team prepared for Melbourne by playing a ten-game exhibition schedule against NIBL and All-Star teams. International crises and domestic tensions were particularly acute. The Suez Crisis and Hungarian Revolution raised thorny issues for the International Olympic Committee. In the United States the South's resistance to the *Brown* decision that declared segregation unconstitutional in public schools and the Montgomery bus boycott signaled the beginning of civil rights activism. As the Olympic team played its exhibition schedule, the team's three black players, according to Russell, were placed "in situation after situation where we were segregated or embarrassed."[41]

The Olympic basketball competition proved a breeze for the United States. Gerald Tucker utilized a pressing defense that befuddled the international teams. American defenders knew that they could gamble, since Russell was a brilliant shot-blocker who could intimidate the opposition on those occasions when they broke the press. The Americans beat the Soviet Union twice by 30 points, while no other nation got within 40 points of the Americans. The Olympics demonstrated once again the clear superiority of the American style of play at this time in history.[42]

TEN

Parity Prevails

While 1957 marked the fiftieth anniversary of the national AAU basketball tournament, it was the first season for the Denver–Chicago Truckers. After the 1956 tournament the Denver Central Bank dropped its sponsorship of a competitive amateur basketball team. The failure of the team to draw well during the regular season troubled Max Brooks, the vice president of Central Bank. While he did not expect the team "to be a money maker or even self supporting," there was a limit to the amount of red ink Central Bank could absorb. Another argument against continuing the sponsorship was that Central Bank believed it received fewer advertising benefits than its NIBL competition.[1]

George Kolowich Jr., the president of the Denver–Chicago Trucking Company, filled the void left by Central Bank. Using the Phillips model, the D-C Truckers established a four-year executive training program for ten basketball players, who reportedly received $400 a month plus $1,200 for hours away from work to play basketball. Although Kolowich estimated that the basketball team cost the company one hundred thousand dollars, he believed, as in the case of the other sponsors, the company would profit from the advertising, good will, and the acquisition of potential employees.[2]

Kolowich hired Johnny Dee, fresh from the University of Alabama and the 1956 tournament, to coach his team. For a variety of reasons the Denver job looked attractive to Dee. For one, Dee's roots were in the Midwest rather than the South. Born in Cedar

Rapids, Iowa, in 1923, Dee grew up in Chicago's North Side where he was a three-sport star at Loyola Academy, which at that time was located near Loyola University. While in high school, he kept score for Loyola University, coached by Leonard Sachs, an innovator who was inducted posthumously into the Naismith Hall of Fame in 1961. After graduating from high school in 1942, Dee's dream of playing for Sachs was short-circuited when the Ramblers' mentor died unexpectedly that year at forty-five. Following two years in the Coast Guard, Dee started two years at Notre Dame, where one of his teammates was Vince Boryla. In 1946–47 Dee returned to Loyola for his senior year. After coaching high school basketball and football in Chicago's Catholic League, Dee returned to Notre Dame, as an assistant to Johnny Jordan, and also earned a law degree before moving to Alabama, where he was also an assistant football coach. By 1956, as the civil rights movement unfolded, Dee also was uncomfortable with Alabama's policy of not scheduling northern basketball teams with black players. Finally, Dee had a law degree and interests in business and politics. He believed that working for Kolowich, who doubled his salary, would give him an opportunity not only to coach but to utilize his legal education.[3] Energetic and engaging, Dee dedicated himself to reviving Denver basketball.

In his first year in the NIBL the D-C Truckers compiled an 11-9 record, which placed them in a tie for second place with three other teams, two games behind Phillips. In building his team Dee started with three players from Central Bank—Dick Eicher, Frank Kuzara, and Ben Gibson. The new coach recruited six-foot-nine, 250-pound Terry Rand—the Marquette star who had played so well for Allen-Bradley in the 1956 tournament—to play center. Rand had led Marquette to its first NCAA appearance in 1955 and had set a Chicago Stadium college scoring record with 43 points against Duquesne in 1956. Jerry Vayda from North Carolina, Joe Capua from Wyoming, Ken Jaksy from DePaul, Bill Logan from Iowa, and Ron Bennink from Washington State were other important additions. In early March, after the Truckers downed Phillips before 5,600 at the Auditorium Arena, local fans looked forward to the 1957 tournament with great anticipation. Terry Rand led the NIBL in rebounding and scoring with a 20.3 average, good enough to give him the league's rookie-of-the-year and most-valuable-player honors.[4]

On Monday March 26, 1957, the fiftieth AAU tournament welcomed twenty-six teams to play in the golden anniversary of this event. Consistent with tradition, all of the twenty-six teams took part in the opening ceremonies, and Willard Greim welcomed the players, coaches, and fans. Two days later Clair Jordan of the *Rocky Mountain News* reported that "the six-year spell that had been woven around Denver's NIBL representative refused to relax its grip" as he described how McDonald Scots of Lake Charles, Louisiana, upset the D-C Truckers. The leader of the little-known Scots was Bill Reigel, an NAIA All-American at McNeese State, who led the nation in scoring with a 33.9 average and carried McNeese to the National Association of Intercollegiate Athletics (NAIA) championship in 1956. In the first seven minutes of the game the Truckers only managed to score 4 points. Down by 10 points at the half, Denver rallied near the end of the game to get within one point. With nine seconds left Joe Capua missed a jumper, and for the fourth time in the last six years of the tournament, Denver failed to move past the second round. D-C's quick exit revived memories of the 1930s when Denver teams seemed doomed by a tournament hex.[5]

Although it was little consolation, other NIBL teams also made early exits from the tourney. Milwaukee's Allen-Bradley and Akron's Goodyear Wingfoots lost their first games, the latter to the Army All-Stars, which featured Carroll Williams, a clever guard from San Jose State; Art Bunte, a strong forward from Denver South High School and the University of Utah; K. C. Jones, ex-San Francisco star and Olympian; and Arnold Short, a deadly shooter from Phillips.

In the quarterfinals the Buchan Bakers spoiled Wichita's bid to reach the semifinals by edging the Vickers. Charlie Koon, Ed Halberg, and Dean Parsons were the only players who returned from Frank Fidler's defending champs. In recasting his team Fidler had added Ron Patnoe and Doyle Perkins, two guards from the University of Washington and, for the tournament, Dick Stricklin, a forward from Seattle University, which had just played in the NIT. His most intriguing pick-up was R. C. Owens, an African American from the College of Idaho, a school of just 450 students in Caldwell, Idaho, which played in the Pacific Northwest Conference. Born in Schreveport, Louisiana, during the depths of the Depression, Owens played sports in California after his parents moved to Santa Monica to find work in the shipyards. A three-sport star at predominantly white Santa Monica High School in California, Owens turned down offers from established university programs to play football and basketball at the College of Idaho with eight friends from Santa Monica. A tremendous leaper, Owens averaged 21 points over four years and in his sophomore year led the nation with 27.6 rebounds per game. Bud Howard successfully recruited Owens to Seattle, because the Bakers, as a result of the 1956 championship, had won the right to play a series of games against European teams preparing for the Olympics, an opportunity Owens could not pass up. In September of 1956 the Bakers toured France and Spain, as well as Poland and Czechoslovakia, the first U.S. team to play behind the Iron Curtain. In Denver Owens immediately impressed the tournament crowd with his athleticism, timing, and leaping ability, which would earn him a spot on the AAU All-America team.[6]

The most stunning upset of the quarterfinals came when Phillips met San Francisco's Olympic Club. The 66ers, with Burdie Haldorson, Jim Walsh, Chuck Darling, and Bill Hougland, had four Olympians, a wealth of tournament experience, and a strong bench. Winner of the NIBL, Phillips was the favorite to win another AAU title. Instead, the Olympic Club blitzed Phillips, 82–61, before a crowd of 7,500 that cheered wildly for the Winged O.[7] As Leonard Cahn observed, fan enthusiasm for the Olympic Club was whetted by watching "the blue bloods of the basketball world . . . chopped apart." He likened the Denver fans to a "blood-thirsty crowd" at a Roman circus. Cahn, obviously repulsed by the fan reaction, praised the 66ers because "[i]n victory or defeat they have something called class."[8]

Until 1955, when it earned a third-place finish, the venerable Olympic Club had not made an appearance in Denver since its loss to Twentieth Century Fox in the 1941 championship game. Carl Minetti, the owner of a San Francisco sporting goods store, was primarily responsible for reviving competitive basketball at the Olympic Club. In 1954 he persuaded the board of directors to make him the club's basketball coach and to support a more competitive program. Minetti had coached and sponsored a number of San Francisco AAU teams for almost twenty years and worked diligently to recruit college stars from the Bay Area. As he recruited players, Minetti offered them a chance to extend their playing careers, an opportunity to play in the Denver tournament, and a membership in the classy Olympic Club for $3.50 a month.[9]

Minetti's 1957 team was an interesting blend of college stars and Tom Meschery, a high school All-American who was a midterm graduate from Lowell High School. Meschery was one of a long line of college and professional stars who played for the legendary Benny Neff, who coached Lowell High School from 1925 through 1965.

Meschery's road to Lowell was more than a little circuitous. Born in Harbin, Manchuria, in 1938 to parents who fled from Russia after the 1917 revolution, Tom, along with his sister and mother, was on his way to join his father, who had found them a home in San Francisco in December of 1941. Just as they were preparing to embark on their voyage, the Japanese bombed Pearl Harbor. The Japanese prevented all ships from leaving China, and because of this bad timing Tom and his family were interned by the Japanese and spent the war years in Tokyo. Meschery was eight years old when his family was reunited on American soil.[10]

The guards for the Olympic Club were Albert "Cappy" Lavin and Phil Vukicevich, University of San Francisco teammates who were local high school stars. Cappy Lavin played at St. Ignatius High School and was a product of the San Francisco schoolyards. Forty years after playing competitive basketball, Lavin confessed that for sheer fun nothing matched the three-on-three game at the Gratton School schoolyard or the Marin Swim and Tennis Club. An excellent ball handler and passer, Lavin could protect the ball and find the open man. At USF he played one year for Pete Newell and two for Phil Woolpert, who also coached him for two years at St. Ignatius.[11] Phil Vukicevich, a Lincoln High School graduate, was one year behind Lavin at USF. A tough defender and good scorer, Vukicevich had an outstanding career for the Dons and continued to develop his game while playing service ball for two years between 1953 and 1955. As Vukicevich recalled, he and his teammates pointed for the Denver tournament and the opportunity to compete against some of the nation's best players. For him it was like playing in the NIT.[12] In the front line, in addition to Meschery, the Olympic Club had Russ Lawler, who had a fine career at Stanford; Barry Brown, another Stanford star; Carl Boldt, a starter for San Francisco's 1956 NCAA championship team; and Ed Romanoff from the College of Pacific.

While the Olympic Club was making history, the Air Force All-Stars were methodically working their way through the tournament. Before the games began, Chet Nelson gave the service team a twelve-to-one shot at winning and thought eight other teams had a better chance of capturing the crown. The All-Stars, however, were not a bunch of players who were unfamiliar with each others' playing styles or the AAU tournament. Five of the players—Dick Boushka, Dick Welch from the University of Southern California, Ray Warren from Texas Christian University, and Don Bragg and Ed White from UCLA—led the Laredo, Texas, Air Force Base to the World Air Force Base Tournament championship held at Lowry Air Force Base in Denver. Boushka, who had played with the Wichita Vickers in 1956, was described by Chet Nelson as "the old prototype, big, rugged, tireless, and a well-rounded ball player."[13] Among those who joined the Laredo Five was Ron Tomsic, a five-foot-eleven shooting guard who had broken Hank Luisetti's single-season and career scoring marks at Stanford. A 1955 AAU All-American with the Olympic Club and a 1956 Olympian, Tomsic knew how to put the ball in the basket. Al Kelley, a star guard at the University of Kansas, who represented Ulm Air Force Base in Germany, had played with Peoria and would play on the 1960 Olympic team. Depth was provided by Jim Coshow of the University of Washington and the 1956 Buchan Bakers, Max Hooper of the University of Illinois, and Henry Mc-Donald, who had no college experience.

The coach of the Air Force team was twenty-six-year-old Ken

Flower, another of Benny Neff's stars at San Francisco's Lowell High School. Flower played for Forrest Twogood at the University of Southern California, where he earned All-Conference honors. Perhaps as memorable as his basketball accomplishments was Flower's brush with a basketball game fixer during his sophomore year in 1950–51. After being offered $1,500 to make sure that USC would lose by more than the point spread in a game against UCLA, Flower called his coaches, who, in turn, called the vice squad, who arrested the fixer. In 1957 Flower played for Ulm, Germany, which had won the European championship and the right to play in the World Air Force Base Tournament in Denver. Although Flower made the Air Force all-tournament team, he had lost his amateur status when, after completing his senior year, he toured with college all-stars against the Harlem Globetrotters. After the tournament at Lowry, Colonel William Stevenson asked Flower to help select and to coach the Air Force's entry in the AAU tournament.[14] Behind the shooting of Dick Boushka and Ron Tomsic, the U.S. Air Force All-Stars rolled over their opposition including an easy semifinal victory over the Buchan Bakers. In the other semifinal the Olympic Club overcame an early 13-point deficit to beat Peoria, as Russ Lawler led all scorers with 16 points.[15]

For thirty-seven minutes the championship game between the Olympic Club and the Air Force All-Stars was a nip-and-tuck affair. Then in the last three minutes the Air Force scored 13 unanswered points for an 87–74 victory. Ironically Ron Tomsic, who had played with the Olympic Club in 1955, scored 26 points to lead the winners. Cappy Lavin dropped in 20 for the Californians followed by Meschery with 18 and Lawler with 15 points.[16]

Despite the early exit of the D-C Truckers, the tournament was a great success and drew standing-room-only crowds for three nights and a record forty-five thousand for six nights.[17] The venerable Jack Carberry called it a "great show" and "looked forward to 1958 with keen anticipation."[18] Before and after the tournament sportswriters had great praise for Johnny Dee, who, wrote Chet Nelson, deserved much of the credit for the "revived interest in AAU basketball" in Denver. Nelson acknowledged that Dee "drew a smattering of criticism for his sideline high jinx" but his team hustled and "they sent spectators out of the Auditorium Arena happy that they were at the game."[19] Jack Carberry thought Dee was "the best thing that has happened to basketball in Denver since William Haraway brought AAU basketball to Denver."[20]

After the tournament Johnny Dee pursued his goal of making the D-C Truckers champions with his customary energy. Between August 17 and September 6 of 1957, Dee took the Truckers on a tour of South America, where they won eight of nine games. In the 1957–58 NIBL campaign the Truckers wound up with a respectable 16-14 mark for a third-place finish in the six-team NIBL. Three of D-C's wins were against Phillips. In his second year at the helm Dee added Harv Schmidt, an All-American forward from the University of Illinois; Joe Belmont, a quick guard from Duke University; Barry Brown, a Stanford University star and 1957 AAU All-American with the San Francisco Olympic Club; Jimmy Ashmore, a sharp-shooting guard from Mississippi State; and Art Bunte, from Denver South High School and the University of Utah. Schmidt averaged 20.1 points per game, which earned him rookie-of-the-year honors and a place on the NIBL All-Star team. Bunte also had an excellent NIBL season as he averaged 14.2 points per game. They joined veterans Terry Rand, Dick Eicher, Frank Kuzara, Ron Bennink, Ken Jaksy, and Jerry Vayda. Rand, Kuzara, and Bennink also scored in double figures for the season.

In addition to coaching, Leonard Cahn reported that Dee was "sandwiching in his off-court role as goodwill ambassador for a sport which has lost some following here in recent years." While Dee had upgraded his team he also recognized that "the tournament is the final word around here. . . . [N]o matter what we do in the league, the tournament provides a happy ending or a hangover."[21]

In the Truckers' first 1958 tournament game, they downed the Marion-Kay Extractors of Brownstown, Indiana, as Harv Schmidt's 20 points led all scorers. The first big upset of the tournament came on a Wednesday, when McDonald Scots, Denver's nemesis in the 1957 tournament, knocked off the seeded Akron Goodyear Wing-foots. Bill Reigel, an AAU All-American in 1957, scored 27 for the

Scots.[22] For the first time since 1954 Denver marched into the semi-finals when the Truckers held off the Air Force All-Stars. The game was tied on fifteen occasions before D-C took command in the final five minutes. Harv Schmidt scored 15 points, Terry Rand 14, and Jimmy Ashmore 10, while Barry Brown snared 13 rebounds for the triumphant Truckers.

In the biggest upset of the quarterfinals, Fort Leonard Wood, Missouri, shocked the Wichita Vickers, 48–45. Wichita had earned a share of the 1958 NIBL championship with Phillips and the Vickers averaged 106.5 points per game in league play. Led by Dick Boushka, back with Wichita, Dan Swartz, Les Lane, and two seven-footers, Wade Halbrook and Don Boldebuck, Vickers had a formidable lineup. Fort Leonard Wood played only five players against Wichita, but two of them were 1956 Olympians and collegiate stars—K. C. Jones and Carl "Sugar" Cain. Two of the other starters were the Judson twins, Paul and Phil, of the University of Illinois. The fifth starter was Ed Crenshaw from Quincy College in Illinois. Fort Leonard Wood played a deliberate game offensively and used a zone defense to slow down the Vickers' offense. In the other quarterfinal games, Burdie Haldorson scored 29 points to lead Phillips past Seattle's Buchan Bakers, and the Peoria Caterpillars relied on their superior size to dump Louisiana's McDonald Scots.[23]

In the semifinals the Denver-Chicago Truckers downed Fort Leonard Wood, making them the first Denver team to reach the AAU finals since 1948. A balanced scoring attack led by Harv Schmidt's 19 points overcame a 20-point, 20-rebound performance by K. C. Jones. In the other semifinal, Peoria crushed Phillips by 37 points, 90–53. In 1957 the 66ers had lost to the Olympic Club by 21, and tournament observers found a second drubbing almost inconceivable. Down by 5 at the half, Phillips lost Burdie Haldorson to fouls and could not find the range offensively, while Peoria shot an impressive 61 percent after the half. Howie Crittenden and Jim Palmer paced Peoria with 19 each.[24]

Denver crowds usually relished every defeat suffered by the AAU Goliaths. This time, Bob Collins reported, "the Auditorium Arena standing-room-only crowd . . . actually felt sorry for the green clad and complexioned warriors."[25] In part the embarrassing defeat was simply a case of a hot Peoria team catching Phillips on a cold night. Bartlesville, however, had lost center Chuck Darling and guard Jim Walsh after the 1957 season. For the first time in twelve years, Bartlesville did not have a center of the stature of Bob Kurland or Chuck Darling. During the NIBL season Burdie Haldorson picked up much of the slack by averaging 26.7 points to lead all scorers and scored a league record 50 points against Akron. Although the 66ers shared the league championships with Wichita, nine league losses demonstrated that Phillips no longer intimidated their opponents. The perplexing loss prompted Jack Carberry to write, "It was like the remark of the Zoo visitor who, seeing his first giraffe, said there ain't no such animal."[26]

The game also reflected the intensity of the rivalry between Phillips and Peoria. Warren Womble recalled that for most of their regular season games, he and his players put in a full work day except when the Cats played Phillips, then the players were given more time to rest and prepare. Between 1955 and 1958 the rivalry between the two teams intensified because there was no love lost between Gerald Tucker and Womble. In their last meeting of the 1958 NIBL season, Phillips beat the Cats in Peoria. To rub it in, Tucker called time-out with seconds left and asked some of his players to carry him off on their shoulders. Womble's players remembered this and several surprised him after their semifinal triumph by hoisting him on their shoulders.[27]

The semifinal debacle was especially difficult for Gerald Tucker, who coached his last game the next night as Phillips defeated Fort Leonard Wood for third place. Before the season the 66ers decided they would return the coaching responsibilities to Bud Browning, who assisted Tucker in the 1957–58 campaign. The Oklahoma All-American played on two Phillips championship teams, was twice named an AAU All-American, coached one team to the AAU championship, and was the coach of the Olympic champions in 1956.

In 1958 Warren Womble's Cats sought their fourth AAU title of the 1950s. He started six-foot-nine B. H. Born, who had starred at the University of Kansas, at center. Flanking Born were Jim Palmer, a six-foot-eight forward from Dayton, whom Womble regarded "as the best board man I ever had"; and Chuck Wolfe, a six-foot-three left-handed forward, from North Dakota and the Armed Services. Womble's starting guards were Howie Crittenden, a Murray State collegian who could shoot and protect the ball; and Dean Kelley, a starter on KU's 1952 NCAA champs and a member of the 1952 Olympic team. Womble's sixth man was Dean's brother, Al, who also starred at KU and played on the 1957 Air Force team, which won the AAU tournament.

While the Caterpillar Company did not make too many exceptions for its basketball players, it allowed Womble to take his team to Denver a week before the tournament. Between Monday and Thursday the team practiced twice a day and ended the week with wind sprints on Friday and Saturday. On Sunday the players went into the mountains for breakfast and to relax. Womble remembered that the tournament "was what the whole year was about" and believed no team would beat him because it was in better condition than the Cats.[28]

In one of the most emotionally draining championship games in AAU history, an overflow crowd of eight thousand watched Peoria survive four overtimes to edge Denver, 74–71. The Truckers had a 44–37 lead at halftime but between turnovers and cold shooting managed only three baskets in the second half. However, they cashed in on enough free throws to take the game into overtime. Peoria's B. H. Born was the game's high scorer with 22, but the hero of the overtime was Chuck Wolfe, who scored 10 of his 17 points after regulation time, including a shot with two seconds left in the second overtime that kept the Cats in the contest. The game reflected a style of play made possible by the absence of a time clock. There were changes of tempo and both teams stalled either to get the last shot or to protect players in foul trouble. Leading the Truckers were Ken Jaksy with 20 and Harv Schmidt, who was the tourney MVP, with 16.[29] Wolfe's performance was especially remarkable because his left toe was broken in the quarterfinals and was heavily taped for the championship game.[30]

For Jack Carberry the championship game stood as "the most

thrill-filled sports spectacle in, at least, our own local history, and one well worthy of rank among the classics in all sports." After the tournament the Denver Basketball Writers and Broadcasters Association named George Kolowich, president of the Denver-Chicago Trucking Company, man of the year in sports, and Carberry endorsed their judgment, declaring, "Basketball has taken on a new stature because of this job well done."[31]

One of the tournament's extra prizes was that the coach of the championship team and six of its players won the right to represent the United States on a six-game tour of the Soviet Union, the first time an American basketball team had visited its Cold War rival. Warren Womble named his starting five plus Al Kelley to the team.[32] Burdie Haldorson and Joe Dean from Phillips, Dick Boushka from Wichita, Bob Jeangerard from the Air Force, and Harv Schmidt and Terry Rand from Denver completed the team. Ralph Moore of the *Denver Post* reported that Lou Wilke, at that time president of the NIBL and a member of the AAU tournament committee, opposed the State Department's decision to send a basketball team to the Soviet Union. The trip, he thought, would only enhance the Soviet technical knowledge of the game, which would be used "to whip us in the 1960 Olympic Games."[33]

For the players, less worried about the Soviets picking up valuable basketball techniques, the trip to the Soviet Union was a memorable adventure. When the team arrived in Moscow, there were ten thousand people to greet them. The Soviets questioned them about basketball and filmed the American practices in Moscow. Almost seventeen thousand watched the Americans defeat the Soviet National team in their two meetings in Moscow. In Tbilisi, twenty-five thousand saw the Americans on an outside court in two games they easily won, the second in the rain. The tour ended with two more victories in Leningrad.[34]

Besides the Cold War, the increasing participation of African Americans in basketball and its relationship to the civil rights movement prompted a column from Harry Farrar, a sports columnist for the *Denver Post*. In "Bias Hoists White Flag," he asserted that "[b]igotry was fouled out in basketball." His evidence was the appearance of four black players on the Associated Press All-America college team and an estimate that 25 percent of the players in the 1958 AAU tournament were black. The achievements of the black basketball players, Farrar wrote, prompted some negative "barroom comments, but most of the remarks seemed to indicate fans have concluded that Negroes earned their honors on the basketball floor."[35] Farrar's belief that athletics provided a merit-based solution for America's racial problems was a widely held idea in American society until 1968, when Harry Edwards led an effort to boycott the Olympics. While only a few athletes boycotted the games, Edwards raised important questions about the exploitation of black athletes. Although the percentage of African Americans competing in the AAU tournament had increased, only a few black players played in the NIBL. In the 1958 tournament, Wichita's Cleo Littleton was the only black NIBL player. In 1958, however, the play of K. C. Jones and other black players caught the attention of Denver writers, who reflected a 1950s optimism about race and sport.

For Denver fans steeped in the history of the AAU tournaments, 1958 was a sorrowful year. They witnessed the untimely deaths of Jack McCracken in January, at forty-six, and Robert "Ace" Gruenig in November, at forty-five. Jack Carberry wrote that McCracken "was in large measure the one man who made the Mile High City the AAU basketball capital of the world." He reminded his readers that in Denver sports history, McCracken and Gruenig were inseparable. Carberry concluded that upon their diverse styles and temperaments Denver "fans built a love and affection which has never been surpassed in any sport."[36] After his playing days were over McCracken went into automobile sales and never pursued a coaching career. Gruenig briefly tried his hand at high school coaching, but was running a small business when he died. In November of 1957 McCracken and Gruenig were among the first inductees to the Helms Amateur Basketball Hall of Fame. In 1962 McCracken was elected to the Naismith Hall of Fame and Gruenig joined him the following year. In 1968, amid much emotion, their friends and admirers celebrated their memory by inducting them posthumously as a single entry in the Colorado Sports Hall of Fame. In death, as in life, Jumping Jack McCracken and Robert "Ace" Gruenig were inseparably linked in the minds of Denver's sports community.[37]

In the 1958–59 NIBL season, the Denver-Chicago Truckers became the first NIBL team other than Phillips to claim exclusive ownership of a league title. In 1957–58 Phillips shared the title with Wichita and in 1953–54 the 66ers and Peoria tied for the championship.[38] Denver had not won a league title since 1939, when the Denver Nuggets claimed the Missouri Valley League championship. Prior to the season Denver made several roster adjustments. Ken Jaksy, a two-year contributor; Dick Eicher, a veteran of many campaigns; and Frank Kuzara, another AAU fixture, retired. To replace them Dee recruited George Bon Salle, a six-foot-nine center from the University of Illinois; and Dennis O'Shea, a starter on Dee's 1956 Alabama team. Bon Salle became the third consecutive Trucker, following Terry Rand and Harv Schmidt, to earn the NIBL rookie-of-the-year honors.

On the eve of the tournament, the experts considered Denver and Wichita the most likely to survive the annual Dribble Derby. The most interesting dark horse was the Baton Rouge Teamsters with Bailey Howell, Mississippi State All-American, and Jackie Moreland of Louisiana Tech. Howell averaged 27.5 points per game in the 1958–59 season and led Mississippi State to an impressive 24-1 mark and the Southeastern Conference championship. Mississippi State elected not to participate in the 1959 NCAA tournament to avoid competition with black players. In Denver, Howell indicated that he had no objection to playing against black athletes.[39] In 1955–56 the six-foot-eight Jackie Moreland had been the object of a fierce recruiting war among Kentucky, North Carolina State, Texas A&M, and Centenary College. A three-time all-state player at Minden High School in Northwest Louisiana, Moreland enrolled at North Carolina State but was declared ineligible to play for the Wolfpack because of assorted recruiting violations. The messy affair would end with Moreland transferring to Louisiana Tech and the NCAA placing N. C. State on probation for four years.[40]

On Wednesday the United States Marines registered the first big upset of the tourney when they edged Seattle's Buchan Bakers.

Jack Sullivan, who played with Peoria the previous year, led the Leathernecks with 20 points. The Army All-Stars, led by Adrian Smith's 25, engineered another surprise when they dumped the Akron Goodyear Wingfoots. In another second-round game the San Francisco Olympic Club's Bob Blake hit a jumper from the corner, his only basket of the game, to give the Winged O's a 72–70 victory over the Air Force. San Francisco's Ron Tomsic scored 34 points to top all scorers.[41]

For Denver the roof caved in on Thursday when Tomsic and the Olympic Club upset the Truckers in the quarterfinals. Tomsic had 29 but the five-foot-ten guard received plenty of help from two Stanford stars, Paul Neumann with 15 and Dick Haga with 13, as well as 13 from AAU veteran Phil Vukicevich. Chuck Garrity of the *Denver Post* wrote that the Truckers played "as though every move meant their life."[42] The defeat left the Truckers in a state of shock, as Leonard Cahn reported that Johnny Dee's first words were, "I'm sorry, George," as he tried to console the company's president.[43] Perhaps the pressure to give Denver its first national title since 1942 was simply too great. Although the Truckers failed to reach the semifinal round, Leonard Cahn, for one, was prepared to be generous. He reminded his readers that D-C won a NIBL championship and "must be credited for reviving basketball interest in our town."[44] While Kolowich and Dee had achieved a great deal in three years, they faced a formidable self-imposed challenge. From the beginning of their relationship Kolowich and Dee thought in terms of winning the 1960 tournament and going to the Olympics. In one sense, they were on schedule with a second-place tournament finish in 1958 and a NIBL championship in 1959. This goal, however, was also shared by other teams.

Denver was not the only upset victim in the quarterfinals, as the Army All-Stars eliminated the 1958 defending champion Peoria Cats. Adrian Smith, former Kentucky star, and Joe Leone of Canisius, led the Soldiers with 15 each. In the third quarterfinal Burdie Haldorson's 20 points led a balanced Phillips scoring attack as the 66ers eliminated the Marines, despite Jack Sullivan's 33 points. Wichita was the fourth team to advance to the semifinals with an easy win over the Baton Rouge Teamsters. Five Wichita players, led by Les Lane's 24, scored in double figures, while Bailey Howell's 27 topped Baton Rouge.[45]

Since their first appearance in 1956, Wichita had been a tournament underachiever. Neither Gene Johnson nor Bruce Drake had been able to lead the Vickers into the semifinals. Drake was especially disappointed after Wichita's quarterfinal loss to Fort Leonard Wood in the 1958 quarterfinals and decided to retire. With his retirement Drake concluded a thirty-year association with basketball that began at the University of Oklahoma in the late 1920s, when he led the Sooners to two Big Six titles and earned All-America honors in 1929. After ten years as the Oklahoma freshman coach, Drake coached the varsity from 1938 to 1955. In 1956 he was the assistant coach for the Olympic team, which was led by Gerald Tucker, the star of Drake's 1947 team, which lost in the NCAA finals to Holy Cross. In 1972 Bruce Drake entered the Naismith Hall of Fame as a coach.[46]

After having hired two veteran coaches with strong ties to the region, the Vickers brothers went in an entirely different direction. They hired thirty-five-year-old Alex Hannum, who had less than two years of head coaching experience. In 1957–58, however, Hannum, in his first full year as a bench coach, led the St. Louis Hawks to an NBA championship in a seven-game series with the Boston Celtics. Afterward Hannum, not able to resolve differences with Hawks owner Ben Kerner, resigned and planned to devote his life to building homes in California. Jim Vickers, however, met Hannum in California and persuaded him to join the Vickers organization. He stressed that Wichita had talent, that the NIBL was a competitive league, and that Wichita had a chance to compete in the 1960 Olympics. All of this was persuasive, especially for a person who admitted: "Once you get the basketball bug, you get it for life."[47] At thirty-five Hannum had an enormous amount of basketball experience. After winning all-city honors at Hamilton High School in Las Angeles, in 1942–43 Hannum played his first year of college basketball at the University of Southern California for Sam Barry, another innovator in that era. After that season Hannum served three years as a medical reconditioning officer in the army. During the war Hannum never stopped playing basketball and eventually hooked up with an AAU team sponsored by J. P. Carroll, the largest paint contractor in Southern California. After the war Hannum returned to USC for his junior and senior years and played in the 1948 AAU tournament with Twentieth Century Fox. The following year the six-foot-seven, 225-pound Californian began an eight-year professional career that ended with a 6-point-per-game scoring average. While he absorbed a great deal from Barry, who played a half-court game, Hannum favored the transition game, which he learned in the NBA.[48]

Hannum's players remembered him as a great motivator who hated to lose. Dick Boushka recalled that, "There was never a night when he did not think we should win." Don Boldebuck, a seven-foot center, described Hannum as a "bearcat" who "knew his stuff." When the team played poorly on the road, Boldebuck remembered a few times when the team returned to Wichita and Hannum found a gym and held a practice at two or three in the morning. While Hannum was tough, as Les Lane observed, he also made "you feel like you were the greatest player in the world."[49]

Hannum inherited a talented and veteran team. While Dick Boushka had won an AAU championship with the Air Force All-Stars in 1957, a championship in a Vickers uniform had eluded him. In 1957 the Vickers added Dan Swartz, a muscular six-foot-four-inch, 215-pound Kentuckian from Morehead State. A hardnosed player who could run over other players, Swartz, in his first four years in the NIBL, averaged almost 21 points, which was exceeded only by Burdie Haldorson and Dick Boushka. With Les Lane as the shooting guard, Hannum asked the speedy Nick Revon to run the offense. Hannum's last words before the Vickers took the court, according to Boushka, were: "Nick—move that ball down the floor and if they can't keep up with you, I will get someone in there who can."[50] In 1959, Swede Halbrook was injured, so the starting center was seven-foot Don Boldebuck from the University of Houston. Slender at 210 pounds, Boldebuck was more graceful, consistent, and gifted offensively than Halbrook. Jerry Mullen from San Francisco; Lionel Smith, a good shooter from Missouri; Lloyd Sharrar from West Virginia; and Joe King from Oklahoma gave the Vickers good depth.

The 1959 semifinalists produced two seesaw battles. In the first game the Olympic Club came back from a 17-point deficit to grab a 54–53 lead against Phillips with ten minutes left to play. The two teams traded baskets until the last ten seconds of the game when Gary Thompson, a former Iowa State star, hit a jump shot, with ten seconds left, to win the game for Phillips, 72–71. Phillips had plenty of heroes as Haldorson bagged 21 and Phil Murrell added 19, all in the second half. Bobby Plump, one of the stars of the Milan High School Indiana State champions—celebrated in the movie *Hoosiers*—scored 9 but held Tomsic to 16. In the other semifinal game Wichita's Vickers barely escaped with a 104–102 victory in overtime over the Army All-Stars. After the end of regulation time, the teams were deadlocked, 89–89. Hot shooting and the pressures of a thirty-second shot clock (this was the first tournament to use a shot clock) produced 28 points in the overtime period. Dick Boushka with 23, Dan Swartz with 20, and Don Boldebuck with 19 led Wichita, while Jack Adams with 31, Adrian Smith with 22, and Ted Savage with 19 were the Army's high scorers. The 206 points scored by both teams set a new tournament record.[51]

In the championship game Bud Browning, beginning his third tour of duty as the 66ers' coach, sought his sixth AAU title, having directed Phillips to five between 1944 and 1948. Wichita had dominated Phillips during the season, winning their last match-up 142–78. Before a capacity crowd of 7,800, Wichita maintained its dominance over Phillips by drubbing the 66ers 105–83, the first team to score 100 or more points in a championship game. Wichita's Les Lane led his team with 29, followed by Boushka's 26 and Swartz's 19, while Boldebuck controlled the boards for Wichita as Vickers out-rebounded Phillips, 65–42. Phillips' Haldorson led all scorers with 31 points. The victory made Alex Hannum the only coach to win AAU and NBA championships. His team's hot shooting coupled with the thirty-second clock produced a record 428 points in four games.[52]

The 1959 tournament was a tremendous success. For Wichita, in particular, the championship struck a nostalgic note as the *Wichita Eagle*'s sports editor, Pete Lightner, connected the Vickers' championship to Wichita's proud basketball heritage when the Wichita Henrys won three consecutive titles between 1930 and 1932. Lightner had covered the 1932 championship game when Mel Miller hit his famous shot with twenty seconds left in the game to give Wichita a 15–14 victory over Henry Iba's Maryville Bearcats.[53]

If other cities wanted to take the tournament away from Denver, Lightner threw cold water on the idea. The tournament's last two nights, he reported, had been sold out a week in advance so "that hundreds of fans were begging for ducats." The AAU, he continued, was "interested only in one item, gate receipts, and no one but Denver can stack in the fans."[54]

In the five tournaments played between 1955 and 1959, there were five different champions. The tournament was well run and the teams were well coached and talented, but Jack Carberry sounded a note of caution. While Carberry believed that the AAU tournament and NIBL teams were the best in amateur basketball, he declared, "from a national standpoint, the NCAA tournament ranks No. 1." His evidence was the limited press coverage given to the AAU tournament outside the area bordered by Kansas City and Salt Lake City. Television coverage and gambling, he thought, were making college basketball a national game. "Don't let us kid ourselves about being a nation that loves sports for sports' sake. We love it for 'action.'"[55]

Following the 1960 Olympic basketball tournament the significance of the AAU in postcollegiate basketball quickly waned. In part AAU basketball was the victim of demographic and technological changes that altered the United States. Americans were moving west and professional leagues were following them. Jet aircraft reduced travel time and made truly national schedules more feasible. Finally television brought professional and collegiate sports into homes throughout the nation. AAU basketball flourished as a midwestern and especially a western phenomenon. In these parts of the country, great distances and relatively small populations had not been conducive to professional sports. This all changed after 1960. Although some NIBL sponsors had their own reasons for dropping their basketball programs, the recognition that they could not compete with the professionals for talent was crucial. Phillips, with its proud tradition, played through 1968, and Akron, which enjoyed success in the 1960s, persisted until 1970.

Rather than a source of pride, Denver gradually viewed the tournament as a houseguest that would not leave. In the 1960s Denver also became a big-league sports town with franchises in the American Football League (1960) and the American Basketball Association (1967). Because of Denver's basketball success in the mid-1970s, it had the leverage to enter the NBA when the established league absorbed four ABL teams in 1975.

The tournament's last year in Denver was in 1968. By that time attendance was limited to a few basketball junkies who attended to see an occasional college star playing his last amateur games before heading to the pros.

Although postcollegiate AAU basketball disappeared into the dustbin of history, it had made a significant contribution to American basketball during its heyday. Perhaps the most important was that it gave many basketball players an opportunity to extend their playing careers and to acquire business skills that would give them some economic security. For a select few, AAU competition made it possible to represent the United States in the Olympic Games as well as other international competitions. The tournament, especially in Denver between 1935 and 1960, was an integral part of basketball's emergence as a major national and international sport. Finally, AAU basketball demonstrated that in the long haul the commitment to amateurism was limited in a market economy where Americans were prepared to bankroll enormous athletic salaries.

ELEVEN

Denver's Last Hurrah

With the exception of 1949 every AAU tournament had been played in Denver since 1935. During that time an AAU coach had directed every one of the four Olympic teams. In Olympic years the national AAU tournament was always the prelude to the Olympic tournament. What made 1960 unique was that for the first time the Olympic tournament was planned for Denver. While Denver's fans had rewarded the tournament with their enthusiastic support, Leonard Cahn wrote that Denver's version of March Madness had not received "national and international appreciation." Because of the Olympic Trials, Cahn observed, "At long last it will have some significance nationally." [1]

In 1959–60, as teams geared up for the AAU tournament, the NIBL expanded to nine teams with the addition of the Cleveland Sweeny Pipers, the San Francisco Investors, and the New York Tuck Tapers. The NIBL season had extra meaning in 1959–60 because the champion earned an automatic spot in the Olympic tourney. In what Leonard Cahn called the NIBL's "finest season," Bud Browning's Phillips 66ers nosed out the Wichita Vickers by two games to win the coveted crown.

The Denver squad that returned for the 1959–60 season was a veteran team. Dee's only additions were George Lee, a six-foot-four forward from the University of Michigan, and Mike Moran, a six-foot-nine center from Marquette University. While Lee made a significant contribution to the team, the Truckers suffered through a miserable season and finished with a 12-20 record, only one place from the cellar. Leonard Cahn offered two theories for D-C's slide. One was that the NIBL was stronger than the previous year; the other was that the players had simply lost their confidence. Regardless of Denver's play, Cahn praised Dee and Kolowich, since no Denver basketball program had approached their "outstanding promotional job." Cahn reported that Dee's "antics on the bench" were the source of some criticism, but other coaches, including Alex Hannum, "were in the same league as thespians."[2]

The other NIBL coaches also fine-tuned their teams as they prepared to make a run at the championship. Peoria's Warren Womble landed the biggest prize of the recruiting season when Bob Boozer, a two-time All-American at Kansas State, agreed to play for Peoria rather than sign with the Cincinnati Royals, who had made him the first pick of the 1959 NBA draft. Boozer had always wanted to play on the United States Olympic team and Cincinnati did not offer him enough money to alter his plans. Given Peoria's basketball success in the 1950s and the business experience it could offer him, Boozer believed that the Caterpillar Company was the best NIBL fit for him.

Bob Boozer was part of the first wave of outstanding African American basketball players of the 1950s who were steadily integrating college basketball teams and making a profound imprint on the game. He was all-state in 1955, his senior year at Omaha Nebraska's Technical High School. Although he dreamed of playing at the University of Iowa, its coach, Bucky O' Connor, wrote Boozer's high school coach, Neal Mosser, that Iowa had filled its quota of black players. With the Iowa door closed, Boozer chose Kansas State, where Tex Winter, the master of the triple post offense, was building a formidable team. Boozer explained to Winter that if KSU played in the South, he expected to room and eat with the team or he would not play. Winter respected Boozer's request and he was never separated from the team. At six-foot-eight and 220 pounds, Boozer established new scoring records at KSU and led the Wildcats to an NCAA final four in 1958 and to a perfect record in the Big Eight as a senior in 1959. The Caterpillars had never had an African American player but Womble and Boozer liked each other immediately and appreciated how they could help each other. The Caterpillars never put Boozer in a racially compromising position.[3]

Paired with Boozer at the other forward was six-foot-four-inch Jack Adams from Eastern Kentucky State who had made the 1959 AAU All-America team with the Army All-Stars. A great competitor, who could drive to the basket, Adams fit in beautifully with Womble's concept of team play and strong defense. John Prudhoe, a six-foot-ten center from Louisville, completed the front line. Prudhoe rebounded well and averaged 10 points per game in four seasons with Peoria.

Peoria had excellent guard play. In 1957 and 1958 Denver sports writers placed Peoria's Howie Crittenden, an outstanding dribbler and ball handler, on the AAU All-America team. Don Ohl, an All-American from the University of Illinois, had a deadly jump shot and averaged 18 points per game the previous year, his first with the Cats. Beginning in 1961 Ohl played ten years in the NBA and played in five all-star games. Al Kelley returned as Womble's reliable sixth man.

Going into the tournament, the Akron Goodyear Wingfoots had never made it into the quarterfinals in the history of the Denver tournament but now were determined to do so. Hank Vaughn, coach of the Wingfoots, picked up Bill Reigel, a six-foot-five high-scoring forward, who had made the AAU All-America teams of 1957 and 1958. With NIBL All-Stars Chuck Slack and George Swyers, Reigel gave Akron more firepower. Jim Francis, a six-foot-nine center from Dartmouth, and Stan Kernan, a teammate of Reigel's at McNeese State and McDonald Scots, completed the starting line-up.

In Seattle Gene Johnson replaced Frank Fidler as the coach of the Buchan Bakers. Johnson traced his AAU roots back to championships with the Wichita Henrys (1930) and the McPherson Globe Refiners (1936). After two years with the Wichita Vickers, the colorful Johnson was nearing the end of a thirty-year coaching career. Royal Brougham, the sports editor of the *Seattle Post-Intelligencer*, described Johnson as "a chatty and chesty man . . . (who) isn't popular in some quarters, but he does a lot with a little."[4] Carroll Williams, one of Johnson's key players, was a favorite of the tournament crowd. Williams made his first tournament appearance in 1956 with the San Jose Green Frogs after he led them to the Pacific Association basketball championship and a free trip to Denver. Don Selby, who covered the PA tournament for the *San Francisco Examiner*, wrote that "Williams doesn't look like a basketball player, he has arms like pine needles and legs like toothpicks, but how the little fellow can go."[5] The former San Jose State star always found a way back to Denver. In 1957 he made the AAU All-America team with the U.S. Army All-Stars and in 1958 played with a service team from San Francisco's Presidio. Frank Fidler, who coached Williams in his first year with Seattle, said he "had more basketball skills than any one guy I ever coached."[6] Pete Gaudin at forward, Bruno Boin at center, and Rolland Todd provided experience and scoring for the Bakers. Dave Mills, a junior forward from Seattle University picked up for the tournament, added strength up front.

In Bartlesville Phillips 66 surrounded Burdie Haldorson with veterans Arnie Short, Gary Thompson, Billy Evans, and Phil "Red" Murrell. Bud Browning hoped that six-foot-eight rookie Tom Robitaille would give the 66ers more strength under the boards and that forward Jerry Shipp, a great scorer at Southeastern State College in Durant, Oklahoma, would provide the 66ers more punch.

Unlike other NIBL teams, the powerful Wichita Vickers chose not to fine tune their roster. They returned to Denver with the identical squad that had won in 1959. Alex Hannum's team had size, speed, and firepower.

Before the tournament a thousand people welcomed the teams at a luncheon in the Lincoln Room of the Shirley Savoy Hotel. Chet Nelson wrote that the event was "graced by the presence of Governor Steve McNichols and Mayor Dick Batterton."[7] With the festivities completed Denver turned to the business of watching basketball. To satisfy the demand for more tickets, the tournament was held at the Denver Coliseum, which provided seating for four thousand more fans than Denver's Auditorium Arena.

The first two days of the competition provided no surprises, but on Wednesday the New York Tuck Tapers, the last place team in the NIBL, shocked the D-C Truckers, 79–75. Incredibly the Truckers made only seven of thirty-six shots from the field in the second half.[8] They seemed to wilt under the burden of bringing to the Mile High City the championship that had eluded a variety of Denver teams since 1942.

The next big surprise came during an interesting quarterfinal when Seattle's Buchan Bakers bumped off the defending champion Wichita Vickers. Pete Gaudin, Dave Mills, and Carroll Williams paced the Seattle team, which had already won two difficult games over the Stars of Storz from Lincoln, Nebraska, and San Francisco's Olympic Club. After the game Gene Johnson wept uncontrollably with joy.[9]

In another quarterfinal game Bob Boozer, who tallied 33 points the previous night, scored the last three of his game-high 29 points with twenty-eight seconds left in the game to secure Peoria's victory over Cleveland's Sweeny Pipers. Johnny McLendon, the Pipers coach, was the NIBL's first black coach. In nineteen years as a coach of a variety of African American college teams, McLendon compiled a remarkable 442-94 record. At Tennessee State McLendon won three consecutive NAIA championships between 1957 and 1959.[10] Three of his Tennessee State stars—John Barnhill, Ron Hamilton, and Ben Warley—followed him to Cleveland. The Pipers also had Johnny Cox, a Kentucky All-American, and Corny Freeman from Xavier.

Phillips also claimed a quarterfinal victory, when it rallied from a 9-point deficit with five minutes left in the game to squeeze by the San Francisco Investors. Former Phillips star Jim Walsh coached the Investors, a team that included such AAU veterans as Ron Tomsic, Paul Neumann, and Russ Lawler. Burdie Haldorson's 20 points led Phillips. Akron's Goodyear Wingfoots became the fourth team to reach the semifinals when it outlasted the New York Tuck Tapers. Bill Reigel with 29, Jim Francis with 25, and Charley Slack with 22 led Akron. The previous night the Wingfoots had broken a six-year streak of early exits when Reigel, Slack, and George Swyers each exceeded 20 points and Akron defeated Marion-Kay Vanilla from Brownstown, Indiana, to reach the quarterfinals for the first time.[11]

In the semifinals Akron kept rolling as Reigel poured in 28 points and the Wingfoots advanced to the finals with a victory over a stubborn Seattle team. Hank Vaughn, the ecstatic Akron Coach, observed candidly, "I didn't hit Denver dreaming that we'd go this far."[12] In the other semifinal game the Peoria Cats clipped Phillips 66, as Bob Boozer, Don Ohl, and Jack Adams turned in fine performances. Red Murrell, Burdie Haldorson, and Jerry Shipp were double-digit scorers for Phillips.[13] The semifinals meant that Akron and Peoria were in the Olympic tournament, along with Phillips, the NIBL champion.

In the championship game Peoria blitzed Akron 115–99 as Bob Boozer, the tournament's MVP, scored 30 and dominated the boards. Don Ohl, who also made the All-America team, pitched in with 28 points. This was Warren Womble's fifth national championship, which tied him with Phillips 66's Omar "Bud" Browning for the record of the most championship titles held by a coach at that time.[14] Since the 1960 AAU tournament was held in the Denver Coliseum, increased attendance produced revenues that reached a record high of seventy-eight thousand dollars.

The excitement generated by the AAU tournament set the stage for the Olympic Trials. There were the three AAU teams, Ohio State University (the 1960 NCAA champion), an Armed Service All-Star team, the NAIA All-Stars, the NCAA University All-Stars, and the NCAA All-Stars. The last team was supposed to represent NCAA small colleges but ended up with seven university players. As in 1956 the AAU teams strengthened their rosters by adding several players from the AAU tournament.

Going into the Olympic tournament one of the favorites, along with Warren Womble's Peoria Caterpillars, was Pete Newell's NCAA University All-Stars. As Newell prepared for the Olympic Trials, he was about to conclude a fourteen-year college coaching career that would earn him a place in the Naismith Hall of Fame. Newell coached the University of San Francisco to an NIT title in 1949 and then moved to Michigan State for four years, before returning to California where he led Cal-Berkeley to an NCAA title in 1959 and a second-place finish in 1960. Despite his success Newell had responded to the tensions of coaching by resorting to a diet of coffee and cigarettes. During the 1959–60 season he decided to accept

Cal's offer to serve as its athletic director and leave the pressures of the game behind him. A master of fundamentals, preparation, and strategy, Newell, like all great coaches, had the ability to persuade his players to play as a team.

After Ohio State beat Cal, to win the 1960 NCAA title, Arthur "Dutch" Lonberg, Kansas athletic director and chairman of the NCAA tournament committee, asked Newell to coach the University All-Star team in the Olympic Trials. Although Newell initially rejected Lonberg's request, after some thought he agreed to one more coaching challenge, made more palatable by a roster of All-Americans. Heading Newell's squad were two of basketball's most gifted players—Oscar Robertson of the University of Cincinnati and Jerry West of West Virginia. Indiana's Walt Bellamy and Cal's Darryl Imhoff gave Newell two six-foot-eleven centers. Purdue's Terry Dischinger and St. Bonaventure's Tom Stith gave Newell two offensive-minded forwards. Robertson and West had played in the 1959 Pan American Games so they were familiar with each other's style of play. Newell, a perfectionist who devoted a great deal of study to preparation, worried about his ability to develop a team concept in only a few days.[15]

Newell was not the only coach with problems. Arad McCutcham, who coached the NCAA All-Stars, was at the midway point of a thirty-one-year career at Evansville University, where he had starred in the 1930s. During his career he won five NCAA college division championships and produced several All-Americans including Jerry Sloan, a record that earned him a place in the Naismith Hall of Fame. Although his team had four college division players, they were overshadowed by players from major university programs, in particular Chet Walker of Bradley, Horace Walker of Michigan State, Herschel Turner of Nebraska, and Wayne Hightower of Kansas.

Milt Jowers, the coach of Southwest Texas, 1960 NAIA champions, directed the NAIA All-Stars. He had three future professional players: Jackie Moreland of Louisiana Tech, Zelmo Beatty of Prairie View A&M, and Charles Hardnett of Grambling.

The Armed Services entered the last of the all-star teams. Hal Fischer, a native of San Francisco who traced his AAU career back to the Oakland Bittners, coached the service team. Adrian Smith, a starter on Kentucky's 1958 NCAA championship team who would go on to play ten years in the NBA, led this team.

The Ohio State Buckeyes, coached by Fred Taylor, another future Hall of Fame coach, had three gifted sophomores: Mel Nowell, John Havlicek, and Jerry Lucas. They joined upperclassmen Larry Siegfried and Joe Roberts. One of Taylor's substitutes was Bobby Knight, who would become one of college basketball's winningest and most controversial coaches.

The AAU teams had four days to recover from the four games they had played the previous week. Peoria's Warren Womble, the 1952 Olympic coach, worried about his team's ability to get up mentally for another big tournament. Since Womble had coached the 1952 Olympic team and Bud Browning the 1948 Olympians, Hank Vaughn was the only AAU coach who had not experienced the pressures of playing for the right to represent the United States in Olympic competition.

As the players, coaches, and spectators prepared for the games, there was no doubt that this was the finest collection of basketball players ever assembled at an Olympic Trials. The task of selecting an Olympic team would pose some interesting problems.

In the opening round of play, before a turnaway crowd, Oscar Robertson scored 23 points to lead the University All-Stars over Phillips. The first evening's biggest surprise came when the NAIA All-Stars surprised Ohio State University by dumping the national champs. Charles Sharp of Southwest Texas used a deadly hook shot to score 15 of his 17 points in the first half. Jackie Moreland scored 12 of his 14 points to lead the way in the second half. Milt Jowers used a 2-1-2 zone defense that limited Jerry Lucas to 13 points, as the Buckeyes were led by John Havlicek with 20. In the third game Akron's Wingfoots used their superior size to best the Armed Forces. Johnny Cox with 15, Dick Boushka with 14, and Wade "Swede" Halbrook with 10, all postseason additions, sparked the Wingfoots. Adrian Smith paced the service team with 21. Vaughn platooned his starting five from Akron with four players picked up from the AAU tournament. In the final game of the opening round Peoria nosed out the NCAA All-Stars. Bob Boozer scored a game high 25 and Jack Adams added 14 for the Cats, while Kansas's Wayne Hightower finished with 24 and Willie Jones of American University sank 18 for the All-Stars.[16]

On the second night Peoria moved into the finals of the Olympic Trials with a convincing victory over the NAIA All-Stars. Bob Boozer had 14 points and 14 rebounds as well as good support from Jack Adams, with 13 points, and tournament additions Dan Swartz with 13 and Tom Meschery with 12. Porter Merriweather of Tennessee State led the collegians with 14. The other finalist was the NCAA University All-Stars, who romped past the Akron Goodyears behind Oscar Robertson with 29, Jerry West with 22, and Walt Bellamy with 17. Dick Boushka led Akron with 19, while Johnny Cox and Swede Halbrook each had 12. In the third game Ohio State handed the NCAA All-Stars their second loss, as John Havlicek led the Buckeyes with 24. Wayne Hightower was high for the All-Stars for the second straight night with 14 points. In the fourth game Burdie Haldorson scored 17 and led Phillips to an easy win over the Armed Forces.[17]

In the championship game Jerry West put on a shooting clinic and popped in 39 points as the University All-Stars blasted Peoria, 124–97. Oscar Robertson added 20 and Terry Dischinger had 18. Tom Meschery's 19 and Bob Boozer's 14 points were high for the Cats. Akron's Goodyear Wingfoots subdued the NAIA All-Stars, to finish third. Dick Boushka and Johnny Cox each had 18 for Akron, while Porter Merriweather had another impressive game as he scorched the nets for 28 points for the losers. The game for fifth place matched the NCAA champs, Ohio State, against the NIBL champs, Phillips 66. After a tight first half, the Buckeyes blew the game open to register a victory. Larry Siegfried, who later played on five Boston Celtic NBA championship teams, led all scorers with 23 points. Jerry Shipp led the 66ers with 16. The Armed Forces finished in seventh place by whipping the NCAA All-Stars. Adrian Smith pumped in 25 for the Armed Forces All-Stars as Wayne Hightower, for the third time, led his team with 16.[18]

The NCAA University All-Stars were the first collegiate team to win the Olympic Trials. The completion of the tournament left the

Olympic Basketball Committee with the difficult task of choosing the twelve-man United States Olympic team. The selection process assured five to seven spots to the winner of the tournament but guaranteed no positions to the second place team and, by inviting eight teams, doubled the number of players to choose from over the 1956 tournament to ninety-six. The committee, chaired by Arthur "Dutch" Lonberg, included athletic administrators from the NCAA and AAU. While the committee inferred that a player's performance in the tournament was the most important of the selection criteria, its work suggests that arriving at some balance between college, AAU, and service representation framed the entire process.

Four players—Oscar Robertson, Jerry West, Walt Bellamy, and Jerry Lucas—were easy choices. They were the dominant collegiate players of the day and had had solid to spectacular games in the tournament. The committee decided to assign six places on the Olympic roster to the University All-Stars and filled these with Robertson, West, Bellamy, Terry Dischinger of Purdue, Darryl Imhoff of the University of California, and Jay Arnette of Texas. All these players had solid tournaments and were identified by the press as deserving consideration. When the committee chose to allot the University All-Stars six rather than seven places, Jim Darrow—a guard from Bowling Green, who had an excellent tournament—was the clearest casualty. The committee was left with six choices from the remaining seven teams. The easiest choice was Jerry Lucas of Ohio State. Another spot on the squad went to Adrian Smith of the Armed Service All-Stars, who had a very good tournament. The final four places went to the AAU, whose officials must have waged a vigorous fight for their players on the basis of past and present contributions to amateur basketball. One of the committee's AAU selections, Bob Boozer from Peoria, had been the MVP in the AAU tournament and was impressive in the Olympic Trials. A second selection was Burdie Haldorson, who had a solid tournament and held just about all of the NIBL's scoring records. Haldorson also became the third American basketball player to play on two Olympic teams, after Bill Hougland and Bob Kurland, also of Phillips. The last two choices were Les Lane, a five-year star for the Wichita Vickers, who played with

Phillips in the Olympic Trials, and Allen Kelley, Warren Womble's all-purpose guard at Peoria. The Olympic Basketball Committee made Pete Newell the first collegiate coach to lead a U.S. basketball team to the Olympics. His assistant was Warren Womble, who was making his second trip to the Olympics.[19]

The harshest critic of the selection process in the media was Leonard Cahn, who wrote: "Politics reared its two-faced head in a smoke-filled room. The AAU Big Domes, NCAA Brass Hats and the military clique took turns in dealing off the bottom of the deck to satisfy each faction." Cahn questioned the selections of Kelley, Haldorson, Lane, and Smith. The Denver writer argued that two players, Jim Darrow of Bowling Green and Dick Boushka of the Wichita Vickers, who played with Akron in the Olympic Trials, were clearly short-changed. Darrow, a guard, outscored Lane and Kelley and was a fan favorite during the tournament. With 51 points Boushka was one of the tourney's high scorers and, in the NIBL, a player who matched Haldorson in stature and was his teammate on the 1956 Olympic team.[20] Cahn did not exhaust the list of disappointed players. Ohio State's Larry Siegfried with 53 points and John Havlicek with 51 had outstanding tournaments and were passed over. Years later Havlicek admitted: "Missing out on the Olympics haunts me to this day; that was my biggest disappointment in sports."[21] No doubt others shared Havlicek's disappointment. Wayne Hightower, from Kansas, scored 54 points, but played on the NCAA All-Stars, a team that failed to win a game or place a player on the Olympic team.

The difficulty of selecting an Olympic team was partially explained by the abundance of talent in the United States. Jack Carberry argued that "no matter who they picked, they would be wrong to some."[22] The framework of the tournament also dictated the composition of the team. Selection of the Olympic team prior to 1956 had been based on identifying not the twelve best players in the United States but the two best amateur teams. By mixing all-star teams with college and AAU teams in 1956 and 1960, the selection committee made the process inherently more difficult. Given the AAU's contribution to amateur basketball and the high level of play in 1960, its claim to four spots on the Olympic team seemed justifiable.

In the cases of Larry Siegfried and John Havlicek, would they have been better served by playing on the University All-Stars instead of Ohio State? If Ohio State had not been invited, would Havlicek and Siegfried have been named to the University All-Star team? The passage of time does not offer easy answers to these questions. With the anxieties of the three-day tournament and selection process behind him, Pete Newell concentrated on preparing his squad for Rome.

In assessing the history of Olympic basketball competition, Arthur Daley, a *New York Times* columnist, thought the 1960 team may have been "the most talented squad ever sent to the Olympics." Daley searched for ways to explain away American advantages. Daley probably spoke for many Americans when he wrote, "A failure in this round-ball tournament would indicate that we've been wasting our time." Since the United States had not lost a game in the Olympics, the pressure to live up to expectations was great, something Newell acknowledged. Another problem was that the tournament was played with a ball of eighteen pieces of seamed leather rather than the one-piece American ball, which was easier to dribble and shoot. The American team practiced with the European ball at their training facility and adjusted to it before settling in at the Olympic Village in Rome. Before the competition Newell still worried about getting the players to jell as a team, but they did not fail him.[23]

Until the Americans played the Soviets, no team came within thirty points of the Yanks. After winning their first five games, the Americans and Soviets met before an overflow crowd in the Little Sports Palace, which sat five thousand. At the half the United States was only up by 7. After the break Newell employed a full-court press, which produced a 28–4 run. With Robertson, Lucas, and West leading the way, the United States won comfortably 81–57. One commentator thought the Soviets "matched the Americans in height and speed, but they lacked the shooting ability to sustain an attack."[24] The game was rough with plenty of elbows thrown by both sides. The Cold War political ramifications of the game clearly influenced the contest's atmosphere. Before the game, Oscar

Robertson recalled, a State Department official reminded the Americans about the game's importance.[25] Bob Boozer remembered the Soviet athletes as being very serious.[26]

When the Americans played their second game against Italy, the Italians were within 8 of the United States at the half, but in the second half the Americans pulled away to an easy victory.[27] The United States crushed Brazil, winning the gold medal and, in Robert Daley's view, "[m]aking one final joke of the competition."[28]

Newell's starting line-up for the tournament was Terry Dischinger and Oscar Robertson at the forwards, Les Lane and Jerry West at the guards, and Jerry Lucas at center. Newell allowed his players to run and freelance, confident that they had the one-on-one moves to beat their defenders. While some nations played the game well, they simply did not have the skill of the Americans. Lucas and Robertson each averaged 17 points a game and West followed with a 13-point average, to lead the team.[29]

When the University All-Stars walloped the Cats, it demonstrated how much the quality of collegiate basketball had changed in twenty-five years. If in any given Olympic year the colleges could produce a team, or several teams, capable of beating the best of the AAU, it would weaken the esteem of the AAU as it sought to maintain its place in amateur basketball competition at the national and international level.

A more serious threat to AAU basketball, however, was the escalation of professional basketball salaries. Until 1960 AAU players rejected professional contracts because they were often in the seven- to ten-thousand-dollar range. Corporations that sponsored basketball could match this by offering an opportunity for advancement in the corporation following a player's career. After 1960 American corporations lost their ability to compete with the professional franchises. Moreover, as the pool of African American players increased, history suggested that large corporate basketball programs would not recruit them.

While the 1960 AAU tournament had been a great success, ironically, the AAU found itself in a precarious position as the colleges challenged its place in amateur basketball and the professionals threatened to dry up its access to the pool of quality basketball talent. Although Jack Carberry described the AAU tournament as "a Denver sport fixture . . . and likely to remain just that through the years ahead," the relentless force of professionalism would quickly prove him a poor fortuneteller.[30]

TWELVE

The National Industrial
Basketball League Collapses

In the aftermath of the 1960 tournament, the Denver press remained supportive of George Kolowich and Johnny Dee. Chet Nelson credited Kolowich and Dee with "restoring interest" to a point where attendance exceeded the era of Gruenig and McCracken.[1] Harry Farrar chose to attribute Denver's basketball misfortunes to a jinx that he traced back to William Haraway's Piggly Wiggly team. Rather than dwelling on disappointments, Farrar focused on the "great sports drama" provided by the Truckers.[2]

The efforts by the media to sugarcoat the disappointing season failed to keep evidence of dissension among the players out of the papers. Dee admitted, "I'm not the Great White father to some, but I don't think they're going to quit me. They have good jobs with a chance to go places."[3] In fact Dee had to reconstruct his team for the 1960–61 season.

In the 1960–61 season the only returning D-C veterans were Joe Belmont, George BonSalle, and Mike Moran. Two of Dee's rookies, Horace Walker of Michigan State and Walt Mangham of Marquette, were the first African American basketball players to play for a postcollegiate Denver team. Lance Olson of Michigan State, Harvey Salz of North Carolina, and Don Ogorek of Seattle were Dee's other first-year men. Dee also gained a valuable veteran with the acquisition of Les Lane, a five-year member of the Wichita Vickers, who had just competed in the Rome Olympics.

In 1960–61 the six-team NIBL split into two three-team divisions.

Each team played its divisional rivals eight times and had six contests with teams in the other division. Denver played in the Western Division with Phillips and Seattle. Cleveland, Akron, and New York played in the Eastern Division. The NIBL suffered a serious blow when it lost two powerhouses, the Peoria Caterpillars and the Wichita Vickers. The third team to drop out was the San Francisco Investors, after having played only one year in the league.

In the case of Peoria a decline in profits and difficult union negotiations persuaded the company that it could no longer justify supporting a competitive basketball program. Between 1951 and 1960 the Cats had won five AAU titles and one Olympic Trials. Warren Womble, the architect of Peoria's success, remained with the Caterpillar Company until he retired and never coached another basketball team.

The Wichita Vickers had a shorter tenure in AAU basketball than Peoria but sponsored one of its strongest teams in the 1950s. After the 1960 tournament Jim Vickers announced that the retirement of six players had forced the company to reconsider its program. He argued that "the NBA was beginning to pay salaries that made it difficult to compete for the top talent necessary to continue having a first-rate team in the NIBL." Forty years later, Vickers recalled that one of the players Wichita hoped to recruit was Jerry West. When it became clear that to sign a player of that caliber was significantly out of line with past player compensation, the Vickers briefly considered buying a professional franchise at $150,000. The plan was initially to divide the home season between Wichita and Denver, with the Mile High City eventually becoming the exclusive location of the team. When the Vickers brothers approached George Kolowich with the idea, he asked to wait a year in order to give Johnny Dee one more crack at an AAU title.[4] The proposal was not far-fetched given NBA expansion to Los Angeles and San Francisco in the early 1960s.

When Vickers dropped its basketball program, Alex Hannum returned to the NBA. After Hannum coached the St. Louis Hawks over the Boston Celtics in the 1958 NBA championship series, the Celtics proceeded to win eight consecutive titles. In 1967 Hannum's Philadelphia 76ers put an end to that streak by defeating the Celtics in the

Eastern Division finals on their way to the 1967 NBA championship. Two years later Hannum guided the Oakland Oaks to an American Basketball Association title. After coaching the ABA's Denver Rockets for three years, 1971–74, Hannum left coaching and an impressive record for private business.

In 1960–61 Johnny Dee's Truckers rebounded from their disastrous season of the previous year. By March the Truckers had clinched the Western Division of the NIBL while the Cleveland Pipers topped the Eastern Division. Dee's success won accolades from the Denver media. Bob Collins wrote that "This may not be Denver's finest AAU team in history, but I believe it is the most interesting one I've ever seen out here." Looking forward to the tournament Collins had a hunch that the Truckers could "bring home the bacon."[5] Chet Nelson was effusive in his praise and thought the 1960–61 Truckers were "the best all-round team ever to represent Denver in top-level AAU competition." As a writer who had covered Denver basketball since the 1930s, Nelson wrote: "Denver never has had a better pair of guards than Joe Belmont and Les Lane, or a better three forwards than Horace Walker, Walt Mangham, and Lance Olsen."[6]

On March 4, 1961, as the Denver media heaped praise on Dee, the volatile coach announced that at the end of the season he planned to resign as coach and assume the duties of general manager of basketball operations. Bob Collins of the *Rocky Mountain News* speculated that Dee and Kolowich entertained ideas of entering a professional league. The latter explained Dee's new assignment as a move to "help in the expansion and improvement of the basketball program . . . to the extent that it equals or betters any basketball organization in either the amateur or professional circuits."[7]

On the Sunday before the tournament, the NIBL'S division champions, Denver and Cleveland, played for the NIBL title. Johnny McLendon still had his three Tennessee State stars, John Barnhill, Ron Hamilton, and Ben Warley. To this trio McLendon added four NIBL veterans: Dan Swartz and Lloyd Sharrar from Wichita, Jack Adams from Peoria, and Roger Taylor from the San Francisco Investors. In a nightmare of a game in which the officials charged Dee and the Denver crowd with technical fouls, the Pipers blasted

Denver 136–100. The experts still expected these two NIBL powers to meet again in the AAU championship game.[8]

In their opening tournament game the Truckers struggled past the University of Dayton freshmen, who played as Pauls' Merchandise. Roger Brown, a legendary high school player at Brooklyn's Wingate High School, led the Dayton freshmen. Along with his high school rival, Connie Hawkins, Brown would never play a varsity college game because of his alleged involvement with basketball gamblers, as the college game struggled through another gambling scandal in 1961. He would later star for the Indiana Pacers in the American Basketball Association. The victory proved a costly one for the Truckers as George BonSalle suffered a broken elbow.[9]

In the quarterfinals, Tony Jackson, an All-American from St. John's University, pumped in 21 as the New York Tuck Tapers dumped the Phillips 66ers. Phillips played without Burdie Haldorson, who retired after the 1960 Olympics as the leading scorer in NIBL history. Haldorson was not only a great scorer, but according to Leonard Cahn, "the last of the AAU rascals." The veteran tournament-watcher put him in the same league as Frank Lubin, Joe Fortenberry, and Bob Kurland. Unlike the others, "Haldorson had an angelic face, but was a smoothie in arousing crowd reaction." If basketball was compared to a dramatic performance, Haldorson, the backbone of the hated 66ers, "could play the role of the varmint" with the best of them. Cahn described him as "an AAU Brando in the melodrama league."[10] In another quarterfinal game the San Francisco Olympic Club beat Clarkson Realty from Des Moines, Iowa. The veteran Ron Tomsic, St. Mary's Tom Meschery, and California's Bill McClintock were the Winged O's high scorers. The Denver Truckers trounced Seattle's Buchan Bakers, with Mike Moran and Horace Walker pacing the Truckers with 22 points each. The fourth team to advance to the semifinals was the Cleveland Pipers, who swamped Washington's Kirk's Pharmacy. Dan Swartz with 33 led all Pipers scorers, and Carroll Williams, two-time AAU All-American, matched him with 33 for the Pharmacists.[11]

In the first semifinal game the Cleveland Pipers squeaked by the New York Tuck Tapers in overtime. In a bruising contest in which

the Denver fans cheered for the New Yorkers, Paul Neumann, former Stanford star, took the game into overtime when he made one
of two free throws after the gun had sounded in regulation time with
the Pipers on top 87–86. If Neumann had made both free throws,
the Tuck Tapers would have won the game for a huge upset. Cleveland's Dan Swartz led all scorers with 29 points, and St. John's All-
American Tony Jackson topped New York with 26. In the nightcap
Denver ripped the Olympic Club, as the Truckers shot almost 50
percent for the game. Horace Walker with 25 paced D-C's balanced
scoring attack, which included 20 from Lane and 18 from Moran.
Tom Meschery's 23 was high for the Winged O.[12]

In his last attempt to win a national AAU championship, Dee did
not have the services of George BonSalle, who had broken his elbow
in the first game of the tournament. An injury in the semifinals to
Ben Warley, Cleveland's star center, however, neutralized the loss
of BonSalle. Before 10,500 at the Coliseum, a partisan crowd saw
the Pipers get hot in the second half and down Denver, 107–96.
Cleveland's Jack Adams, the tournament MVP, was the game's high
scorer with 28 but he had great support from John Barnhill with 21,
Dan Swartz with 19, Lloyd Sharrar with 16, and Roger Taylor with
15. The coach of the Pipers, John McLendon, was the first African
American coach to win the national AAU tournament. Horace Walker
with 25, Mike Moran with 23, and Les Lane with 18 led the D-C
scorers.[13]

In addition to winning the championship, Johnny McLendon
won the right to lead a U.S. amateur basketball team on an eight-
game tour of the Soviet Union. With African American college students leading sit-ins against segregation throughout the South, a
coach who established his reputation at all-black colleges was about
to lead an integrated team to the Soviet Union. Ironically, two days
after the Pipers had won the tournament and the right to represent amateur basketball, George Steinbrenner, the team's president
and future owner of the New York Yankees, announced the Pipers'
intention to join the American Basketball League. Since ABL play
would not begin until the fall of 1961, the AAU allowed McLendon
and his players to make the trip.[14]

A day after the tournament, George Kolowich named Les Lane to replace Johnny Dee as the Denver team's coach. While D-C seemed committed to amateur basketball, the erosion of the NIBL continued. Two months after Cleveland bolted from the NIBL, Paul Cohen of the New York Tuck Tapers terminated his basketball program.[15] The third team to drop out of the NIBL was Seattle's Buchan Bakers. After fourteen years of play the NIBL had folded. While the 1961 tournament's gross revenue was a respectable $72,379, just $6,000 below the 1960 figure, the collapse of the NIBL was a severe blow to amateur basketball and the AAU tournament. It left the Denver–Chicago Trucking Company, Phillips 66, and the Goodyear Tire and Rubber Company as the only major amateur teams, but without a league. Chuck Garrity considered Denver's commitment to amateur ball limited and believed that Johnny Dee's "main job" as a general manager "will be seeking a pro (NBA) franchise for Denver."[16] George Kolowich was not interested in the American Basketball League.

According to the Truckers' promotional literature, in the fall of 1961 George Kolowich "decided to sponsor the team another year when Denver fans raised such clamor after the league suspension was announced." The team lost George BonSalle, Horace Walker, Walt Mangham, Lance Olson, and Les Lane, who was to be strictly a bench coach. To replace them the Truckers recruited Chuck Rask from Oregon and two former Denver high school stars—Dennis Boone, a high-scoring guard from Manual High School who also starred at Regis College, and Carney Crisler, a standout center at North High School who played collegiately at the University of Utah. Two more additions were Ron Heller and Al Tate, forwards from Wichita University. Joe Belmont, Mike Moran, Harvey Salz and Don Ogorek returned from the previous year. In 1961–62 the Truckers played a thirty-two-game exhibition schedule and won twenty-five of them.

Beginning in 1962 the character of the tournament changed. Denver, Phillips, and Akron were the only teams that evoked memories of the tournament's glory days. The other major attraction of the 1962 and remaining tournaments was the occasional All-American playing one last tournament before signing a professional contract.

In 1962 Bill "the Hill" McGill, University of Utah All-American, played with Sander's State Line out of Salt Lake City with his Utah teammates and Utah State's future Dallas Cowboy football star Cornell Green. McGill, who had led the nation in scoring with an average of 38.8 points per game, scored 77 points in two games, before his team fell in the quarterfinals to the Akron Goodyear Wingfoots, 81–76.[17] Roger Brown, who played with Dayton University as a freshman in 1961, played for the Inland Manufacturing Company of Dayton, Ohio, a team composed of ex-high-school players. Brown scored 46 points in two games, including 29 in a tough loss to Phillips.[18]

Going into the tournament, the Denver Truckers added Wilky Gilmore, who helped to lead the University of Colorado to a conference championship in 1962 and an NCAA regional final, which the Buffs lost to Cincinnati. The Truckers won their first three tournament games, which placed them in the finals against their historic rival, Phillips 66. Mike Moran, in his third year with Denver, led the Truckers in scoring in all three games as he blossomed into the team's star. Phillips had not won a title since 1955 but had a veteran squad anchored by guard Gary Thompson, forward Jerry Shipp, and center Tom Robitaille. Coach Browning's most important addition was Don Kojis, a former Marquette All-American and future NBA star. Wally Frank, a star at Kansas State in the Bob Boozer years, started as the other forward. Denny Price from the University of Oklahoma complemented Thompson in the backcourt. Although the tournament had been a drab affair, the finalists were quality teams and the rivalry rich with tradition. While the Denver media and fans hoped the Truckers would end the twenty-year championship drought, the 66ers continued their dominance over Denver in title play, 70–59, before eight thousand fans. Don Kojis led Phillips with 13, followed by Charley Bowerman with 11, and Gary Thompson, the tournament MVP, with 11. Joe Belmont, the Truckers' popular floor general, led all scorers with 17 and made the All-America team in his last tournament.[19] The title was Bud Browning's sixth, a record for AAU coaches.

The tournament grossed about $59,000, which was $13,000 below the previous year. Chet Nelson described the week as "the next thing to an illuminated dud." Two years of declining attendance, revenues, and quality of play prompted speculation about the tournament's future. Nelson recommended a return to the Auditorium Arena, after three years at the Coliseum, and then either a return to a "mass competition of more than sixty teams or at the other extreme a selective sixteen."[20] Bill Greim, the tournament's director reflected the general pessimism by observing, "If the quality of teams is not good enough for Denver we might let it go somewhere else."[21] Two weeks after the tournament, Denver's amateur basketball suffered another blow when George Kolowich announced that, after six years, the Denver–Chicago Trucking Company had decided to drop its sponsorship of amateur basketball. In the past when this happened, another sponsor had always been found, and Denver amateur basketball had always continued to flourish. This time, as Chuck Garrity noted, a new sponsorship "would only be a sham. Amateur basketball as we native Denverites knew and loved it is dead."[22]

With the AAU tournament on a respirator, rumors swirled about Johnny Dee and his future in basketball. In the fall of 1962, Dee accepted an offer to coach the Kansas City Steers in the ABL. With the Steers in first place with a 25-9 record in January of 1963, the ABL collapsed and Dee returned to Denver as manager of Parks and Recreation. Then, in March of 1964, Notre Dame named Dee to replace Johnny Jordan as its basketball coach. Dee coached the Fighting Irish for seven years and then returned to Denver where he practiced law and served a term as auditor of the City and County of Denver.[23]

While the D-C Truckers were essentially out of the basketball business, in March of 1963 Les Lane organized a team that the Denver–Chicago Trucking Company sponsored for the twelve-team tournament. D-C's roster included such familiar names as Dennis Boone, Joe Capua, Al Tate, Carney Crisler and Wilky Gilmore. The Truckers bolstered their roster when they added Bill Green, an All-American from Colorado State University, and All-American Ken Charlton plus his teammates Milt Mueller and Eric Lee from the University of Colorado's Big Eight champions, who had lost to Cincinnati in the

NCAA regionals. Phillips remained remarkably competitive. In 1963 Mike Moran joined Phillips and with Dan Kojis, Jerry Shipp, and Wally Frank gave the 66ers a strong front line. Bobby Rascoe, an All-American from Western Kentucky, and Del Ray Mounts from Texas Tech joined Denny Price and Charley Bowerman to give Phillips a strong backcourt. The Akron Goodyear Wingfoots also managed to return a strong cast of players. Pete McCaffrey was an AAU All-American, Lloyd Sharrar an experienced center, and Dick Davies, Bennie Coffman, and Thornton Hill were talented players.

While there were some other college stars sprinkled throughout the teams, Bob Collins of the *Rocky Mountain News* wrote that the tournament's players were generally "just a bunch of guys named Joe." More evidence of the tournament's declining stature was the San Francisco Olympic Club's decision not to send a team because the expenses were no longer justifiable. Now instead of worrying about losing the tournament, Collins told his readers to relax because "who in the world wants it? I'm afraid it's as much a part of Denver as are the chuckholes in the streets after a heavy dew." Before the tournament became a part of history, Collins urged Denver fans to "give it a chance the next four days." Maybe, he thought, Denver "would catch the brass ring with a team assembled a day before the tournament?"[24] Leonard Cahn agreed with his colleague and reported that with the exception of Phillips, Akron, and the Armed Forces All-Stars, the entrants were a collection of "bobtailed teams or nonentities."[25]

After an easy opening round win, the Truckers benefited from the hot shooting of Bill Green, who hit his first seven shots, and outlasted the Akron Goodyears, 72–62. With this victory, the Truckers found themselves in the championship game against the Phillips 66ers, who had squeaked by the Armed Forces All-Stars in their semifinal game, 80–78. Don Kojis led Phillips with 24, while Cleveland McKinney dumped in 22 for the servicemen.[26] Phillips possessed too much firepower and experience for Denver in the finals and crushed the Truckers, 100–70. Ken Charlton with 20 and Bill Green with 15 were the only Truckers in the double figures. Jerry Shipp with 22, Wally Frank with 16, and Don Kojis with 10 paced Phillips, which won its eleventh title, and seventh under Bud Browning.[27] The tournament attracted a mere fifteen thousand fans and grossed about thirty-five thousand dollars, the lowest figure since 1949. Leonard Cahn rated the tournament "a real stinker" and held out "little hope for the future."[28] Ralph Moore of the *Denver Post* agreed that the tournament had lost its charm and that unfortunately there was "nothing to look forward to next year."[29] Chuck Garrity called the tourney "a cheap imitation of previous AAU meets."[30] With only Phillips and Goodyear sponsoring teams, there was no likelihood that other major corporations would see amateur basketball as a useful investment.

Although the national AAU tournament faded as an event, 1964 was an Olympic year, which meant that the Denver tournament had international implications. This time Denver's hopes for a national title rested with Capitol Federal Savings and Loan, a team organized by Maceo Brodnax Sr., who came to Denver from Kansas City in 1940 to play for a black baseball team called the Denver White Elephants. Brodnax persuaded Bill Heimer of Capitol Federal Savings and Loan to sponsor a team, which played about thirty games in the region and then picked up a few regional college stars for the tournament. Brodnax recruited Joe B. Hall, who had just resigned as Regis College's basketball coach, to guide the team. Hall was about to return to Kentucky, as an assistant to Adolph Rupp. Hall would guide the Wildcats to an NCAA title in 1978, their first since 1958. The Capitol Federal roster included a collection of area stars, which featured Flynn Robinson, Wyoming's great scorer; Lonnie Wright, a sophomore star at Colorado State; Dennis Boone and Carney Crisler, former Truckers; George Parsons, CU guard; and Cozel Walker from Regis College.[31]

In 1964 the sixteen teams that competed for the AAU championship returned to the Auditorium Arena after four years at the Coliseum. Smaller crowds nullified the need for the Coliseum's seating capacity, while the Auditorium Arena, with its 7,500 seats, was a great place to view a game and very accessible to those who worked in downtown Denver. For the first time in its history the four-day tournament ended with the championship game on Wednesday evening. Before the eight games scheduled for Sunday, Leonard Cahn predicted, "this will be the last time Denver plays host to what once carried the Chamber of Commerce label of basketball's blue-ribbon event."[32]

In its second game Denver fell to the Akron Goodyears, 68–64, as Lonnie Wright with 18 points and Flynn Robinson with 16 points were the only Denver players who reached double figures. The difference in the game was five-foot-eleven Larry Brown, former North Carolina star, who scored 18 of his 22 points in the second half. Brown would go on to coach the Denver Nuggets in the 1970s as part of his long, successful, and sometimes enigmatic coaching career, which included an NCAA championship with Kansas in 1988 and a second-place finish in the 2001 NBA finals with the Philadelphia 76ers.[33]

In the semifinals Akron remained hot as it dumped the Tennessee State Tigers. Pete McCaffrey with 20 points, Hunter Beckman with 16, and Larry Brown with 15 paced Goodyear. Tennessee State was the first college team, playing under its own name, to make the semifinals of the AAU tournament since the University of Wyoming and Denver University in 1943. In the other semifinal game, Phillips 66, led by Jerry Shipp's 23 points, easily disposed of Seattle's Federal Old Line Insurance, 91–76.[34]

The championship game matched Phillips and Goodyear, the only AAU teams with links to former traditions in AAU basketball. While Phillips returned Jerry Shipp, Denny Price, and Mike Moran, the 66ers lost Don Kojis, who signed an NBA contract. They were the favorites against Goodyear, who had never won an AAU championship. Before three thousand fans, the smallest crowd to watch a championship game, Akron claimed its first national AAU title in the fiftieth-anniversary year of the Goodyear basketball program by dropping Phillips, 86–78. The victory was particularly rewarding for Hank Vaughn, who was in his twelfth season as the Akron coach. Pete McCaffrey, former All-American from St. Louis University, led all scorers with 24 points. Dick Davies with 18, Larry Brown with 17, and Lloyd Sharrar with 10 also scored in double figures for Goodyear. Jerry Shipp, with 22 points, was high man for Phillips.[35]

The past Olympic years had always energized the AAU tournament. This trend ended in 1964 when only 13,197 attended the event. Gross revenues amounted to twenty-two thousand dollars, a ten-thousand-dollar drop from the 1963 tournament. Sportswriters, who expected that the 1964 event was Denver's last, delivered their funeral orations. While all the writers shared fond memories of the tournament's past, they offered different interpretations of its collapse. Leonard Cahn sharply criticized AAU officials, who, Cahn argued, had consistently resisted advice and were victims of their own hubris. They had failed to promote the tournament properly and, in its most profitable years, alienated sponsors with a tight-fisted policy regarding expense money. Cahn, however, recognized that no matter what the AAU had done, "the emergence of the pro game" had killed AAU ball as it had been played between 1935 and 1960. This veteran writer resented any suggestion that somehow Denver sports fans had failed the event. Cahn thought that Denver was a good sports town and bet that, with good management, the Denver Broncos, a struggling American Football League franchise, would draw well.[36] Chet Nelson argued that the tournament had "outlived its usefulness" because of competition from other sports and recreation activity, the absence of a local team, and changing habits of a busy populace. The chances of reviving amateur basketball were slim, Nelson thought, but concluded "it was fun while it lasted."[37]

Following the AAU tournament, AAU officials picked two twelve-man all-star teams. Hank Vaughn coached the AAU Stars, which included six Akron players. Joe B. Hall directed the AAU Stripes, after Bud Browning declined to accept this coaching opportunity. Hall's team had five Phillips 66ers and three of his players from Capitol Federal—Lonnie Wright, Carney Crisler, and Cozel Walker. A former D-C Trucker, Terry Rand, who played with Save-One Stores from Ogden, Utah, in the 1964 tournament, was also on the roster.

The Olympic Trials in New York City provided an interesting postscript to the 1964 national AAU tournament. The eight-team tournament was played at St. John's University's Alumni Hall in New York City. Given the perception that the AAU competition had declined, the experts did not expect much from the AAU teams. In its opening game Hank Vaughn's AAU Stars edged the NCAA Blues. The Blues looked formidable because the core of their team was from UCLA, which had just won its first NCAA title under John Wooden. Gale Goodrich, Walt Hazzard, Doug McIntosh, Jack Hirsch, Fred Slaughter, and Kenny Washington were either starters or key substitutes with the 1964 Bruins. Akron's Pete McCaffrey led the AAU Stars with 29, and George Wilson, a six-foot-ten star at the University of Cincinnati who played in Denver with Chicago's Jamaco Saints, pitched in with 12.[38]

In their second game the AAU Stars squeaked by the NCAA Whites, a squad that included Joe Caldwell from Arizona State, Cotton Nash of Kentucky, Ron Bonham of Cincinnati, and Paul Silas of Creighton. Pete McCaffrey remained hot with 22, Larry Brown scored 20, and Jerry Shipp canned 18 to help the AAU Stars register a victory.[39] This set up a championship game with the NCAA Reds, an all-star team loaded with talent. Rick Barry of the University of Miami, Bill Bradley of Princeton, Jim "Bad News" Barnes of Texas Western, Jeff Mullins of Duke, Wally Jones of Villanova, and Dave Stallworth of Wichita State were All-Americans. The underdog AAU All-Stars, with five players scoring in double figures, upset the NCAA Reds.[40] At the end of his coaching career, Akron's Hank Vaughn had the satisfaction of winning two big tournaments in two weeks.

Russ Lyons, who had a long association with AAU basketball in Denver, chaired the twenty-man Olympic Selection Committee. The challenge, once again, was formidable. The committee rewarded Vaughn's AAU All-Stars for their fine play by naming Pete McCaffrey, George Wilson, Jerry Shipp, Dick Davies, and Larry Brown to the Olympic squad. Bill Bradley of Princeton, Mel Counts of Oregon State, Jim Barnes of Texas Western, and Jeff Mullins of Duke, all from the NCAA Reds, made the final squad. The final three players were Lucious Jackson of Pan American, Walt Hazzard of UCLA, and Joe Caldwell of Arizona State.[41]

The selection met with fewer raised eyebrows than in the past. The most conspicuous omission was the absence of Villanova's Wally Jones from the list of alternates. Gordon S. White Jr., who covered the games for the *New York Times*, reported that, after his first game,

Jones "seemed assured of a spot on the team" but it was "believed that Jones, who has a knack for fancy play, was turned down because of his 'clowning.' "[42] Willis Reed of Grambling, a future star of the New York Knicks, had a good tournament but also failed to make even the list of alternates. In addition to the problem of selection the all-star format created the dilemma of adequate exposure. In the final night of the tournament fans booed Amory "Slats" Gill, coach of the NCAA Reds, when he played Mel Counts, his center at Oregon State, all of the first half and most of the second, which kept Providence College's John Thompson glued to the bench. When Gill decided to put Thompson in the game, the Providence star reportedly waved him off in disgust and remained on the bench.[43] After playing with the Boston Celtics, Thompson won an NCAA championship coaching Georgetown University in 1984 and coached the 1988 Olympic team.

In organizing the 1964 Olympic team, the Olympic Selection Committee broke with precedent when it named Henry Iba of Oklahoma State to coach the team. One of the most respected college coaches in the game's history, Iba, at sixty, was nearing the end of a brilliant career, which included two NCAA championships. As Iba looked forward to the challenges of the Tokyo Games, he worried that "the American people will think this will be easy. It won't." Iba took seriously reports of increasing skill levels as foreign countries studied American play. On the bright side, Iba observed that "No one can shoot with the American boys." Arthur Daley noted, however, that Iba "has been a coach who stressed artful maneuvering and few wasted shots." One might speculate that the choices of Larry Brown, Walt Hazzard, and Bill Bradley met Iba's emphasis on players who fit into a passing game. Whatever Iba's approach to offense would be, he said, "I still intend to insist on defense."[44]

At Tokyo, Iba started Joe Caldwell, Bill Bradley, Lucious Jackson, Jerry Shipp, and Walt Hazzard. With the exception of a 69–61 victory over Yugoslavia, and a tough first half against Puerto Rico, no nation seriously challenged the United States until it met the Soviet Union in the championship game. Before a capacity crowd the Soviets took an early lead, but the Americans rallied to take a halftime lead and controlled the second half to win the gold medal, 73–59. After the game, Coach Iba observed: "Americans had better get serious about this because these foreign countries are playing better basketball all the time."[45]

While the number of quality AAU teams had declined considerably since 1960, AAU players made a significant contribution to the 1964 Olympic team. Jerry Shipp of Phillips led the U.S. team in scoring, while his four AAU teammates also made significant contributions. Iba's comments that "Americans had better get serious" suggested that the United States could not take Olympic basketball gold for granted. As the pool of talent contracted, the AAU's role in Olympic basketball looked bleak. The same was true of the Denver tournament. Although AAU officials struggled to find some way of reviving AAU basketball, they could not reverse the forces that worked against them.

THIRTEEN

The Dribble Derby Passes into History

In 1965 Maceo Brodnax Sr. once again assembled a Denver team under the banner of Capitol Federal Savings and Loan and recruited Horace Walker, former D-C Trucker star, to coach the players. Walker's team included two Wyoming stars, Flynn Robinson and Randy Richardson; two Denver University standouts, Dennis Hodge and Frank Mixon; and Al Dillard from the American University; George Parsons from the University of Colorado; and former Trucker Terry Rand, who played his first tournament in 1956. As the event continued to struggle, its directors asked, "[W]ouldn't it be nice if Denver and the area sports fans got behind the AAU this year in a manner partially as overwhelming as they are supporting the Broncos?"[1]

Led by Flynn Robinson and Al Dillard, Capitol Federal won its first two games to reach the semifinals. Joining them were Hal Fischer's Armed Forces All-Stars, who out-hustled Marion-Kay from Brownstown, Indiana. Vern Benson, from Miami of Ohio, and Calvin Fowler, from St. Francis, two quick guards, were the top scorers and sparked the team's full-court press. The Akron Goodyear Wingfoots, led by Larry Brown, topped Opinion Research from Long Beach, California, and the San Francisco Athletic Club defeated Phillips to complete the semifinal lineup.[2] Carl Minetti, who had coached some excellent Olympic Club teams in the late 1950s, directed the San Francisco Athletic Club. His team was a collection of University of San Francisco, Cal, and Stanford players led by Ollie

Johnson, a six-foot-eight All-American center from the University of San Francisco.

The 1965 tournament was Gary Thompson's first as the coach of the 66ers. After the 1962 season, Thompson left Bartlesville to become a district representative for Phillips in Cedar Rapids, Iowa. In the 1950s Thompson had been one of Iowa's most celebrated athletes. In 1951, as a five-foot-six sophomore, Thompson led tiny Roland High School to the state finals where they lost to Davenport. Thompson's 2,042 points established a new Iowa high-school career scoring record, and another 1,253 at Iowa State set a new career high for the Cyclones. At Iowa State, Thompson's coach was Bill Strannigan, who was a star at the University of Wyoming and on Denver's last AAU championship team in 1942. One of the most memorable moments of the Strannigan-Thompson era was a 39–37 victory in 1957 over Kansas and Wilt Chamberlain in which Thompson edged Chamberlain for scoring honors, 18–17. In five years with Phillips, Thompson collected another 2,348 points, which placed him sixth on the list of the 66er's top scorers. Two years after playing, Thompson could not get the idea of coaching out of his blood. As he explored his options, Bud Browning, who had been a valued mentor, indicated that he was ready to retire and offered Thompson the opportunity to replace him at Phillips. As it turned out, he would be the 66ers' last coach.[3]

In the semifinals 4,540 excited fans watched Capitol Federal defeat the defending champion Akron Goodyear Wingfoots. Flynn Robinson relied on a feathery jump shot to pace Denver with 24 points and received great help from Randy Redwine with 16 and Randy Richardson with 15. Larry Brown and Al Tuttle from Georgetown each scored 22 to top Akron's scorers. In another surprise the shorter Armed Forces All-Stars nipped San Francisco Athletic Club. Little Vern Benson, the top scorer in the tournament, led his team with 17 points. Ollie Johnson scored 20 points and snagged 21 rebounds in defeat.[4]

With the future of the tournament in doubt, Denver recognized that there were not many opportunities remaining to capture another title. Since 1942, eight Denver teams had reached the finals but none had claimed the champion's crown. In many ways, Capitol Federal was a throwback to the tournament's origins with three college players—Flynn Robinson, Randy Richardson, and Frank Mixon—and a bunch of ex-collegians who were working regular eight-hour days, or in the case of George Parsons, attending pharmacy school. During the regular season the Savers played nineteen games but only one was at home. The remainder of the games were weekend jaunts into Wyoming and Nebraska, a much different preparation from the NIBL experience.

In the championship game, before 5,800 screaming fans, substitute Richard Peloff scored the last 3 points of the game, his only points, to secure a 77–75 victory for the Armed Forces All-Stars. For Hal Fischer, the winning coach, this was his first championship in twelve attempts. Little Vern Benson, who played two years of basketball with Oscar Robertson on Indianapolis's Crispus Attucks state championship team in 1955 and 1956, popped in 22 points to win tournament scoring honors and the most valuable player award. Flynn Robinson with 17 and Terry Rand with 14 were the top scorers for Capitol Federal.[5]

Because of the exciting performances by Capitol Federal the AAU grossed almost six thousand dollars more than in 1964 and for the first time since 1961 the AAU had reversed the downward spiral at the gate. This modest improvement at the cash register encouraged AAU officials to ponder the possibility of reviving an amateur industrial basketball league as part of a plan to rebuild postcollegiate amateur basketball in the United States. Cliff Buck of Denver, who was the national AAU president, hoped to find corporate sponsors like Phillips Petroleum and Akron Goodyear who would subsidize a basketball program. Buck said the AAU was considering hiring a full-time executive director "to foster, promote, and develop industrial sports" rather than relying on volunteers. But what would rekindle an interest among corporate sponsors who had jumped out of basketball between 1960 and 1962?[6]

While the AAU obviously did not want to surrender its role in postcollegiate basketball, it was dependent on large corporations to save amateur basketball. Chuck Garrity of the *Denver Post* speculated that there were two major reasons why corporations would not provide a bailout for the AAU. One was the cost, estimated by Garrity at twenty-five thousand dollars a year. But what sort of justification could the AAU offer to justify even this sort of modest investment? The second reason, Garrity admitted, was harder to get on the public record but was discussed "when the doors closed for executive sessions."[7] The issue that was too difficult to talk about openly was the role of African American players in any projected effort to revive amateur basketball. Through the 1950s the longstanding corporate teams such as Phillips, Akron, and Peoria were able to recruit outstanding white players but had almost never reached out to the African American athletes. By the mid-1960s white and black players were going to follow the money, which was increasing exponentially, as professional sports appeared more frequently on television.

The period between 1960 and 1965, with the passage of the 1964 Civil Rights law and the Voting Rights Act of 1965, was the peak of the civil rights movement in post–World War Two America. In basketball these years also marked the emergence of African Americans as a new force in the sport. They were responsible for increasing the size of the gap between NBA and AAU basketball. White fans and coaches had some difficulty adjusting to the change in the composition of talent in basketball. At the end of the 1965 AAU tournament, the *Denver Post*'s Harry Farrar, a political moderate who generally praised the accomplishments of racial integration in sports, wrote an emotionally powerful column on this subject. Just before the semifinals Farrar reported that a college coach remarked, "Our team can whip most other white teams, but we can't beat the Niggers." Another member of this casual group of conversationalists chimed in: "The AAU is turning into the African Olympics"— which was a reference to all-star teams with black players. Stunned by the depth of this racism and the absence of a rebuttal, Farrar apologized "now for my own cowardice as a silent witness." Clearly uncomfortable about preaching to his readers, Farrar stressed that his "remarks are made only to deplore the pockets of sports bigotry in the United States." While Farrar feared that calling attention to race risked greater tensions, he thought it "shameful to remain silent in gatherings of alleged sports men when 'Nigger jokes' are told by whites, who seem to fear a challenge to Caucasian virility."[8]

The 1965 tournament was the last managed by Willard "Big Bill" Greim. He had helped bring the national AAU tournament to Denver in 1935 and his name was synonymous with it. He had played an integral role in every tournament and was officially designated the director in 1943. Greim's involvement with sports began in Warrensburg, Missouri, where he grew up and played football, basketball, and track at Warrensburg State College (now Central Missouri State). After earning a master's degree in physical education from Springfield College in Springfield, Massachusetts, Greim coached briefly in Lathrop, Missouri, before moving to Denver in 1924 to direct health and physical education for the Denver public schools and to manage prep sports. After mandatory retirement in 1955, Greim served as Denver's director of Parks and Recreation until replaced by Johnny Dee in 1963. While Greim was often on the hot seat and frequently considered dictatorial, Denverites respected his integrity and administrative skills. Greim's impact on amateur sports extended well beyond Denver. For twelve years he was president of the International Federation of Amateur Basketball (FIBA), which governed world basketball competition. Between 1945 and 1947 Greim was president of the AAU and from 1946 to 1966 he served on the United States Olympic Committee. While Greim was closely identified with amateur basketball, he was also a popular starter in track meets at all levels of competition. In April of 1966 Colorado honored Greim by inducting him into the Colorado Sports Hall of Fame.[9] For the last three years of play L. W. "Pete" Seipel directed the tourney.

As play opened in March of 1966 the spotlight focused on the Ford Mustangs from Detroit, Michigan, and their star player, Cazzie Russell, three-time All-American from the University of Michigan, who lost to UCLA in the 1965 championship game. The Mustangs, coached by Horace Walker, Denver's coach in 1965, had four other Wolverines—Oliver Darden, Larry Tregoning, John Clawson, and John Thompson—and three Spartans from Michigan State—Lance Olsen, Stan Washington, and Bill Curtis. His center was Ollie Johnson, of the University of San Francisco, who had played in 1965 with the San Francisco Athletic Club. The presence of Russell as well as a sprinkling of other All-Americans led to a record Sunday crowd of 8,500, some of whom saw the Mustangs register an easy first-round win. Capitol Federal also won easily in the first round with Bill Peay, who played at the University of Denver, in charge of the team. Lonnie Wright from Colorado State University, Chuck Gardner of the University of Colorado, and Leon Clark of the University of Wyoming joined five players from the 1965 team.[10]

In the second round of play the Akron Goodyear Wingfoots squeezed by Contac Caps of Knoxville, Tennessee, as Vern Benson, the MVP of the 1965 tournament when he played with the Armed Forces All-Stars, and Jay Miller of Notre Dame led the Wingfoots scorers. All-Americans Clyde Lee of Vanderbilt and Jack Marin of Duke were the top scorers for the Caps. In another quarterfinal game Lonnie Wright scored 24 and Chuck Gardner neutralized Walt Wesley, All-American at the University of Kansas, as Capitol Federal pulled out a 66–65 victory over May Builders of Arkansas City, Kansas, on a basket by Gardner with four seconds left. Hal Fischer's Armed Forces All-Stars lost an 11-point lead in the second half as Cazzie Russell with 23, and Oliver Darden with 21, helped the Ford Mustangs to victory. The fourth semifinalist was Phillips 66, which dominated the McDonald Company from Torrance, California. Harold Sergent, a rookie from Morehead State, led all scorers with 22, one more than McDonald's John Block, who would go on to play in the NBA.[11]

In the semifinals the Ford Mustangs turned back the Akron Goodyear Wingfoots, 84–81. Down by 15 points with three minutes left in the game, Akron stormed back to get within 2 points before Larry Tregoning's free throw sealed the victory for the Mustangs. Russell once again led all scorers with 25, and Al Tuttle was high man for Akron with 20. In the other semifinal game Phillips employed a swarming defense and an error-free offense to pull away from Denver Capitol Federal in the last four minutes of play. Phillips's Harold Sergent led the 66ers for a second night with 20, followed by Bobby Rascoe's 17. Leon Clark with 20 and Chuck Gardner with

16 were the double-digit scorers for Denver.[12] Gary Thompson had eight veterans from the previous year plus newcomers Kendall Rhine, a six-foot-ten center from Rice University; Warren Rustand, a guard from Arizona; and Harold Sergent.

In the championship game, with most of the 6,800 fans cheering their every move, the Ford Mustangs, behind Russell's 25, won a tight contest, 71–67. Russell, the tournament's MVP and leading scorer, topped all scorers with 25. Phillips had played well, but Denver fans, resorting to decades of habit, booed the 66ers heartily when they received their second-place trophy. Classy Cazzie Russell observed, "I don't like that. They don't deserve it."[13]

Russell had an electrifying impact on the tournament, which grossed forty thousand dollars and produced an eighteen-thousand-dollar profit, the best gate since 1962. The short-term effect was to give the illusion that the AAU tournament's future was not as bleak as predicted by the doomsayers. Articles appeared in the Denver papers that predicted that several corporations planned to jump into amateur basketball for the 1966–67 season. Boulder's Russ Lyons, the AAU's national basketball chairman, announced that the AAU would also allow a player who tried out but failed to make a professional team to keep his amateur status. Another carrot extended to collegiate players was the promise of more international travel.[14]

In 1967 the AAU organized a four-team league, the National AAU Basketball League, that included Phillips, Akron, Airmatic Valves of Cleveland, and the Jamaco Saints of Chicago. This league was a shell of the National Industrial Basketball League and a belated effort to revive amateur basketball. Russ Lyons, AAU basketball chairman, hoped that Denver companies would sponsor players like they did in the 1930s and that he could find one more corporate team to increase the league to six teams. Interestingly, he was unable to find a sponsor. Leonard Cahn thought "[t]hat type of support went out the window long ago. Too many persons got burnt."[15]

Twenty teams entered the 1967 tournament as the AAU hoped to build on the enthusiasm generated by Cazzie Russell in 1966. Although Capitol Federal Savings made it to the semifinal round, the 1967 national AAU tournament generated little excitement. Capitol

Federal's most productive players were Byron Beck, a Denver University star who would become a popular Denver Rocket and Denver Nugget, and Bob Rule from Colorado State University, who would play in the NBA for eight years. There was no Cazzie Russell to serve as a lightning rod for the tournament, so the teams played before sparse crowds.

In the semifinals, in what would have been a sure-fire sellout in the tournament's heyday, three thousand fans watched Phillips knock out Capitol Federal. Down by 20 points at the beginning of the second half, Bob Rule scored 19 of his game high 24 after the intermission to keep the Savers in the game. Harold Sergent, Phillips's outstanding guard, matched Rule's offensive outburst by hitting eight baskets from all over the court. The Akron Goodyears kept pace with Phillips by beating Chicago's Jamaco Saints. Akron's tight defense and balanced scoring attack led by Vern Benson with 22 were too much for the Chicagoans.[16]

For the second time in the 1960s Akron defeated Phillips to win the AAU championship. Akron limited Harold Sergent to 6 points, while five Goodyears scored in double figures to give the Wingfoots the victory. Hank Vaughn, Akron's jubilant coach, summed up the game very simply: "We shot well and they didn't." Gary Thompson agreed with Vaughn's assessment and pointed to two long 66er scoring droughts that made it difficult for his team to get any closer than 3 points in the second half. For the second consecutive year Phillips found itself unable to win the all-important final game.[17]

While the coaches analyzed their team's performances, the tournament's future in Denver was in doubt. A mere 3,500 attended the championship game, a graphic illustration of the tournament's obscurity. The tournament's fate was sealed in 1967 when Denver secured a franchise in the newly formed American Basketball Association (ABA). This was Denver's second effort to establish a professional team and it stumbled out of the gate. When it turned out that the first investors did not have the financial resources to compete, it looked as if the Denver Rockets franchise might not get off the ground. In an effort to save the franchise, interested citizens persuaded Bill Ringsby, the wealthy owner of a local trucking company, to purchase ownership of two-thirds of the team. Ringsby's decision was influenced by his friendship with George Kolowich, who had sponsored the D-C Truckers. One of Ringsby's first moves was to name Dick Eicher, who starred for Central Bank and the Truckers, his vice president, general manager, and chief operating officer.

In its first year the Rockets had a winning season and the second-best league attendance. In the franchise's early years, it had some interesting AAU connections. Byron Beck of the University of Denver played some AAU ball before enjoying a fine career with the Rockets and Nuggets. In the 1969–70 season, John McLendon, whose Cleveland Pipers won the 1961 tournament, coached the Rockets for twenty-eight games before he was replaced by Joe Belmont, the popular guard for the D-C Truckers. Between 1971 and 1974 Alex Hannum, who had an AAU championship in his résumé, ran the team. For the next five years Larry Brown, who played with Akron, coached Denver as it became the Nuggets and moved into the NBA.[18]

In 1968 Denver hosted its last AAU tournament. As basketball fans turned their attention to the Denver Rockets and the American Basketball Association, interest in the tournament hit rock bottom. The only hook the AAU had to attract fan interest was the connection between the Denver tourney and the Olympic Trials, which were scheduled for Albuquerque, New Mexico, in early April. Because it was an Olympic year, the National Collegiate Athletic Association allowed all collegians to play in the AAU tournament. The hope that top collegians would flock to Denver did not materialize. Prior to the tournament Capitol Federal persuaded Gordon "Shorty" Carpenter, a former Phillips star and 1948 Olympian, to coach a hastily assembled team of collegians. Team members included Carl Ashley and Harry Hall from Wyoming; Harry Hollines, Denver University's all-time leading scorer; plus Pat Frink and Chuck Williams from the University of Colorado. In their second game Capitol Federal, despite Pat Frink's 27, lost a heartbreaker to the San Francisco Athletic Club, 99–97. The Phillips 66ers also fell in the second round to Vaughn Realty of Spokane, Washington.[19]

In the semifinal Vaughn Realty surprised Carl Minetti's San Francisco Athletic Club. Gary Lechman from Gonzaga and Rod Mc-

Donald from Whitworth combined for 42 points for the winners. The Armed Forces All-Stars, paced by Mike Barrett's 26, were too strong for Akron and registered an easy victory.[20] Before a mere 2,200 Hal Fischer's All-Stars jumped out to a 16-point first-half lead and turned back two comeback efforts by Vaughn Realty to win the last AAU championship in Denver. Mike Barrett, the tournament MVP, topped all scorers with 26 points.[21]

Hosting its last national tournament, Denver lost over $3,300, its second consecutive year in red ink. In September of 1968 the Rocky Mountain AAU voted unanimously against seeking to host the 1969 AAU tournament. It recognized that Denver had lost interest in it. The immediate cause of the tournament's demise was the establishment of the Denver Rockets, but the old Dribble Derby had been living on borrowed time for its last seven years. It was not just the Rockets but a combination of the professionalization of American sports and television's ability to make professional and college basketball accessible nationally that killed postcollegiate amateur basketball. In 1935, when Denver hosted its first national AAU tournament, this was the biggest sporting event in town. By 1968 the Denver Broncos, the Rockets, minor league baseball, and nationally televised sports simply overwhelmed amateur basketball. As newcomers poured into the Denver metropolitan area, Chet Nelson wrote they "couldn't care less about the event's traditions and many contributions to the local sports scene in past years."[22]

Following the conclusion of the 1968 tournament, Phillips Petroleum Company dropped its basketball program. Going back to the 1930s Phillips had been the model for the industrial basketball teams. For a variety of reasons amateur basketball no longer made sense for Phillips. By 1967 the 66ers were having difficulty retaining their best players as they were picked off by professional teams. Phillips had always prided itself on keeping a high percentage of its players as employees, but this was no longer the case. This problem plus the increasing difficulty of recruiting blue-chip players, meant that Phillips was destined to field a second-rate team, which had no appeal to the company. The recruiting problem was exacerbated by the inability of Phillips to recruit an African American player at a time when African Americans were changing the game. Finally the demise of the NIBL and the Denver tournament meant that Phillips, if it had continued, would have been a barnstorming team with no event left to measure the team's quality.

Two years later the Akron Goodyear Company also dropped its program. Akron's basketball team preceded the Phillips program but never had the same competitive success until the 1960s. Nonetheless, it had a carefully structured training program and took pride in the number of employees who stayed with the company.

The AAU tournament, which had been identified with Denver, fell off the sports radar screen as it moved from one small city to another. The AAU sponsored its last national championship in 1976 without media comment. While the AAU would have no impact on postcollegiate basketball after the 1968 Olympics, that was a memorable year in Olympic basketball and American History.

The year 1968 was among the most divisive in the history of the United States. Anti–Vietnam War protests, the assassinations of Martin Luther King Jr. and Robert Kennedy, and the chaos of the Democratic Party's convention in Chicago were among the most troubling events of that year. Sports did not escape the tensions of a divided society. Although an effort to boycott the Olympic Games in Mexico City failed to enlist many black athletes, Lew Alcindor (Kareem Abdul-Jabbar), who had just completed his junior year, chose not to play on the 1968 U.S. Olympic team. He thought that this was one way that he could protest against the history of racial discrimination in the United States.[23] Alcindor was not the only collegiate star to decide not to play in 1968. Wanting to take advantage of a bidding war between the NBA and ABA for the nation's best talent, Elvin Hayes, Wes Unseld, Bob Lanier, Neil Walk, and Don May also passed on participating at the Olympic Trials. Given the intensity of the Cold War and the self-imposed pressure to maintain its unbeaten streak in Olympic competition, this was not welcome news to the U.S. Olympic Basketball Committee.

In Albuquerque, New Mexico, the Olympic Trials were patterned after the 1964 Trials with some interesting modifications. In 1968 the United States Olympic Committee allotted the AAU and Armed

Forces one representative each rather than two as in 1964. This decision reflected recognition of the declining strength in AAU and Armed Forces basketball. In addition, there were three NCAA university teams, one NAIA squad, one NCAA College Division team, and a junior college team.

The AAU team surprised the experts in 1964. Could Akron's Hank Vaughn manufacture another surprise in 1968? Vaughn had four of his Akron players—Calvin Fowler, Tom Black, Mike Patterson, and Jim King. Steve Kuberski from Bradley, Harold Sergent and Gary Schull from Phillips, Edgar Lacey from UCLA, Jim Tillman from Loyola of Chicago, and Ted McLain and Ed Johnson of Tennessee A&I completed the team, which had plenty of size. In the first round Vaughn's team got off to an excellent start by cruising past the NCAA College Division team.[24] On the following night the AAU stars remained hot and topped the Armed Forces All-Stars.[25] This set up a championship match up between the AAU stars and the NAIA stars, who had beaten the NCAA White team with Charlie Scott and Dan Issel, as well as the Junior College All-Stars, who featured Spencer Haywood. Plagued by some cold shooting, the AAU stars fell to the NAIA, 64–59.[26]

In selecting the Olympic team, as in the past, the U.S. Olympic Basketball Committee paid attention to distributing some slots to the various teams. Calvin Fowler and James King, both of the Akron Goodyears, represented the AAU. The committee selected John Clawson, Mike Barrett, and Mike Silliman from the Armed Forces All-Stars. One of Detroit's most gifted high school players, Spencer Haywood, was the sole selection from the Junior College All-Stars. Glynn Saulters from Northeast Louisiana and Don Dee from St. Mary of the Plains in Kansas won spots from the NAIA All-Stars. The four spots left to the University All-Stars were awarded to Jo Jo White of Kansas, Charlie Scott of North Carolina, Bill Hosket of Ohio State, and Ken Spain of Houston. There were no representatives from the College Division.[27] The list of players passed over by virtue of limiting the NCAA to four spots was impressive and included Pete Maravich, Dan Issel, Rick Mount, and Calvin Murphy.

There was one irony associated with the selection of this team. During the 1960s there was a battle royal between the AAU and the NCAA over control of amateur sports in the United States and representation on the IOC. Bill Reed, Big Ten commissioner and chairman of the NCAA's Olympic Committee, announced that the NCAA was thinking about withdrawing from the United States Olympic Committee unless it received more representation on that committee. The one area that pleased Reed was the NCAA's representation at the Olympic Basketball Trials.[28] Ironically the four NCAA players on the 1968 team were two fewer than in 1964.

Going into the Olympics at Mexico City, some experts thought that the Soviet Union and Yugoslavia had better teams than the United States. Repeating the formula of 1964, the U.S. Olympic Basketball committee named Henry Iba to coach the U.S. team with Hank Vaughn serving as his assistant. After routing Spain in its first game, Iba observed, "We have the fewest number of NCAA major college players we ever had. These small college players make some errors, but all in all it was a good game for us."[29] After two more easy wins against Senegal and the Philippines, the United States survived its first big test with a relatively easy win over Yugoslavia. Jo Jo White of Kansas led all scorers with 24.[30] After another two easy victories, over Panama and Italy, the United States found itself in a dogfight with a hot team from Puerto Rico. In the second half Puerto Rico closed within 3 points but came no closer as the United States posted a 61–56 victory. Spencer Haywood topped all scorers with 21 points.[31] The United States notched its eighth victory by easily beating Brazil. On the same day, Yugoslavia upset the Soviet Union, 63–62, before twenty-two thousand approving fans, which meant the championship game would be a rematch between the United States and Yugoslavia.[32] Before an overflow crowd of twenty-five thousand Spencer Haywood and Jo Jo White broke the gold medal game open in the second half as the United States won its seventh gold medal in basketball. At the beginning of the contest the fans supported the Yugoslavs, but Haywood and White won them over to the American side in the second half.[33]

Although Coach Henry Iba had enjoyed many great moments

as a coach, the 1968 Olympic Championship had to be among the most satisfying of his career. Because so many blue-chip players elected not to participate in the Olympic Trials, the experts were not optimistic about America's chances of winning a gold medal. Arthur Daley thought the absence of marquee performers played into Iba's "highly disciplined style of play. . . . He was the alchemist who turned a ragtag collection into a slick purposeful unit." As Daley thought, the victory probably indicated "how deep the supply of talent is back home." Despite the 1968 team's success, Daley recommended that the United States send nothing but the "best to future Olympics because the brand of basketball displayed by the rest of the world keeps improving steadily and markedly."[34] The AAU would not be a part of this future. In 1972, in response to the declining quality of AAU competition, the International Basketball Federation withdrew its recognition of the AAU as the institution responsible for organizing U.S. basketball teams, which it had done since 1936.

When James Naismith invented basketball just over a hundred years ago, he had no idea that it would become a big business. Unlike AAU basketball, the history of professional basketball began in the Northeast and Midwest, where sports entrepreneurs hustled to build franchises that could turn a profit. In the first six decades of the twentieth century, in the wide-open spaces west of the Mississippi River, professional basketball was absent. In this vast region of the United States, Kansas City and Denver provided the venues for teams to compete for national championships and players to earn All-America honors. While basketball today is commonly referred to as the City Game, it is important to remember that the small towns and mid-sized cities of the West produced their fair share of quality players who filled the rosters of the AAU teams after completing their college careers. As long as professional salaries remained low, the pro game had limited appeal.

Between 1921 and 1934, Kansas City succeeded in making the tournament a popular event. It was there that traditions were established and teams like the Kansas City Athletic Club, the Cook Paint Company, the Hillyards, the Wichita Henrys, and the Tulsa

Diamond DX Oilers made an imprint on the region. These teams
barnstormed to the Pacific Coast and helped to connect teams from
California and Washington to the tournament.

In the depths of the Great Depression, Denver, desperate for
some claim to athletic distinction, succeeded in its bid to host the
AAU tournament. Sportswriters and local athletic administrators got
behind the effort, and it succeeded beyond expectations.

Crucial to the success of Denver's tournament was the ability
of Robert "Ace" Gruenig and Jack McCracken to lead Denver's
team through the gauntlet of a single-elimination tournament to
capture the championship trophy. Between 1937 and 1942, Denver
won three championships and thought of itself as the "basketball
capital of the U.S." During these years Gruenig and McCracken
were the stars, and their teammates, however capable, the supporting cast. Sportswriters elaborated upon their achievements, and they
became Denver's first sports heroes. Although successful, Gruenig
and McCracken created no dynasty. Instead, from 1943 through
1948, it was the Phillips Petroleum Company, reflecting the energy
and enthusiasm of Kenneth "Boots" Adams, which did. Initially the
rivalry between Denver and Bartlesville made the "dribble derby"
tournament an exciting event. In every one of its three championship
years, Denver edged the 66ers for the title. By 1943 the superior
resources and corporate efficiency of Phillips simply wore down
Denver, which had to rely on an aging Gruenig and McCracken and
makeshift sponsorships. By 1948 Phillips had won six consecutive
championships and threatened to make the tournament dull and
predictable. Just the reverse occurred.

From 1949 through 1960, while Phillips was always a threat, it
won only two championships as compared to seven in its first twelve
years. During this period the Peoria Caterpillars won five championships, a remarkable record given the parity among the teams
that competed in Denver. Although George Kolowich and Johnny
Dee gave Denver well-organized, competitive teams, they lost their
only appearance in a championship game to Peoria in 1958. In 1960
twelve years of exciting competition culminated with the Olympic
tournament, which made even the skeptics think of Denver momen-

tarily as a basketball mecca. The exhilaration of 1960 quickly faded as professional basketball flourished and, with the benefit of television, changed the economics of basketball. Corporations, such as Phillips Petroleum, the Caterpillar Corporation, and others recognized that there was no longer a place for their brand of basketball in the United States.

In the twenty-first century the legacy of AAU basketball and the tournaments in Kansas City and Denver are recognized only in limited ways. Some AAU players and coaches are enshrined in the Naismith Hall of Fame or the state halls of fame that dot the country. The tournament deserves to be remembered for its contribution to basketball history, Olympic basketball history, and the pleasure it gave to players, coaches, and fans. It was a well-run event with unique traditions and colorful players. Some like Red DeBernardi, Melvin Miller, Ace Gruenig, Jack McCracken, Frank Lubin, Chuck Hyatt, and Les O'Gara seemed ageless. Products of the Great Depression, they were legends who played until their bodies no longer could respond to the competition. In the 1940s Phillips produced superb teams built around Scat McNatt, Shorty Carpenter, and Bob Kurland. They matched their skills against those of California's Hank Luisetti, Jim Pollard, and Don Barksdale, some of the finest players of their time. In the 1950s there was an explosion of talent as Chuck Darling, Burdie Haldorson, Howie Williams, Ron Bontemps, George Yardley, Dick Boushka, Ron Tomsic, and Bob Boozer, to name a few, battled in the Denver tournament. Every March the fans religiously returned—looking for a dark horse, hoping for an upset, especially if Phillips was on the floor, comparing new players to the stars of yesteryear, and hoping that a Denver team would claim one more national championship. Then it all came to an end. It is hard to disagree with Chet Nelson, who covered all the tournaments for the *Rocky Mountain News* who simply said: "It was fun while it lasted."[35]

Summary of AAU Championship Finals and Winning Coaches, 1921–1968

1921
QUARTERFINALS
Kansas City Athletic Club over University of Nevada, Reno (40–19)

Lowe & Campbell, Kansas City, over Northwestern Normal, Alva OK (49–35)

Atlanta Athletic Club over Los Angeles Athletic Club (21–20)

Southwestern College, Winfield KS, over Des Moines College (51–12)

SEMIFINALS
Kansas City Athletic Club over Lowe & Campbell (42–31)

Southwestern College over Atlanta Athletic Club (36–31)

THIRD PLACE
Atlanta Athletic Club over Lowe & Campbell (34–23)

CHAMPIONSHIP
Kansas City Athletic Club (Coach Henry Ashley) over Southwestern College (42–36)

1922
QUARTERFINALS
Lowe & Campbell over Washburn College, Topeka KS (39–24)

Southwestern College over Kentucky & Indiana Terminals, Louisville KY (46–30)

Indianapolis YMCA over Newton Athletic Club, Newton KS (28–26)

Kansas City Athletic Club over Union Club, Belvedere IL (50–28)

SEMIFINALS
Lowe & Campbell over Southwestern College (29–25)

Kansas City Athletic Club over Indianapolis YMCA (58–27)

THIRD PLACE

Southwestern College over Indianapolis YMCA (35–32).

CHAMPIONSHIP

Lowe & Campbell (Coach Harry Mudd) over Kansas City Athletic
Club (42–28)   1923

QUARTERFINALS

Two Harbors All-Stars, Two Harbors MN, over Southeastern State
Teachers, Durant OK (25–21)

Kansas City Athletic Club over Kansas City Tabernacles (35–15)

Hillyard Chemical, St. Joseph MO, over Southwestern College (42–
23)

Larry Semon Athletic Club, Hollywood CA over Fairmont College,
Wichita KS (32–28)   SEMIFINALS

Kansas City Athletic Club over Two Harbors All-Stars (42–24)

Hillyard Chemical over Larry Semon Athletic Club (46–31)

THIRD PLACE

Two Harbors All-Stars over Larry Semon Athletic Club (20–10)

CHAMPIONSHIP

Kansas City Athletic Club (Coach Henry Ashley) over Hillyard
Chemical (31–18)   1924

QUARTERFINALS

Lombard College, Galesburg IL, over University Club, Brooklyn NY
(43–22)

Kansas City Athletic Club over Washburn College (58–25)

Hillyard Chemical over San Francisco Olympic Club (31–30)

Butler University, Indianapolis, over Kansas City Schooleys (34–29)

SEMIFINALS

Kansas City Athletic Club over Lombard College (38–21)

Butler University over Hillyard Chemical (35–29)

THIRD PLACE

Hillyard Chemical over Lombard College (28–15)

CHAMPIONSHIP

Butler University (Coach Pat Page) over Kansas City Athletic Club
(30–26)

1925

QUARTERFINALS

Washburn College over St. Phillips Athletic Club, Chicago (34–11)

Monon Athletic Club, Lafayette IN, over Southern Surety, Des Moines IA (44–41)

Hillyard Chemical over Kansas City Schooleys (38–33)

Kansas City Athletic Club over Lombard College (34–26)

SEMIFINALS

Washburn College over Monon Athletic Club (45–33)

Hillyard Chemical over Kansas City Athletic Club (19–14)

THIRD PLACE

Kansas City Athletic Club over Monon Athletic Club (29–16)

CHAMPIONSHIP

Washburn College (Coach Arthur "Dutch" Lonberg) over Hillyard Chemical (42–30)

1926

QUARTERFINALS

Hillyard Chemical over Southside Turners, Indianapolis (38–18)

Emporia Teachers, Emporia KS, over Pittsburg Teachers, Pittsburg KS (27–23)

Kansas City Athletic Club over Werner-Werner, St. Louis MO (44–28)

Akron Goodyear, Akron OH, over Kansas City Schooleys (40–19)

SEMIFINALS

Hillyard Chemical over Emporia Teachers (43–31)

Kansas City Athletic Club over Akron Goodyear (33–16)

THIRD PLACE

Akron Goodyear over Emporia Teachers (38–25)

CHAMPIONSHIP

Hillyard Chemical (Coach George Levis) over Kansas City Athletic Club (25–20)

1927

QUARTERFINALS

Hillyard Chemical over Phillips University, Enid OK (23–21)

Washburn College over Emporia Teachers, Emporia KS (23–17)

Ke-Nash-A, Kenosha WI, over Monon Athletic Club (28–23)

Wichita University over St. Joseph Missouri Boosters (37–26)

SEMIFINALS
Hillyard Chemical over Washburn College (34–29)
Ke-Nash-A over Wichita University (36–33)
THIRD PLACE
Wichita University over Washburn College (31–18)
CHAMPIONSHIP
Hillyard Chemical (Coach George Levis) over Ke-Nash-A (29–10)

1928

QUARTERFINALS
Hillyard Chemical over McPherson College, McPherson KS (35–17)
Sterling Milk, Oklahoma City, over Pittsburg Teachers, Pittsburg
    KS (26–25)
Cook Paint, Kansas City MO, over Cudahy Athletic Club, Sioux City
    IA (39–21)
Kansas City Athletic Club over Rockhurst College, Kansas City MO
    (36–23)
SEMIFINALS
Kansas City Athletic Club over Sterling Milk (28–15)
Cook Paint over Hillyard Chemical (41–17)
THIRD PLACE
Sterling Milk over Hillyard Chemical (31–30)
CHAMPIONSHIP
Cook Paint (Coach Hugh McDermott) over Kansas City Athletic
    Club (25–23)

1929

QUARTERFINALS
Southside Turners over Phillips University (31–28)
Cook Paint over Central Normal College, Danville IN (40–18)
Ke-Nash-A over Denver University (23–11)
Wichita Henrys over McPherson College (34–26)
SEMIFINALS
Cook Paint over Southside Turners (32–19)
Wichita Henrys over Ke-Nash-A (23–12)
THIRD PLACE
Ke-Nash-A over Southside Turners (21–16)
CHAMPIONSHIP
Cook Paint (Coach J. R. "Bob" Mosby) over Wichita Henrys (51–35)

1930
QUARTERFINALS
Bethany College, Lindsborg KS, over Southside Turners (21–15)
San Francisco Olympic Club over Kansas City Athletic Club (30–25)
East Central Teachers, Ada OK, over Murphy-Did-It, Omaha NE (44–33)
Wichita Henrys over Ke-Nash-A (26–21)
SEMIFINALS
San Francisco Olympic Club over Bethany College (23–21)
Wichita Henrys over East Central Teachers (27–22)
THIRD PLACE
East Central Teachers over Bethany College (42–21)
CHAMPIONSHIP
Wichita Henrys (Coach Gene Johnson) over San Francisco Olympic Club (29–16)

1931
QUARTERFINALS
Wichita Henrys over Bethany College (34–19)
Los Angeles Athletic Club over East Central Teachers (43–30)
Young Men's Institute, San Francisco, over Big Four Athletic Association, Cincinnati (28–21)
Kansas City Athletic Club over Lowe & Campbell (25–21)
SEMIFINALS
Wichita Henrys over Los Angeles Athletic Club (33–20)
Kansas City Athletic Club over Young Men's Institute (23–17)
THIRD PLACE
Los Angeles Athletic Club over Young Men's Institute (33–13)
CHAMPIONSHIP
Wichita Henrys (Coach George Gardner) over Kansas City Athletic Club (38–14)

1932
QUARTERFINALS
Wichita Henrys over Sugar Creek Creamery, St. Louis MO (27–20)
Schuessler Athletic Club, Chicago, over Dakota Wesleyan, Mitchell SD (39–35)
Maryville Teachers, Maryville MO, over San Francisco Olympic Club (26–14)

Southern Kansas Stage Lines, Wichita KS, over Young Men's Institute (38–18)

SEMIFINALS

Wichita Henrys over Schuessler Athletic Club (32–26)

Maryville Teachers over Southern Kansas Stage Lines (22–18)

THIRD PLACE

Schuessler Athletic Club over Southern Kansas Stage Lines (26–24)

CHAMPIONSHIP

Wichita Henrys (Coach Jim Gardner) over Maryville Teachers (15–14)

1933

QUARTERFINALS

Wichita Henrys over West Texas Teachers (37–17)

Diamond DX Oilers, Tulsa OK, over Phillips University (30–17)

Rosenberg-Arvey, Chicago, over Pasadena Majors (34–28)

Southern Kansas Stage Lines, Kansas City KS, over Reno Creamery, Hutchinson KS (23–18)

SEMIFINALS

Diamond DX Oilers over Wichita Henrys (34–20)

Rosenberg-Arvey over Southern Kansas Stage Line (34–28)

THIRD PLACE

Wichita Henrys over Southern Kansas Stage Lines (26–24)

CHAMPIONSHIP

Diamond DX Oilers (Coach Bill Miller) over Rosenberg-Arvey (25–23)

1934

QUARTERFINALS

Diamond DX Oilers over Lifeschultz Fast Freight, Chicago (40–38)

San Francisco Olympic Club over Denver Piggly Wiggly (31–30)

Reno Creamery over Southern Kansas Stage Lines (16–11)

University of Wyoming over Gridley Chieftains, Wichita KS (28–25)

SEMIFINALS

Diamond DX Oilers over San Francisco Olympic Club (38–26)

University of Wyoming over Reno Creamery (30–27)

THIRD PLACE

San Francisco Olympic Club over Reno Creamery (38–34)

CHAMPIONSHIP

Diamond DX Oilers (Coach Bill Miller) over University of Wyoming (29–19)

1935

QUARTERFINALS

Diamond DX Oilers over Denver Athletic Club (36–27)

Southern Kansas Stage Lines over Denver Piggly Wiggly (30–28)

Universal Pictures over Reno Creamery (44–36)

McPherson Globe Refiners, McPherson KS, over Italian Athletic Club, Seattle (51–26)

SEMIFINALS

Southern Kansas Stage Lines over Diamond DX Oilers (36–27)

McPherson Globe Refiners over Universal Pictures (40–36)

THIRD PLACE

Diamond DX Oilers over Universal Pictures (42–33)

CHAMPIONSHIP

Southern Kansas Stage Lines (Coach Frank "Buck" Weaver) over McPherson Globe Refiners (45–26)

1936

QUARTERFINALS

Santa Fe Trailways, Kansas City, over Warrensburg State MO (34–23)

McPherson Globe Refiners over Greeley State Teachers (67–30)

Hutchinson KS Western Transits over Kansas City Life, Denver (37–36)

Universal Pictures over Denver Safeway Stores (31–30)

SEMIFINALS

McPherson Globe Refiners over Santa Fe Trailways (54–41)

Universal Pictures over Hutchinson Western Transits (45–16)

THIRD PLACE

Santa Fe Trailways over Hutchinson Western Transits (35–33)

CHAMPIONSHIP

McPherson Globe Refiners (Coach Gene Johnson) over Universal Pictures (47–35)

1937

QUARTERFINALS

Laemmle Stars, Hollywood, over Antlers Hotel, Colorado Springs (53–34)

Denver Safeway Stores over Long Island University NY (49–26)

Santa Fe Trailways over Kansas City Life, Denver (43–42)

Phillips 66ers over Golden State Creamery, Oakland (56–26)

SEMIFINALS

Denver Safeway Stores over Laemmle Stars (49–32)

Phillips 66ers over Santa Fe Trailways (43–35)

THIRD PLACE

Santa Fe Trailways over Laemmle Stars (47–42)

CHAMPIONSHIP

Denver Safeway Stores (Coach Everett Shelton) over Phillips 66ers
 (43–38)

1938

QUARTERFINALS

Denver Safeway Stores over Hollywood Athletic Club (76–44)

Wichita Gridleys over Parks Clothiers, Oklahoma City (45–25)

Healey Motors, Kansas City, over Warrensburg State (42–38)

Phillips 66ers over Antlers Hotel (56–36)

SEMIFINALS

Denver Safeway Stores over Wichita Gridleys (45–34)

Healey Motors over Phillips 66ers (45–39)

THIRD PLACE

Phillips 66ers over Wichita Gridleys (45–32)

CHAMPIONSHIP

Healey Motors (Coach Frank "Buck" Weaver) over Denver Safeway
 Stores (40–38)

1939

QUARTERFINALS

Denver Nuggets over Alpine Dairy, Seattle (38–21)

San Francisco Olympic Club over Harmon Demons, Chicago (46–
 19)

Phillips 66ers over Antlers Hotel (28–24)

Metro-Goldwyn-Mayer, Hollywood, over Parks Clothiers (44–38)

SEMIFINALS

Denver Nuggets over San Francisco Olympic Club (46–34)

Phillips 66ers over Metro-Goldwyn-Mayer (53–30)

THIRD PLACE

San Francisco Olympic Club over Metro-Goldwyn-Mayer (34–30)

CHAMPIONSHIP

Denver Nuggets (Coach Jack McCracken) over Phillips 66ers (25–22)

1940

QUARTERFINALS

Denver Nuggets over Idaho Southern (43–26)

Golden State Creamery over St. Louis Rangers (37–19)

Phillips 66ers over Twentieth Century Fox (40–32)

S. L. Savidge, Seattle, over Acme Steel, Chicago (75–46)

SEMIFINALS

Denver Nuggets over Golden State Creamery (46–32)

Phillips 66ers over S. L. Savidge (43–31)

THIRD PLACE

Golden State Creamery over S. L. Savidge (50–36)

CHAMPIONSHIP

Phillips 66ers (Coach Chuck Hyatt) over Denver Nuggets (39–36)

1941

QUARTERFINALS

Phillips 66ers over Clifton's Cafeteria, Los Angeles (42–21)

Twentieth Century Fox over Morris-Dickson, Shreveport LA (47–38)

San Francisco Olympic Club over S. L. Savidge (58–36)

Athens Club, Oakland, over Dallas Wilsons (48–36)

SEMIFINALS

Twentieth Century Fox over Phillips 66ers (27–24)

San Francisco Olympic Club over Athens Club (42–36)

THIRD PLACE

Phillips 66ers over Athens Club (49–36)

CHAMPIONSHIP

Twentieth Century Fox (Coach G. J. "Bud" Fischer) over San Francisco Olympic Club (47–34)

1942

QUARTERFINALS

Twentieth Century Fox over San Francisco Athletic Club (65–32)

Denver American Legion over Clifton's Cafeteria (60–42)

Golden State Creamery over Alpine Dairy (37–21)

Phillips 66ers over YMCA Clippers, Chicago (66–33)

Denver American Legion over Twentieth Century Fox (38–31)

Phillips 66ers over Golden State Creamery (43–32)

Golden State Creamery over Twentieth Century Fox (45–43)

Denver American Legion (Coach Jack McCracken) over Phillips
66ers (45–32)

1943

Denver American Legion over Allen-Bradley, Milwaukee (83–51)

University of Wyoming over Poudre Valley Creamery, Ft. Collins
CO (64–27)

Denver University over Williams Field AZ (54–44)

Phillips 66ers over Eckers, Salt Lake City (34–33)

Denver American Legion over University of Wyoming (41–33)

Phillips 66ers over Denver University (40–36)

University of Wyoming over Denver University (58–45)

Phillips 66ers (Coach Jack McCracken) over Denver American Legion (57–40)

1944

Phillips 66ers over Fircrest Dairy, Bellingham WA (44–39)

Colorado Springs Army over Boeing, Wichita KS (49–43)

Ft. Warren WY over Twentieth Century Fox (45–43)

Denver Ambrose-Legion over Allen-Bradley (56–37)

Phillips 66ers over Colorado Springs Army (72–48)

Denver Ambrose-Legion over Ft. Warren (52–35)

Colorado Springs Army over Ft. Warren (59–52)

CHAMPIONSHIP

Phillips 66ers (Coach Omar "Bud" Browning) over Denver Ambrose-Legion (50–43)

1945

QUARTERFINALS

Phillips 66ers over San Francisco Athletic Club (47–40)

Twentieth Century Fox over Allen-Bradley (39–33)

Cessna Aircraft, Wichita KS, over Ft. Lewis WA (55–40)

Denver Ambrose Jellymakers over Camp Robinson AR (51–43)

SEMIFINALS

Phillips 66ers over Twentieth Century Fox (62–52)

Denver Ambrose Jellymakers over Cessna Aircraft, (43–28)

THIRD PLACE

Cessna Aircraft over Twentieth Century Fox (55–48)

CHAMPIONSHIP

Phillips 66ers (Coach Omar "Bud" Browning) over Denver Ambrose Jellymakers (47–46)

1946

QUARTERFINALS

Phillips 66ers over Marimer CA Marines (54–35)

Twentieth Century Fox over Simplot-Deserets, Salt Lake City (40–32)

Denver Ambrose Jellymakers over Phillips Lee Tires (56–49)

San Diego Dons over San Francisco Dardis (41–35)

SEMIFINALS

Phillips 66ers over Twentieth Century Fox (45–36)

San Diego Dons over Denver Ambrose Jellymakers (46–42)

THIRD PLACE

Denver Ambrose Jellymakers over Twentieth Century Fox (44–36)

CHAMPIONSHIP

Phillips 66ers (Coach Omar "Bud" Browning) over San Diego Dons (45–34)

1947

QUARTERFINALS

Phillips 66ers over Coors Brewery, Golden CO (66–26)

Alpine Dairy over Los Angeles Shamrocks (34–31)

Oakland Bittners over Majors & Majors, Dallas (74–42)

Denver Nuggets over Twentieth Century Fox (65–58)

SEMIFINALS

Phillips 66ers over Alpine Dairy (47–23)

Oakland Bittners over Denver Nuggets (55–40)

THIRD PLACE

Denver Nuggets over Alpine Dairy (58–36)

CHAMPIONSHIP

Phillips 66ers (Coach Omar "Bud" Browning) over Oakland Bittners (62–41)

1948

QUARTERFINALS

Phillips 66ers over Eckers (54–41)

Oakland Bittners over Kokomo IN All-Stars (64–46)

Denver Murphy Mahoney over Naval Academy (70–55)

Denver Nuggets over Twentieth Century Fox (64–50)

SEMIFINALS

Phillips 66ers over Oakland Bittners (41–37)

Denver Nuggets over Denver Murphy Mahoney (60–56)

THIRD PLACE

Oakland Bittners over Denver Murphy Mahoney (69–43)

CHAMPIONSHIP

Phillips 66ers (Coach Omar "Bud" Browning) over Denver Nuggets (62–48)

1949

QUARTERFINALS

Phillips 66ers over Los Angeles Police (75–38)

Alpine Dairy over Denver Chevrolet (57–44)

Oakland Bittners over Clifton's Cafeteria (62–48)

Peoria Cats over Oklahoma City University (43–40)

SEMIFINALS

Phillips 66ers over Alpine Dairy (77–45)

Oakland Bittners over Peoria Cats (62–59)

THIRD PLACE

Peoria Cats over Alpine Dairy (53–44)

CHAMPIONSHIP

Oakland Bittners (Coach Bob Alameida) over Phillips 66ers (55–51)

1950
QUARTERFINALS

Oakland Blue 'n Gold over Alpine Dairy (54–37)

Denver Chevrolet over Allen-Bradley (70–48)

Stewart Chevrolet, San Francisco, over Peoria Cats (60–53)

Phillips 66ers over Santa Maria Golden Dukes (83–48)

SEMIFINALS

Oakland Blue 'n Gold over Denver Chevrolet (64–53)

Phillips 66ers over Stewart Chevrolet (64–47)

THIRD PLACE

Denver Chevrolet over Stewart Chevrolet (58–50)

CHAMPIONSHIP

Phillips 66ers (Coach Jesse "Cab" Renick) over Oakland Blue 'n Gold (65–42)

1951
QUARTERFINALS

Phillips 66ers over Dayton Air Gems (76–50)

Stewart Chevrolet over Jamcos, Sioux City IA (88–42)

Peoria Cats over Denver Chevrolet (78–53)

Poudre Valley Creamery over Vandergriff Motors, Dallas (62–47)

SEMIFINALS

Stewart Chevrolet over Phillips 66ers (66–63)

Poudre Valley Creamery over Peoria Cats (59–57)

THIRD PLACE

Phillips 66ers over Peoria Cats (72–55)

CHAMPIONSHIP

Stewart Chevrolet (Coach Hank Luisetti) over Poudre Valley Creamery (76–57)

1952
QUARTERFINALS

Fibber McGee & Molly, Hollywood, over Stewart Chevrolet (43–41)

Peoria Cats over Riggles Plaza Bowl, Warrensburg MO (66–43)

Air Force All-Stars over Oakland Atlas Pacific Engineers (40–34)

Phillips 66ers over REA Travelers, Artesia NM (70–52)

SEMIFINALS

Peoria Cats over Fibber McGee & Molly (49–34)

Phillips 66ers over Air Force All-Stars (66–49)

THIRD PLACE

Air Force All-Stars over Fibber McGee & Molly (48–47)

CHAMPIONSHIP

Peoria Cats (Coach Warren Womble) over Phillips 66ers (66–53)

1953

QUARTERFINALS

Peoria Cats over Ada Oilers, Houston (61–57)

Grihalva Buick, San Diego, over Quantico Marines (63–55)

Los Alamitos Naval Air Station CA, over Sampson NY AFB (58–56)

Everybody's Drug Store, Eugene OR over Ritz Café, Carbondale IL (70–52)

SEMIFINALS

Peoria Cats over Grihalva Buick (67–53)

Los Alamitos Naval Air Station over Everybody's Drug Store (56–49)

THIRD PLACE

Grihalva Buick over Everybody's Drug Store (56–48)

CHAMPIONSHIP

Peoria Cats (Coach Warren Womble) over Los Alamitos Naval Air Station (73–62)

1954

QUARTERFINALS

Peoria Cats over Young Men's Institute (56–55)

Denver Central Bank over Kirby's Shoes, Los Angeles, (68–65)

Fort Sill OK over Ogden Utah Food Stores (80–58)

Grihalva Buick over Phillips 66ers (63–58)

SEMIFINALS

Peoria Cats over Denver Central Bank (61–59)

Grihalva Buick over Fort Sill (63–50)

THIRD PLACE

Denver Central Bank over Fort Sill (87–72)

CHAMPIONSHIP

Peoria Cats (Coach Warren Womble) over Grihalva Buick (63–55)

1955

QUARTERFINALS

Luckett-Nix, Boulder CO, over Peoria Cats (70–67)

Quantico Marines over Kirby's Shoes, Los Angeles (81–72)

San Francisco Olympic Club over North Carolina State (70–60)

Phillips 66ers over Gregory Clothing, Greeley CO (58–44)

SEMIFINALS

Luckett-Nix over Marines All-Stars (63–56)

Phillips 66ers over San Francisco Olympic Club (53–51)

THIRD PLACE

San Francisco Olympic Club over Quantico Marines (78–69)

CHAMPIONSHIP

Phillips 66ers (Gerald Tucker) over Luckett-Nix (66–64)

1956

QUARTERFINALS

Phillips 66ers over Ranier Comets, Chicago (106–90)

Ada Oilers, Mobile AL over Wichita Vickers (79–74)

Allen-Bradley over Denver Central Bank (79–77)

Buchan Bakers, Seattle, over Pasadena Mirror Glaze (68–64)

SEMIFINALS

Phillips 66ers over Ada Oilers (71–69)

Buchan Bakers over Allen-Bradley (85–75)

THIRD PLACE

Ada Oilers over Allen-Bradley (77–76)

CHAMPIONSHIP

Buchan Bakers (Coach Frank Fidler) over Phillips 66ers (59–57)

1957

QUARTERFINALS

Buchan Bakers over Wichita Vickers (67–63)

Air Force All-Stars over McDonald Scots, Lake Charles LA (79–68)

Peoria Cats over Army All-Stars (82–67)

San Francisco Olympic Club over Phillips 66ers (82–61)

SEMIFINALS

Air Force All-Stars over Buchan Bakers (84–63)

San Francisco Olympic Club over Peoria Cats (70–61)

THIRD PLACE

Peoria Cats over Buchan Bakers (76–71)

CHAMPIONSHIP

Air Force All-Stars (Coach Ken Flower) over Olympic Club (87–74)

1958

QUARTERFINALS

Phillips 66ers over Buchan Bakers (71–61)

Peoria Cats over McDonald Scots (70–59)

Denver-Chicago Truckers over Air Force All-Stars (74–63)

Fort Leonard Wood over Wichita Vickers (48–45)

SEMIFINALS

Peoria Cats over Phillips 66ers (90–53)

Denver-Chicago Truckers over Fort Leonard Wood (76–48)

THIRD PLACE

Phillips 66ers over Fort Leonard Wood (93–66)

CHAMPIONSHIP

Peoria Cats (Coach Warren Womble) over Denver-Chicago Truckers (74–71; 4 overtimes)

1959

QUARTERFINALS

Army All-Stars over Peoria Caterpillar (81–75)

Wichita Vickers over Baton Rouge Teamsters (120–82)

Phillips 66ers over U.S. Marines (86–80)

San Francisco Olympic Club over Denver-Chicago Truckers (91–80)

SEMIFINALS

Wichita Vickers over Army All-Stars (104–102)

Phillips 66ers over San Francisco Olympic Club (72–71)

THIRD PLACE

Army All-Stars over San Francisco Olympic Club (102–79)

CHAMPIONSHIP

Wichita Vickers (Coach Alex Hannum) over Phillips 66ers (105–83)

1960

QUARTERFINALS

Buchan Bakers over Wichita Vickers (93–83)

Akron Goodyear over Tuck Tapers, New Rochelle NY (111–97)

Peoria Cats over Cleveland Pipers (84–82)

Phillips 66ers over San Francisco Investors (80–78)

Akron Goodyear over Buchan Bakers (95–90)

Peoria Cats over Phillips 66ers (90–83)

Buchan Bakers over Phillips 66ers (82–73)

Peoria Cats (Coach Warren Womble) over Akron Goodyear (115–99)

1961

Denver-Chicago Truckers over Buchan Bakers (107–81)

San Francisco Olympic Club over Clarkson Reality, Des Moines IA (96–86)

Tuck Tapers over Phillips 66ers (87–84)

Cleveland Pipers over Kirks Pharmacy, Burien WA (120–90)

Denver-Chicago Truckers over San Francisco Olympic Club (101–86)

Cleveland Pipers over Tuck Tapers (97–94)

Tuck Tapers over San Francisco Olympic Club (103–75)

Cleveland Pipers (Coach John McLendon) over Denver-Chicago Truckers (107–96)

1962

Denver-Chicago Truckers over Al Maroone Bachelor Arms, Buffalo NY (83–55)

U.S. Marines over Port of San Diego (82–59)

Akron Goodyear over Sanders State-Line, Salt Lake City (81–76)

Phillips 66ers over B&W Lumber, Vallejo CA (89–63)

Denver-Chicago Truckers over U.S. Marines (83–70)

Phillips 66ers over Akron Goodyear (82–72)

THIRD PLACE

Akron Goodyear over U.S. Marines (84–74)

CHAMPIONSHIP

Phillips 66ers (Coach Omar "Bud" Browning) over Denver-Chicago Truckers (70–59)

1963

QUARTERFINALS

Phillips 66ers over State Line–Wendover Motel, Wendover UT (120–82)

Armed Forces All-Stars over Marion-Kay Vanilla, Brownstown IN (102–84)

Akron Goodyear over May Builders, Arkansas KS (106–56)

Denver-Chicago Truckers over Prince Electric, Enid OK (72–63)

SEMIFINALS

Phillips 66ers over Armed Forces All-Stars (80–78)

Denver-Chicago Truckers over Akron Goodyear (72–62)

THIRD PLACE

Akron Goodyear over Armed Forces All-Stars (75–69)

CHAMPIONSHIP

Phillips 66ers (Coach Omar "Bud" Browning) over Denver-Chicago Truckers (100–70)

1964

QUARTERFINALS

Phillips 66ers over Sav-On, Ogden UT (106–85)

Federal Old Line Insurance, Seattle WA, over Al Maroone Ford, Buffalo NY (84–78)

Tennessee State University Club over Service Jets USA, Nashville (86–84)

Akron Goodyear over Denver Capitol Federal (68–64)

SEMIFINALS

Phillips 66ers over Federal Old Line (91–76)

Akron Goodyear over Tennessee State U. C. (89–71)

THIRD PLACE

Tennessee State U. C. over Federal Old Line (90–85)

CHAMPIONSHIP

Akron Goodyear (Coach Hank Vaughn) over Phillips 66ers (86–78)

1965

QUARTERFINALS

Akron Goodyear over Opinion Research, Long Beach CA (77–67)

Denver Capitol Federal over May Builders (95–88)

Armed Forces All-Stars over Marion-Kay Vanilla (84–70)

San Francisco Athletic Club over Phillips 66ers (80–67)

SEMIFINALS

Denver Capitol Federal over Akron Goodyear (77–67)

Armed Forces All-Stars over San Francisco Athletic Club (77–75)

THIRD PLACE

Akron Goodyear over San Francisco Athletic Club (86–71)

CHAMPIONSHIP

Armed Forces All-Stars (Coach Hal Fischer) over Denver Capitol Federal (77–75)

1966

QUARTERFINALS

Ford Mustangs, Detroit MI, over Armed Forces All-Stars (75–71)

Akron Goodyear over Contac Caps, Knoxville TN (77–72)

Phillips 66ers over McDonald Company, Torrance CA (69–54)

Denver Capital Federal over May Builders (66–65)

SEMIFINALS

Ford Mustangs over Akron Goodyear (84–81)

Phillips 66ers over Denver Capital Federal (69–57)

THIRD PLACE

Denver Capitol Federal over Akron Goodyear (77–74)

CHAMPIONSHIP

Ford Mustangs (Coach Horace Walker) over Phillips 66ers (71–67)

1967

QUARTERFINALS

Phillips 66ers over Armed Forces All-Stars (94–79)

Denver Capitol Federal over Group Productions, New York City (79–70)

Akron Goodyear over Vaughn Realty, Spokane (66–62)

Jamaco Saints, Chicago, over San Francisco Athletic Club (84–82)

SEMIFINALS

Phillips 66ers over Denver Capitol Federal (76–71)

Akron Goodyear over Jamaco Saints (81–70)

Denver Capitol Federal over Jamaco Saints (93–83)

Akron Goodyear (Coach Hank Vaughn) over Phillips 66 (77–62)

1968

Akron Goodyear over Kitchen Fresh Chippers, Los Angeles (89–70)

Armed Forces All-Stars over National Zip Codes, Milwaukee (92–70)

San Francisco Athletic Club over Denver Capitol Federal (99–97)

Vaughn Realty over San Francisco Athletic Club (57–52)

Armed Forces All-Stars over Akron Goodyear (78–65)

Vaughn Realty over San Francisco Athletic Club (81–74)

Akron Goodyear over San Francisco Athletic Club (92–64)

Armed Forces All-Stars (Coach Hal Fischer) over Vaughn Realty (73–69)

AAU All-Americans, 1921–1968

1921

Milton Singer and Forrest "Red" DeBernardi of the Kansas City Athletic Club; Edmund Cairns and Vincent Keyes of Southwestern College, Winfield KS; Bonnie Stewart of Northwestern Normal, Alva OK.

1922

Forrest "Red" DeBernardi and George Hess of the Kansas City Athletic Club; George "Pidge" Browning, George Reeves, and George Williams of Lowe & Campbell, Kansas City MO.

1923

George Reeves, Milton Singer, George Williams, Robert Sanders, and George "Pidge" Browning of the Kansas City Athletic Club.

1924

Haldane Griggs and Paul Jones of Butler University, Indianapolis; George Reeves, George Browning, and George Williams of the Kansas City Athletic Club; Richard Berndt of the San Francisco Olympic Club.

1925

Forrest "Red" DeBernardi and George Starbuck of Hillyard Chemical, St. Joseph MO; Arthur Brewster of Washburn College, Topeka KS; Tusten Ackerman of the Kansas City Athletic Club; George Hess of the Kansas City Schooleys.

1926

Forrest "Red" DeBernardi, John Wulf, and George Starbuck of Hillyard Chemical, St. Joseph MO; Tusten Ackerman and Verne Wilkins of the Kansas City Athletic Club.

1927
Forrest "Red" DeBernardi, Harold Hewitt, and George Starbuck of Hillyard Chemical, St. Joseph MO; Ross McBurney of Wichita University; Elmer Hooker of Ke-Nash-A, Kenosha WI.

1928
Albert Peterson and Victor Holt of Cook Paint, Kansas City MO; Ed Hogue and Frank "Buck" Weaver of the Kansas City Athletic Club; George Starbuck of Hillyard Chemical, St. Joseph MO.

1929
Frank Harrigan, Albert Peterson, Floyd Burk, and Victor Holt of Cook Paint, Kansas City MO; Berry Dunham and Ross McBurney of Henry Clothiers, Wichita KS.

1930
Melvin Miller and Floyd Burk of the Wichita Henrys; Raymond Maloney and Frank Wilson of the San Francisco Olympic Club; Bart Carlton of East Central Teachers, Ada OK.

1931
Melvin Miller, Merle Alexander, and Berry Dunham of the Wichita Henrys; Chuck Hyatt of the Los Angeles Athletic Club; Paul Burks and Frank Weaver of the Kansas City Athletic Club.

1932
Tom Pickell and Berry Dunham of the Wichita Henrys; Jack Mc-Cracken and Tom Merrick of Maryville Teachers (Northwest Missouri State), Maryville MO; William Young of the Schuessler Athletic Club, Chicago.

1933
Chuck Hyatt and Carl Larson of the Tulsa Diamond DX Oilers; Joseph Reiff of Rosenberg-Arvey, Chicago; Berry Dunham of the Wichita Henrys; Paul Burks of Southern Kansas City Stage Lines, Kansas City.

1934
Chuck Hyatt, Bart Carlton and Tom Pickell of the Tulsa Diamond

DX Oilers; Ed McGinty and Arthur Hamon of the University of Wyoming.

1935

Chuck Hyatt of Universal Pictures; Francis Johnson and Joe Fortenberry of McPherson Globe Refiners; Omar "Bud" Browning and Herman Fischer of Southern Kansas Stage Lines.

1936

Carl Knowles of Universal Pictures; Omar "Bud" Browning and Jay Wallenstrom of Santa Fe Trailways, Kansas City; Bill Wheatley and Joe Fortenberry of McPherson Globe Refiners.

1937

Robert "Ace" Gruenig, Tex Colvin, and Jack McCracken of Denver Safeway Stores; Jack Ozburn of Santa Fe Trailways, Kansas City; Jay Wallenstrom of Phillips 66.

1938

Robert "Ace" Gruenig and Jack McCracken of Denver Safeway Stores; Dick Smith of the Gridley Chieftains, Wichita KS; Frank Groves and Herman Fischer of Healey Motors, Kansas City.

1939

Robert "Ace" Gruenig, Jack McCracken, and Dick Wells of the Denver Nuggets; Ray Ebling of Phillips 66; Jack Hupp of Metro-Goldwyn-Mayer.

1940

Robert "Ace" Gruenig and Tee Connelley of the Denver Nuggets; Don Lockard, Joe Fortenberry, and Grady Lewis of Phillips 66.

1941

Hank Luisetti and Ralph Giannini of the San Francisco Olympic Club; Carl Knowles and Frank Lubin of Twentieth Century Fox; Chet Carlisle of the Athens Athletic Club, Oakland.

1942

Robert "Ace" Gruenig, Jack McCracken, and Bill Strannigan of Denver American Legion; Hank Luisetti and Bill Martin of Phillips 66.

1943
Robert "Ace" Gruenig and Bob Doll of Denver American Legion; Jimmy McNatt and Gordon "Shorty" Carpenter of Phillips 66; Kenny Sailors of the University of Wyoming.

1944
Robert "Ace" Gruenig, George Hamburg, Bob Marsh, and Chuck Hyatt of Denver Ambrose-Legion; Jimmy McNatt, Fred Pralle, and Gordon "Shorty" Carpenter of Phillips 66; Ed Beisser of Colorado Springs Army; Jules Rivlin of Fort Warren WY; Gale Bishop of Fircrest Dairy, Bellingham WA.

1945
Robert "Ace" Gruenig, Jack McCracken, and George Hamburg of Denver Ambrose Jellymakers; Paul Lindemann, Jimmy McNatt, and Gordon "Shorty" Carpenter of Phillips 66; Frank Lubin of Twentieth Century Fox; Gale Bishop of the Fort Lewis Warriors WA; Dick Smith of Cessna Aircraft, Wichita KS; Frank Fullmer of Idaho Simplots, Burley ID.

1946
Robert "Ace" Gruenig of Denver Ambrose Jellymakers; Marty Nash, Bill Martin, Gordon "Shorty" Carpenter, and Jimmy McNatt of Phillips 66; Tee Connelley, Jim Pollard, and Kenny Sailors of the San Diego Dons; Art Mollner of Twentieth Century Fox; Andy Phillip of Fleet Marine Force.

1947
Vince Boryla and Jimmy Darden of the Denver Nuggets; Marty Nash, Gordon "Shorty" Carpenter, Bob Kurland, and Jesse "Cab" Renick of Phillips 66; Jim Pollard, Paul Napolitano, Ron Livingstone, and Bill Calhoun of the Oakland Bittners.

1948
Vince Boryla, Ray Lipscomb, and Jimmy Darden of the Denver Nuggets; Robert "Ace" Gruenig, Murphy Mahoney, Bob Kurland, R. C. Pitts, and Jesse "Cab" Renick of Phillips 66; Les O'Gara, Don Barksdale, and Warren Taulbee of the Oakland Bittners.

1949
Harold Howey of Denver Chevrolet; Don Barksdale, Les O'Gara,

and Chuck Hanger of the Oakland Bittners; Bob Kurland, Gerald Tucker, Roy Lipscomb, and Johnny Stanich of Phillips 66; Bill Vandenburgh of Alpine Dairy, Seattle; Paul Whalen of the Peoria Cats.

1950

Thornton Jenkins and Gordon "Shorty" Carpenter of Denver Chevrolet; Don Barksdale, Chuck Hanger, and Dave Minor of Oakland Blue 'n Gold; Bob Kurland, Gerald Tucker, and Roy Lipscomb of Phillips 66; Les O'Gara of Los Angeles Police; Andy Wolfe of Stewart Chevrolet, San Francisco.

1951

George Yardley, Cliff Crandall, and Frankie Kuzara of Stewart Chevrolet, San Francisco; Glen Anderson and Bill Gosset of Poudre Valley Creamery, Fort Collins co; Bob Kurland and Ken Pryor of Phillips 66; Howie Williams and Frank McCabe of the Peoria Cats; Don Barksdale of Oakland Blue 'n Gold.

1952

Howie Williams, Frank McCabe, and Dan Pippin of the Peoria Cats; Bob Kurland, Ken Pryor, and Bus Whitehead of Phillips 66; Bobby Wallace and Bryce Heffley of Air Force All-Stars; Jack Stone and Billy Donovan of Fibber McGee & Molly.

1953

Dan Pippin, Ron Bontemps, Howie Williams, and Frank McCabe of the Peoria Cats; George Yardley and Johnny Arndt of Los Alamitos Naval Air Station; Jim Hoverder, Glen Anderson, and Hugh Faulkner of Grihalva Buick, San Diego; Chet Noe of Everybody's Drug Store, Eugene OR.

1954

Ron Bontemps, Dick Retherford, and Frank McCabe of the Peoria Cats; Glen Smith and Frankie Kuzara of Denver Central Bank; Jim Hoverder, Glen Anderson, Joe Stratton, and Ken Leslie of Grihalva Buick, San Diego; Chuck Darling of Phillips 66.

1955

Burdie Haldorson, Bob Jeangerard, and Charlie Mock of Luckett-Nix, Boulder co; Chuck Darling, Jim Walsh, and Arnie Short of

Phillips 66; Ron Tomsic and Ken Sears of the San Francisco Olympic Club; Richie Guerin and Jim Bingham of U.S. Marine All-Stars.

1956

Dick Eicher of Denver Central Bank; Charlie Koon and George Swyers of Seattle Buchan Bakers; Burdie Haldorson, Chuck Darling, and Jim Walsh of Phillips 66; Terry Rand and Dick Miller of Allen-Bradley, Milwaukee; George Linn and Jerry Harper of the Ada Oilers, Mobile AL.

1957

Ron Tomsic, Dick Boushka, and Dick Welsh of Air Force All-Stars; Barry Brown and Russ Lawler of the San Francisco Olympic Club; B. H. Born and Howie Crittenden of the Peoria Cats; R. C. Owens of Seattle Buchan Bakers; Carroll Williams of Army All-Stars; Bill Reigel of McDonald Scots, Lake Charles LA.

1958

Harv Schmidt, Barry Brown, and Jimmy Ashmore of Denver-Chicago Truckers; Burdie Haldorson and Gary Thompson of Phillips 66; B. H. Born, Jim Palmer, and Howie Crittenden of the Peoria Cats; K. C. Jones of Fort Leonard Wood; Bill Reigel of McDonald Scots, Lake Charles LA.

1959

Dick Boushka, Dan Swartz, Don Boldebuck, and Les Lane of Wichita Vickers; Burdie Haldorson and Gary Thompson of Phillips 66; Jack Sullivan of U.S. Marine All-Stars; Ron Tomsic of the San Francisco Olympic Club; Jack Adams and Adrian Smith of U.S. Army All-Stars.

1960

Bob Boozer, Don Ohl, and Howie Crittenden of the Peoria Cats; Bill Reigel, Chuck Slack, and Jim Francis of Akron Goodyear; Phil Murrell of Phillips 66; Ben Warley of Cleveland Pipers; Carroll Williams and Rolland Todd of Seattle Buchan Bakers.

1961

Jack Adams, Dan Swartz, Roger Taylor, and Ben Warley of Cleveland Pipers; Horace Walker, Les Lane, and Mike Moran of Denver-Chicago Truckers; Paul Neumann and Tony Jackson of New York

Tuck Tapers; Tom Meschery of the San Francisco Olympic Club.

1962

Pete McCaffrey and Bill Reigel of Akron Goodyear; Mike Moran, Dennis Boone, and Joe Belmont of Denver-Chicago Truckers; Dennis Price, Jerry Shipp, and Gary Thompson, Phillips 66; Billy McGill of Sanders State Line, Salt Lake City; Roger Brown of Inland Manufacturing, Dayton OH.

1963

Pete McCaffrey and Bennie Coffman of Akron Goodyear; Don Kojis, Jerry Shipp, and Dennis Price of Phillips 66; Carney Crisler, Dennis Boone, and Bill Green of Denver-Chicago Truckers; Cleveland McKinney of Armed Forces All-Stars; Jim Hagan of Tennessee Tech.

1964

Larry Brown, Pete McCaffrey, and Lloyd Sharrar of Akron Goodyear; Jerry Shipp, Jim Hagan, and Charlie Bowerman of Phillips 66; Edwin Correll of Seattle Federal Old Line; Willie Porter and Bill Bradley of Tennessee State; Jim Lyon of Save-on Store of Ogden UT.

1965

Vern Benson and Don Reid of Armed Forces All-Stars; Flynn Robinson, Rod Holst, Al Dillard, and Randy Richardson of Denver Capitol Federal; Larry Brown and Cecil Tuttle of Akron Goodyear; Dave Stallworth of May Builders, Arkansas City KS.

1966

Cazzie Russell and Oliver Darden of Ford Mustangs, Detroit MI; Leon Clark and Lonnie Wright of Denver Capitol Federal; Harold Sergent, Bobby Roscoe, Bobby Carey, and Kendell Rhine of Phillips 66; Clyde Lee of Contac Caps, Knoxville TN; Vern Benson of Akron Goodyear.

1967

Don Freeman and Steve Jones of Jamaco Saints, Chicago; Jim King, Vern Bensen, Cal Fowler, and Edwin Correll of Akron Goodyear; John Beasley and Harold Sergent of Phillips 66; Byron Beck and Bob Rule of Denver Capitol Federal.

1968

Mike Barrett, John Clawson, Michael Silliman, and George Carter of Armed Forces All-Stars; Jerry Skaife, Gary Lechman, and Rod McDonald of Vaughn Reality, Seattle WA; Carl Ashley of Denver Capitol Federal; Calvin Fowler and Tom Black of Akron Goodyear.

Notes

1. EVERYTHING IS UP-TO-DATE IN KANSAS CITY

1. Alexander M. Weyand, *The Cavalcade of Basketball* (New York: Macmillan, 1960), 191–208.

2. Elliot J. Gorn and Warren Goldstein, *A Brief History of American Sports* (New York: Hill and Wang, 1993), 169–77.

3. Robert W. Peterson, *Cages to Jump Shots: Pro Basketball's Early Years* (New York: Oxford University Press, 1990), 55–61, 69–79.

4. Peterson, *Cages to Jump Shots*, 4–6, 110–12.

5. Forrest C. Allen, *My Basketball Bible* (Kansas City MO: Smith-Grieves, 1924), 180.

6. Howard "Ham" Beresford, "Huddles with Ham," *Rocky Mountain News*, February 8, 1934.

7. Chester "Red" Nelson, "This Morning," *Rocky Mountain News*, December 20, 1934.

8. S. W Pope, *Patriotic Games: Sporting Traditions in the American Imagination, 1876–1926* (New York: Oxford University Press, 1997), 22–32.

9. Pope, *Patriotic Games*, 40, 54–58.

10. Weyand, *Cavalcade of Basketball*, 193–95.

11. Weyand, *Cavalcade of Basketball*, 192–93.

12. *Kansas City Star*, April 2, 1993, 14A.

13. *Kansas City Star*, March 6, 1921, 14A.

14. Peter C. Bjorkman, *Hoopla: A Century of College Basketball* (Indianapolis: Masters Press, 1996), 33–38, 48–50.

15. *Kansas City Star*, March 10, 1921, 16.

16. *Kansas City Times*, March 14, 1921, 14.

17. C. E. McBride, "Review of the AAU Season: 1921–1922," *Spalding Official Basketball Guide* (New York: American Sports, 1922), 7.

18. Maury White, "Coach Outfoxed Quigley," *Des Moines Register*, February 10, 1925, 45.

19. McBride, "Review of the AAU Season," 7.

20. *Kansas City Star*, "Basketball," March 8, 1922, 14.

21. *St. Joseph Gazette*, December 10, 1922, and March 20, 1923, Scrapbooks, Hillyard Archives, St. Joseph, Missouri.

22. *Kansas City Journal Post*, February 25, 1923, Scrapbooks, Hillyard Archives.

23. *St. Joseph's News Press*, February 23, 1923, Scrapbooks, Hillyard Archives.

24. *St. Joseph's News Press*, March 10, 1923, Scrapbooks, Hillyard Archives.

25. *St. Joseph Gazette*, March 17, 1923, Scrapbooks, Hillyard Archives.

26. *Kansas City Star*, March 18, 1923, 16A.

27. *St. Joseph Gazette*, January 25, 1924, Scrapbooks, Hillyard Archives.

28. *St. Joseph Gazette*, March 16, 1924, Scrapbooks, Hillyard Archives.

29. *Kansas City Star*, March 16, 1924, 8A.

30. *Kansas City Star*, March 16, 1924, 8A.

31. Ronald L. Mendell, *Who's Who in Basketball* (New Rochelle: Arlington House, 1973) 141.

32. Loren V. "Red" Brown, "The National AAU Basketball Tournament—1925," *Converse Basketball Yearbook—1925*, 21–25.

33. Editorial, "The Hillyard Team," *St. Joseph Gazette*, March 16, 1925, Scrapbooks, Hillyard Archives.

34. Mendell, *Who's Who in Basketball*, 11.

35. "Just the Jist and Jest of It," Scrapbooks, Hillyard Archives.

36. G. P. Wendell, "Basketball Committee Report," *Spalding Official Basketball Guide* (New York: American Sports, 1925), 129–30.

37. George W. Levis, "Basketball as played by the Hillyard Shine Alls," 63, undated in Scrapbooks, Hillyard Archives.

38. Leslie Blair, "Harold Hewitt: An Overnight Sensation" in *The Lure and the Lore of Basketball in Missouri*, ed. George Sherman (Virginia Beach: Donning, 1994), 114–15. During his career Hewitt made six AAU All-America teams and in 1974 was inducted into the Helms Basketball Hall of Fame.

39. "National Basketball Title to Hillyards," *The Blue Diamond*, April 1926, 10, 27, Scrapbooks, Hillyard Archives.

40. *Kansas City Times*, March 9, 1926, *St. Joseph Gazette*, March 9, 1926, Scrapbooks, Hillyard Archives.

41. Undated articles, Scrapbooks, Hillyard Archives.

42. *Kansas City Star*, March 21, 1926, 2B.

43. Undated articles, Scrapbooks, Hillyard Archives.

44. G. P. Wendell, "Report of Basketball Committee, *Spalding Official Basketball Guide*, (New York: American Sports, 1926), 150.

45. "City Pays Tribute to Hillyard Team at Banquet," undated, Scrapbooks, Hillyard Archives.

46. *St. Joseph News-Press*, November 1926, Scrapbooks, Hillyard Archives.

47. Harold Slater, "DeBernardi and Hillyard: A Championship Combination," in Sherman, *Lure and Lore of Basketball*, 113.

48. Letter, Jim Houck to George Sherman, in Sherman, *Lure and Lore of Basketball*, 110.

49. "Hillyards All Set for Cage Tourney," March 1927, Scrapbook, Hillyard Archives.

50. Letter, Forest C. Allen to Tusten Ackerman, February 18, 1927, Kansas University, Spencer Research Library Archives, Allen Letter File.

51. *Kansas City Times*, March 7, 1927, 10.

52. *Kansas City Star*, March 20, 1927, 16A.

53. Levis, "Basketball as played by the Hillyard Shine Alls," 53.

54. Jerry Thrailkill, *St. Joseph Gazette*, March 17, 1928, Scrapbooks, Hillyard Archives.

55. *St. Joseph Gazette*, February 3, 1928, and March 8, 1928. One of the Hillyard victories during this trip was a 34–32 win over the

San Francisco Olympic Club before 5,500 fans at the Kezar Pavillion (San *Francisco Examiner*, January 24, 1928). Scrapbooks, Hillyard Archives.

56. *Kansas City Times*, March 17, 1928, 18.

57. *Kansas City Star*, March 18, 1928, 14A.

58. *St. Joseph Gazette*, February 29, 1929, Scrapbooks, Hillyard Archives.

59. "The End of an Era," *Wichita Eagle*, July 24, 1993, 6.

60. "End of an Era," *Wichita Eagle*, July 24, 1993, 1.

61. *Kansas City Star*, March 17, 1929, B1.

62. J. Lyman Bingham, "Basketball Committee Report," *Spalding Official Basketball Guide* (New York: American Sports, 1929), 99–100.

63. Bingham, "Basketball Committee Report," 99–100.

64. *Kansas City Star*, March 16, 1930, 1B.

65. *Kansas City Star*, March 16, 1930, 2B.

66. "The Sport Dial," *Kansas City Star*, March 16, 1930.

67. Hal Middlesworth, "On the Level," *Daily Oklahoman*, March 10, 1949.

68. Jeff Tuttle, "High-Test Hoops: Industrial Basketball and the Phillips Petroleum Company" (master's thesis, University of San Diego, 1995), 61–64.

69. *Wichita Eagle*, August 24, 1930. This full-page ad included copies of correspondence.

70. *Wichita Eagle*, August 24, 1930, full-page ad.

71. *Kansas City Times*, March 14, 1931, 20.

72. *Kansas City Star*, March 15, 1931, B2.

73. *Kansas City Times*, March 8, 1932, 8.

74. *Kansas City Times*, March 10, 1932, 10.

75. Bill Mokray, "The Incredible Maryville Bearcats," *Sports Review*, 1953, 18–22.

76. *Kansas City Times*, March 11, 1932, 10.

77. *Kansas City Times*, March 12, 1932, 18.

78. *Wichita Eagle*, March 11, 1932, 4.

79. *Wichita Eagle*, March 13, 1932, 7.

80. *Wichita Eagle*, March 16, 1932, 6.

81. C. E. McBride, "The National AAU Tournament," *Converse Basketball Yearbook*, 1933, no page.

82. *Kansas City Times*, March 11, 1936, 16.

83. "The Sport Dial," *Kansas City Times*, March 8, 1933.

84. Pete Lightner, "Just in Sports," *Wichita Eagle*, March 12, 1933.

85. Pete Lightner, "Just in Sports," *Wichita Eagle*, March 13, 1933.

86. Pete Lightner, "Just in Sports," *Wichita Eagle*, March 12, 1933.

87. Pete Lightner, "Just in Sports," *Wichita Eagle*, March 13, 1933.

88. "Men's Basketball Committee Report," *Spalding Official Basketball Guide* (New York: American Sports, 1934), 100.

89. *Kansas City Star*, March 14, 1934, 11.

90. *Denver Post*, March 15, 1934, 11.

91. *Kansas City Star*, March 16, 1934, 14; March 17, 1934, 16.

92. *Kansas City Star*, March 18, 1934, 1B.

93. *Kansas City Star*, March 16, 1934, 2B.

94. John M'Manmon, "Denver Gets Basketball Classic," *Rocky Mountain News*, December 8, 1934.

2. THE AAU TOURNAMENT IN DENVER

1. Jack Carberry, "The Second Guess," *Rocky Mountain News*, January 27, 1933. Jack Carberry, one of the legends of Denver journalism, established a national reputation as a crime and political reporter before turning to sports journalism. Born in Denver on October 17, 1892, Carberry worked for the *Kansas City Post*, and *New York Daily Mirror*. In 1932 Carberry returned to Denver and worked for the *Rocky Mountain News* until 1934. From that year to his death on November 22, 1962, Carberry wrote for the *Denver Post* and served as its sports editor from 1941 until 1959 when he retired except to write a Sunday column. In his column, "The Second Guess," Carberry not only pronounced what was good and bad about athletics, but also used his influence to promote every level of sports. William N. Haraway was a major figure in Denver sports until his death on October 30, 1939. He was born February 12, 1882 in Center Hill, Mississippi. He played baseball and boxed at the University of Tennessee and remained an avid sports fan all his

life. Along with basketball, Haraway sponsored baseball and bowling teams and provided trophies for amateur athletics in the Rocky Mountain region (*Rocky Mountain News*, March 2, 1933, 11).

2. Frank Haraway, interview with the author, May 22, 1990. Until he retired in 1982 Frank Haraway covered sports for the *Denver Post* for forty-four years. He followed AAU basketball during the period of this study and his clearly written articles were an invaluable aid to me. After his retirement from sports journalism, Haraway filled a variety of assignments for Denver's professional franchises and was the official scorer for the Colorado Rockies in 1993. In 1994 he was inducted into the Colorado Sports Hall of Fame.

3. Volney Walsh, "As Volney Walsh Sees It," *Denver Post*, March 12, 1932; March 8, 1932.

4. *Rocky Mountain News*, November 1, 1932, 12.

5. *Rocky Mountain News*, November 1, 1932, 12.

6. *Longmont Daily Times-Call*, undated, Hal Davis Scrapbooks.

7. *Rocky Mountain News*, January 3, 1933, 10.

8. *Rocky Mountain News*, February 21, 1933, 21.

9. *Rocky Mountain News*, March 9, 1933, 9.

10. *Rocky Mountain News*, November 28, 1933, 11.

11. *Rocky Mountain News*, November 24, 1933, 20.

12. Howard "Ham" Beresford, "Huddles with Ham," *Rocky Mountain News*, December 21, 1933.

13. *Denver Post*, March 1 1934, 23.

14. *Denver Post*, March 2, 1934, 37. Henry Iba coached at the University of Colorado for one year before moving to Oklahoma A&M where he would establish himself as one of the most successful coaches in basketball history.

15. *Denver Post*, March 1, 1934, 23.

16. *Denver Post*, March 4, 1934, 5.

17. *Rocky Mountain News*, March 16, 1934, 20.

18. *Rocky Mountain News*, November 20 1933, 9.

19. *Denver Post*, March 20 1934, 23.

20. *Denver Post*, March 19, 1934, 17.

21. Howard "Ham" Beresford, "Huddles with Ham," *Rocky Mountain News*, December 30, 1934.

22. Chester "Red" Nelson, "This Morning," *Rocky Mountain News*, December 3, 1934.

23. John M'Manmon, "Denver Gets Basketball Classic: Men's Tournament," *Rocky Mountain News*, December 8, 1934.

24. *Rocky Mountain News*, February 6, 1934, 9.

25. Howard "Ham" Beresford, "Huddles with Ham," *Rocky Mountain News*, February 8, 1934.

26. Chester "Red" Nelson, "This Morning," *Rocky Mountain News*, December 20, 1934.

27. Stephen J. Leonard and Thomas J. Noel, *Denver: Mining Camp to Metropolis* (Niwot: University Press of Colorado, 1990), 203–4.

28. Frederick J. Augustryn Jr., "Gruenig, Robert F. 'Bob,'" *Biographical Dictionary of American Sports: Basketball and Other Indoor Sports*, ed. David L. Porter (Westport CT: Greenwood Press, 1989), 105–6.

29. Frank Haraway, interview with the author.

30. *Rocky Mountain News*, Sports Section, January 6, 1935, 3.

31. *Rocky Mountain News*, January 7, 1935, 11.

32. Chester "Red" Nelson, "This Morning," *Rocky Mountain News*, December 20, 1934.

33. John J. M'Manmon, "When McCracken Cracks the Pigs Crack Too: He Is Team's Star," *Rocky Mountain News*, Sports Section, December 30, 1934.

34. Dick Wells, interview with the author, June 5, 1990.

35. John J. M'Manmon, *Rocky Mountain News*, January 6, 1935, 3.

36. Chester "Red" Nelson, "This Morning," *Rocky Mountain News*, March 15, 1935.

37. *Rocky Mountain News*, January 23, 1935, 10.

38. Chester "Red" Nelson, "This Morning," *Rocky Mountain News*, January 24, 1935.

39. *Rocky Mountain News*, February 3, 1935, 1.

40. *Rocky Mountain News*, February 7, 1935, 1, 12–13.

41. *Rocky Mountain News*, February 26, 1935, 12.

42. *Rocky Mountain News*, February 29, 1935, 12.

43. *Rocky Mountain News*, March 17, 1935, 12.

44. *Denver Post*, March 17, 1935, Sports Section, 1.

45. Harry Farrar, "AAU Bedlam Begins Again," *Denver Post*, March 18, 1951.

46. *Rocky Mountain News*, March 18, 1935, 16.

47. Farrar, "AAU Bedlam," 13.

48. Jack Gray, interview with the author, February 22, 1994.

49. C. L. "Poss" Parsons, "JABS," *Denver Post*, sec. 5, March 17, 1935.

50. Editorial, "The Champions Arrive," *Rocky Mountain News*, March 18, 1935, 8.

51. Chester "Red" Nelson, "This Morning," *Rocky Mountain News*, March 14, 1935.

52. *Denver Post*, March 22, 1935, 39.

53. *Denver Post*, March 22, 1935, 39.

54. *Denver Post*, March 23, 1935, 10; *Denver Post* Sports Section, March 24, 1935, 1.

55. C. L. "Poss" Parsons, "JABS," Sports Section, *Denver Post*, March 24, 1935.

56. C. L. "Poss" Parsons, "JABS," Sports Section, *Denver Post*, March 24, 1935.

57. C. L. "Poss" Parsons, "JABS," *Denver Post*, March 27, 1935.

58. *Denver Post*, Sports Section, March 24, 1935, 2.

59. *Rocky Mountain News*, December 3, 1935, 11.

60. Chester "Red" Nelson, "This Morning," *Rocky Mountain News*, December 6, 1935.

61. *Rocky Mountain News*, Sports Section, December 15, 1935, 3.

62. Chester "Red" Nelson, "This Morning," *Rocky Mountain News*, December 6, 1935.

63. Chester "Red" Nelson, "This Morning," *Rocky Mountain News*, January 8, 1936.

64. Chester "Red" Nelson, "This Morning," *Rocky Mountain News*, January 17, 1936.

65. Chester "Red" Nelson, "This Morning," *Rocky Mountain News*, January 8, 1936.

66. *Rocky Mountain News*, February 4, 1936, 10.

67. *Rocky Mountain News*, February 8, 1936, 10.

68. *Rocky Mountain News*, March 2, 1936, 18.

69. C. L. "Poss" Parsons, "JABS," *Denver Post*, March 10, 1935.

70. Walter Judge, "Naismith Receives Thrills as Thousands Pay Tribute," *Denver Post*, March 17, 1936.

71. C. L. "Poss" Parsons, "JABS," *Denver Post*, March 13, 1936.

72. Mal Elliot, "Johnson's Maverick Style Made Waves," *Wichita Eagle-Beacon*, May 8, 1986.

73. Arthur J. Daley, "Awesome Kansas Giants Reverse Basketball Lay-up Shot Process," *New York Times*, March 10, 1936.

74. Arthur J. Daley, "McPherson Oilers Conquer All-Stars," *New York Times*, March 12, 1936.

75. *Denver Post*, March 20, 1936, 36.

76. Chester "Red" Nelson, "This Morning," *Rocky Mountain News*, March 21, 1936.

77. *Rocky Mountain News*, Sports Section, March 22, 1936, 2.

78. *Rocky Mountain News*, Sports Section, March 22, 1936, 2.

79. "AAU National Basketball Championships: Receipts and Expenditures." This is a table in the author's possession that summarizes the receipts and expenditures for the tournament between 1929 and 1965.

80. C. L. "Poss" Parsons, "JABS," *Denver Post*, March 23, 1936.

3. FORREST C. ALLEN AND THE
POLITICS OF OLYMPIC BASKETBALL

1. There is no published book-length study of the battle between the AAU and the NCAA for control of amateur sport in the United States. The best discussion of this complicated history is John Lucas's unpublished manuscript, "The Amateur Athletic Union of the United States 1888–1988: A Century of Power and Progress," 1989.

2. Arthur F. McClure, "Forrest Clare 'Phog' Allen," *Bibliographical Dictionary of American Sports: Basketball and other Indoor Sports*, ed. David L. Potter (Westport CT: Greenwood Press, 1989) 4–6.

3. Dr. Forrest C. Allen, "The International Growth of Basketball," original manuscript, University of Kansas, Spencer Research Library, Archives, Allen Letter File.

4. Letter, Avery Brundage to Dr. Forrest C. Allen, October 7, 1936, University of Kansas, Spencer Research Library, Archives, Allen Letter File.

5. Letter, Dr. Forrest C. Allen to F. B. Eagleson, October 8, 1931, Secretary Treasurer Canadian Amateur Basketball Association, University of Kansas, Spencer Research Library, Archives, Allen Letter File.

6. J. Lyman Bingham, "Olympic Basketball Tryouts," *Spalding's Official Basketball Guide, 1936–37* (New York: American Sports, 1936), 38.

7. Bingham, "Olympic Basketball Tryouts," 39.

8. Letter, Floyd A. Rowe to Forrest C. Allen, October 15, 1935, University of Kansas, Spencer Research Library, Archives, Allen Letter File. Rowe was a member of the Olympic Basketball Committee and director of the Bureau of Physical Welfare for the Cleveland Board of Education.

9. Letter, Forrest C. Allen to Major John L. Griffith, January 22, 1936, University of Kansas, Spencer Research Library, Archives, Allen Letter File. Griffith was the president of the NCAA.

10. Letter, L. W. St. John to Walter E. Meanwell, January 24, 1936, University of Kansas, Spencer Research Library, Archives, Allen Letter File. St. John was the director of athletics at Ohio State University and Meanwell, who had been a successful basketball coach at the University of Wisconsin, was chair of the Olympic Basketball Committee.

11. Letter, Floyd A. Rowe to Forrest C. Allen, February 7, 1936, University of Kansas, Spencer Research Library, Archives, Allen Letter File.

12. *Denver Post*, March 22, 1936, 7.

13. *Denver Post*, March 28, 1936, 20.

14. *New York Times*, April 2, 1936, 32.

15. *New York Times*, March 4, 1936, 29; March 30, 1936, 25.

16. Bingham, "Olympic Basketball Tryouts," 41–42.

17. *Denver Post*, March 29, 1936, 25.

18. *New York Times*, April 2, 1936, 2.

19. *New York Times*, April 4, 1936, 20.

20. *New York Times*, April 5, 1936, 20.

21. *New York Times*, April 6, 1936, 25.

22. Richard D. Mandell, *The Nazi Olympics* (New York: Ballentine, 1971), 90.

23. Bingham, "Olympic Basketball Tryouts," 45.

24. Bingham, "Olympic Basketball Tryouts," 45.

25. Letter, Forrest C. Allen to Major John L. Griffith, April 24, 1936, University of Kansas, Spencer Research Library, Archives, Allen Letter File.

26. Letter, Major John L. Griffith to Forrest C. Allen, May 1, 1936, University of Kansas, Spencer Research Library, Archives, Allen Letter File.

27. Letter, Forrest C. Allen to Dr. W. E. Meanwell, May 5, 1936, University of Kansas, Spencer Research Library, Archives, Allen Letter File.

28. Letter, Allen to Meanwell, May 5, 1936.

29. *Denver Post*, May 6, 1936, 21.

30. C. L. "Poss" Parsons, "JABS," *Denver Post*, May 7, 1936. Parsons was the sports editor of the *Denver Post*. He was also one of the AAU members of the Olympic Basketball Committee and was very interested in this controversy.

31. Letter, Allen to Meanwell, May 5, 1936.

32. Copies of the *Topeka Daily Capitol* for April 10 and 11 are in the Allen Letter File.

33. Letter, Allen to Meanwell, May 5, 1936.

34. C. L. "Poss" Parsons, "JABS," *Denver Post*, May 6, 1936.

35. Frank L. Lubin, interview with the author, July 6, 1995.

36. *McPherson Daily Republic*, June 16, 1936, 19.

37. *McPherson Daily Republic*, July 11, 1936, 5.

38. *McPherson Daily Republic*, July 11, 1936, 5.

39. Sam Balter, "Olympic Basketball," *The Amateur Athlete*, October 1936, 12.

40. Arthur J. Daley, "Olympic Basketball at Berlin," *Spalding Official Basketball Guide, 1936–37* (New York; American Sports, 1937), 46–47.

41. Balter, "Olympic Basketball," 10–12.

282   NOTES TO PAGES 52–59

42. *New York Times*, August 28, 1936, 2.

43. Sam Balter, "Olympic Basketball," *Spalding's Athletic Library* (New York: American Sports, 1937), 46.

44. *Topeka Daily Capital*, August 28, 1936, 2.

45. William J. Baker, *Jesse Owens: An American Life* (New York: Free Press, 1986), 109–38.

46. *Topeka Daily Capital*, August 28, 1936, 2.

47. Letter, John L. Griffith to Dr. Forrest C. Allen, May 1, 1936, University of Kansas, Spencer Research Library, Archives, Allen Letter File.

48. *Denver Post*, April 2, 1952, 38.

49. Adolph H. Grundman, "Frank John Lubin," *Biographical Dictionary of American Sports: 1942–1995 Supplement*, ed. David L. Porter (Westport CT, 1995), 278–79.

4. GRUENIG AND McCRACKEN TRIUMPHANT

1. *Denver Post*, March 22, 1937, 19.

2. Jerry Jaye Wright, "Shelton, Everett F. 'Ev,'" *Biographical Dictionary of American Sports: Basketball and Other Indoor Sports*, ed. David L. Porter (Westport CT: Greenwood Press, 1989), 105–6.

3. *Rocky Mountain News*, December 1, 1936, 10.

4. William C Wertz, *Phillips: The First 66 Years* (Bartlesville OK: A Public Affairs Publication of Phillips Petroleum Company, 1983), 66–72.

5. *Rocky Mountain News*, March 7, 1937, 2.

6. *Denver Post*, March 19 1937, 37–38.

7. *Denver Post*, March 19, 1937, 37–38.

8. *Denver Post*, March 20, 1937, 13.

9. *Denver Post*, March 20, 1937, 13.

10. *Denver Post*, sec. 5, March 21, 1937, 1.

11. *Rocky Mountain News*, March 21, 1937, 1–3.

12. Frank Haraway, "Willard N. Greim: An Honorable Legend," *Denver Post*, March 30, 1966, 64. In 1966 Willard N. Greim was inducted to the Colorado Sports Hall of Fame for his contribution as an administrator to state, national, and international sports organization. In 1924 he was named director of health education for the

Denver Public Schools. As secretary of the Rocky Mountain AAU, he was one of those responsible for bringing the national AAU basketball tournament to Denver, and he was on the tournament committee or directed it from 1935 through 1966. Beginning in 1944 Greim served as national president for the AAU for three years. He served as president for the International Federation of Basketball (FIBA) from 1948 to 1956 and on various Olympic Committees.

13. *Denver Post*, March 30 1937, 19.

14. Chester "Red" Nelson, "The Morning After," *Rocky Mountain News*, March 23, 1937.

15. "AAU National Basketball Championships: Receipts and Expenditures."

16. C. L. "Poss" Parsons, "JABS" *Denver Post*, March 21, 1937.

17. *Rocky Mountain News*, December 14, 1937, 17.

18. *Denver Post*, December 30, 1937, 9.

19. *Rocky Mountain News*, January 9, 1938, 9; January 9, 1938, 11.

20. *Rocky Mountain News*, January 20, 1938, 11.

21. Chester "Red" Nelson, "The Morning After," February 5, 1938.

22. *Rocky Mountain News*, December 14, 1937, 11.

23. *Rocky Mountain News*, March 14, 1938, 11–13.

24. *Rocky Mountain News*, March 17, 1938, 1.

25. *Rocky Mountain News*, March 18, 1938, 18.

26. *Rocky Mountain News*, March 19, 1938, 9.

27. *Rocky Mountain News*, March 19, 1938, 1–3.

28. *Denver Post*, Sports Section, March 20, 1938, 10.

29. *Denver Post*, sec. 5, March 19, 1939, 1.

30. *Denver Post*, March 21, 1939, 19.

31. *Rocky Mountain News*, March 21, 1938, 10.

32. "AAU" National Basketball Championships: Receipts and Expenditures"

33. Chester "Red" Nelson, "The Morning After," *Rocky Mountain News*, March 22, 1938.

34. *Rocky Mountain News*, December 11, 1938, 9.

35. *Rocky Mountain News*, December 4, 1938, 7.

36. *Rocky Mountain News*, March 4, 1939, 9.

37. C. L. "Poss" Parsons, "JABS," *Denver Post*, March 16, 1939.

38. *Denver Post*, March 18, 1939, 13.

39. *Rocky Mountain News*, March 19, 1939, 8.

40. *Denver Post*, sec. 5, March 19, 1939, 1.

41. *Denver Post*, March 20, 1939, 16.

42. *Denver Post*, March 20, 1939, 16.

43. *Denver Post*, sec. 5, March 19, 1939, 1.

44. *Denver Post*, March 18, 1939, 13.

45. *Rocky Mountain News*, March 20, 1939, 10.

46. *Denver Post*, sec. 5, March 19, 1939, 3.

47. *Rocky Mountain News*, March 17, 1939, 17.

48. Art Unger Scrapbooks.

49. *Denver Post*, sec. 4, March 8, 1942, 15.

50. *Denver Post*, sec. 5, February 4, 1940, 1.

51. C. L. "Poss" Parsons "JABS," *Denver Post*, February 15, 1940.

52. *Denver Post*, sec. 5, March 3, 1940, 2.

53. *Denver Post*, sec. 5, February 18, 1940, 2.

54. *Denver Post*, February 20, 1940, 18.

55. C. L. "Poss" Parsons, "JABS," *Denver Post*, Sports Section, March 3, 1940.

56. *Denver Post*, March 14, 1940, 28.

57. *Rocky Mountain News*, March 18, 1940, 2.

58. *Denver Post*, March 3, 1940, 2.

59. *Rocky Mountain News*, March 18, 1940, 2.

60. *Rocky Mountain News*, March 23, 1940, 9.

61. *Denver Post*, March 23, 1940, 3.

62. *Rocky Mountain News*, Sports Section, March 24, 1940, 1.

63. *Denver Post*, March 21, 1940, 26.

64. *Denver Post*, March 12, 1941, 21.

65. Jay Langhammer, "Luisetti, Angelo Joseph 'Hank,'" *Biographical Dictionary of American Sports: Basketball and Other Indoor Sports*, ed. David L. Porter (Westport CT: Greenwood Press, 1989), 105–6.

66. Bill Lieser, "As Bill Sees It," *San Francisco Chronicle*, March 15, 1941.

67. *Rocky Mountain News*, March 21, 1941, 11.

68. Chester "Red" Nelson, "Sports This Morning," *Rocky Mountain News*, March 19, 1941.

69. "AAU National Basketball Championships: Receipts and Expenditures."

70. *Rocky Mountain News*, March 23, 1941, 14.

71. Chester "Red" Nelson, "Sports This Morning," *Rocky Mountain News*, March 19, 1941.

72. *Denver Post*, March 19, 1941, 19.

73. *Rocky Mountain News*, March 22, 1941, 11.

74. Paul Zimmerman, "Sports Post Scripts," *Los Angeles Times*, March 24, 1941.

75. *Rocky Mountain News*, March 23, 1941, 14–15.

76. *Rocky Mountain News*, March 23, 1941, 14–15.

77. Chester "Red" Nelson, "Sports This Morning," *Rocky Mountain News*, July 30, 1941.

78. Jack Gray, interview with the author.

79. *Denver Post*, Sports Section, January 8, 1942, 2.

80. Chester "Red" Nelson, "Sports This Morning," *Rocky Mountain News*, March 15, 1942.

81. Bill Strannigan, interview with the author, February 22, 1994.

82. Chester "Red" Nelson, "Sports This Morning," *Rocky Mountain News*, March 16, 1942.

83. Fred Scolari, interview with the author, June 25, 1997.

84. *Rocky Mountain News*, March 16, 1942, 10.

85. *Rocky Mountain News*, March 17, 1942, 9.

86. Fred Scolari, interview with the author.

87. Chester "Red" Nelson, "Sports This Morning," *Rocky Mountain News*, March 17, 1942.

88. *Rocky Mountain News*, March 17, 1942, 9–10.

89. *Rocky Mountain News*, March 19, 1942, 9.

90. *Rocky Mountain News*, March 20, 1942, 9.

91. *Rocky Mountain News*, March 21, 1942, 11.

92. *Rocky Mountain News*, March 22, 1942, 14.

93. *Rocky Mountain News*, March 22, 1942, 15.

94. *Denver Post*, March 22, 1942, 12–17.

95. *Rocky Mountain News*, March 23, 1942, 10.

96. Chester "Red" Nelson, "Sports This Morning," *Rocky Mountain News*, March 24, 1942.

97. *Denver Post*, August 27, 1942, 1.

5. PHILLIPS 66 AND AAU BASKETBALL

1. Wertz, *Phillips*, 66–72.

2. Paul Endacott, interview with the author, July 2, 1993.

3. Elmer Sark, "The History of Phillips 66 Basketball" (unpublished manuscript), 6, Phillips Archives.

4. Sark, "History of Phillips 66 Basketball," 7.

5. *Denver Post*, March 20, 1937, 13.

6. Allen recommended Pralle to Adams in a letter from Forrest C. Allen to Kenneth S. Adams, February 25, 1938, University of Kansas, Spencer Research Library, Archives, Allen Letter File. Allen's description of Pralle's skills is in Forrest C. Allen to Jerry Brondfield, NEA *Sports Writer*, March 3, 1938, Spencer Research Library Archives. Shields and Troutwine are described in "They're Out to Win," PHILNEWS, January 1939, 7–9.

7. Grady Lewis, interview with the author, March 20, 1994.

8. *Rocky Mountain News*, March 24, 1940, 6.

9. Official Program, Orhbach AAU vs. Phillips 66 Oilers, Phillips Petroleum Corporate Archives, Bartlesville OK.

10. "Team Work—For More Sales," *Selling 66*, December 1939, 7.

11. "Team Work," *Selling 66*, December 1939, 7.

12. "They're Out to Win," PHILNEWS, January 1939.

13. "Team Work—For More Sales," December 1939.

14. Frank Phillips, "Way Back When—This Game Called Basketball," PHILNEWS, 1937.

15. "Championship Teamwork," PHILNEWS, May 1940, 10–11.

16. Tuttle, "High-Test Hoops," 97.

17. Tuttle, "High-Test Hoops," 97, and Wertz, *Phillips*, 165.

18. Tuttle, "High-Test Hoops," 99.

19. Tuttle, "High-Test Hoops," 99.

20. Tuttle, "High-Test Hoops," 101.

21. Tuttle, "High-Test Hoops," 100.

22. Tuttle, "High-Test Hoops," 100, and Wertz, *Phillips*, 71.

23. Letter, Bob Kurland to Arilee Pollard, undated, Jim Pollard Scrapbooks, in possession of Arilee Pollard. Arilee Pollard is the wife of Jim Pollard, one of the outstanding players of the 1940s and 1950s. Following her husband's death in 1993, Arilee Pollard solicited comments from players who played with or against her husband. Bob Kurland's are particularly useful in capturing the atmosphere of Phillips basketball in the late 1940s.

24. Burdie Haldorson, interview with the author, September 5, 1993.

25. Will Rothman, interview with the author, March 10, 1994.

26. Letter, Forrest C. Allen to Kenneth S. Adams, March 30, 1938, University of Kansas, Spencer Research Library, Archives, Allen Letter File.

27. Chester "Red" Nelson, "Sailors Must Use Mirrors," *Rocky Mountain News*, March 19, 1943.

28. *New York Times*, November, 20, 1942, 41.

29. *New York Times*, November 25, 1942, 34.

30. Chester "Red" Nelson, "Clay One-Man Gang," *Rocky Mountain News*, March 11, 1943. Clay was a 1994 inductee in the Colorado Hall of Fame. World War Two interrupted his college career, and after the service he played professional football with the Chicago Rockets in the All-American Conference rather than return to the University of Colorado.

31. Nelson, "Sailors Must Use Mirrors," March 19, 1943.

32. Nelson, "Sailors Must Use Mirrors," March 19, 1943.

33. Bob Wilson, interview with the author, December 30, 1999.

34. Joe Hendrickson, "Jim Pollard—In Mikan's Shadow," *Sport*, December 1951, 16–70, 80.

35. *Rocky Mountain News*, March 17, 1943, 25; March 18, 1943, 21.

36. *Rocky Mountain News*, March 17, 1943, 24–25.

37. Chester "Red" Nelson, "Kick Over Dope Bucket," *Rocky Mountain News*, March 18, 1943.

38. Jack Carberry, "The Second Guess," *Denver Post*, March 20, 1943.

39. *Rocky Mountain News*, March 19, 1943, 23.

40. Carberry, "Second Guess," March 20, 1943.

41. Carberry, "Second Guess," March 20, 1943.

42. Chet Nelson, "Gruenig the Difference," *Rocky Mountain News*, March 21, 1943.

43. "1943 Champs," PHILNEWS, May 1943, 12–13.

44. Jack Carberry, "The Second Guess," *Denver Post*, March 28, 1943.

45. Jack Carberry, "The Second Guess," *Denver Post*, March 21 1944.

46. Carberry, "Second Guess," March 21, 1944.

47. *Denver Post*, March 24, 1944, 13.

48. Chester "Red" Nelson, "Good Fast Breaks," *Rocky Mountain News*, March 24, 1944.

49. *Rocky Mountain News*, March 22, 1944, 18.

50. *Denver Post*, March 24, 1944, 12.

51. *Rocky Mountain News*, March 25, 1944, 12.

52. *Rocky Mountain News*, March 25, 1944, 12.

53. *Rocky Mountain News*, March 26, 1944, 32.

54. Jack Carberry, "The Second Guess," *Denver Post*, March 27, 1944.

55. Carberry, "Second Guess," March 27, 1944.

56. Chester "Red" Nelson, "The Morning After," *Rocky Mountain News*, March 27, 1944.

57. Jack Carberry, "The Second Guess," *Denver Post*, March 28, 1944.

58. Bob Considine, "College Basketball Threatened With a Black Sox Scandal," *Denver Post*, March 26, 1944, sec. 4.

59. *Denver Post*, April 5, 1944, 19.

60. Jack Carberry, "The Second Guess," *Denver Post*, December 27, 1944.

61. *Rocky Mountain News*, March 23, 1945, 24.

62. *Rocky Mountain News*, March 24, 1945, 14.

63. *Rocky Mountain News*, March 25, 1945, 39.

64. Jack Carberry, "The Second Guess," *Denver Post*, March 26, 1945, sec. 4.

65. Leonard Cahn, "McCracken and Gruenig Will Quit," *Rocky Mountain News*, March 26, 1945.

6. The Rich Get Richer

1. James Patterson, *Grand Expectations* (New York: Oxford University Press, 1996), 61–81.

2. Charles Hyatt, "Pinch Hitting for Second Guess," *Denver Post*, March 18, 1946.

3. "League for World's Fastest Basketball," *American Basketball League Official Program*, 1945–46, 5.

4. Richard Green, "The Peacemaker," *Journal of Chickasaw History* 4 (1998): 8–16.

5. *Rocky Mountain News*, March 21, 1946, 25; *Denver Post*, March 22, 1946, 15.

6. *Rocky Mountain News*, March 23, 1946, 20.

7. Chester "Red" Nelson, "Sports," *Rocky Mountain News*, March 24, 1946.

8. *Rocky Mountain News*, March 23, 1946, 20.

9. "Two Men and a Team," *American Basketball League Official Program*, 1945–46, 13.

10. *Rocky Mountain News*, March 24, 1946, 40.

11. Jack Carberry, "The Second Guess," *Denver Post*, March 25, 1946.

12. Leonard Cahn, "Pro and Cahn," *Rocky Mountain News*, March 25, 1946.

13. Jack Carberry, "The Second Guess," *Denver Post*, March 26, 1946.

14. Jack Carberry, "The Second Guess," *Denver Post*, March 30, 1946.

15. *Rocky Mountain News*, March 24, 1946, 40.

16. Chester "Red" Nelson, "Sports," *Rocky Mountain News*, March 23, 1946.

17. *Rocky Mountain News*, March 24, 1946, 40.

18. Jack Carberry, "The Second Guess," *Denver Post*, March 24, 1946.

19. Bob Kurland, interview with the author, July 1, 1993.

20. "Lou Bittner Dies at Seventy-two," *Oakland Tribune*, May 31, 1980, D2.

21. Jim Pollard Scrapbooks.

22. Jim Pollard Scrapbooks.

23. *Denver Post*, December 12, 1946, 22.

24. Hal Davis, interview with the author, January 20, 1994.

25. "Basketball a la Nugget," *Denver Nuggets vs. Phillips "66" Official Program*, January 22, 1947, 3.

26. Davis, interview with the author.

27. Don Williams, interview with the author, January 13, 2000.

28. Jim Pollard Scrapbooks.

29. *Bartlesville Examiner*, February 27, 1947, Bob Kurland Scrapbooks.

30. Jack Carberry, "The Second Guess," *Denver Post*, March 8, 1947.

31. Chester "Red" Nelson, "Sports: Bishop the Difference," *Rocky Mountain News*, March 9, 1947.

32. *Denver Post*, March 9, 1947, 15.

33. *Rocky Mountain News*, March 20, 1947, 17.

34. *Rocky Mountain News*, March 21, 1947, 24–25.

35. *Rocky Mountain News*, March 22, 1947, 16.

36. *Rocky Mountain News*, March 23, 1947, 37.

37. Leonard Cahn, "Pro and Cahn," *Rocky Mountain News*, March 25, 1946.

38. Jack Carberry, "The Second Guess," *Denver Post*, March 19, 1947.

39. Jack Carberry, "The Second Guess," *Denver Post*, March 18, 1947; March 10, 1947.

40. Chester "Red" Nelson, "Sports," *Rocky Mountain News*, March 26, 1947.

41. Jack Carberry, "The Second Guess," *Denver Post*, March 21, 1947.

42. Jack Carberry, "The Second Guess, *Denver Post*, March 18, 1947.

43. *Rocky Mountain News*, March 27, 1947, 21.

44. Jack Carberry, "The Second Guess," *Denver Post*, March 12, 1947.

45. *Bartlesville Examiner*, March 21, 1947, Bob Kurland Scrapbooks.

46. *Denver Post*, March 29, 1947.

47. Chester "Red" Nelson, "Sports," *Rocky Mountain News*, March 31, 1947.

48. Jack Carberry, "The Second Guess," *Denver Post*, March 16, 1947.

49. Leonard Cahn, "Pro and Cahn," *Rocky Mountain News*, September 12, 1947.

50. Jack Carberry, "The Second Guess," *Denver Post*, January 15, 1948.

51. Jack Carberry, "The Second Guess," *Denver Post*, December 10, 1948.

52. Hal Davis, "Pinch-hitting for the Second Guess," *Denver Post*, June 16, 1947, Hal Davis Scrapbooks.

53. Jack Carberry, "The Second Guess," *Denver Post*, Hal Davis Scrapbooks.

54. Chester "Red" Nelson, "Nugs Will Do Alright," *Rocky Mountain News*, January 13, 1948, Hal Davis Scrapbooks.

55. *Rocky Mountain News*, February 12, 22, and 23, 1948, Hal Davis Scrapbooks.

56. Chester "Red" Nelson, *Rocky Mountain News*, March 9, 1948, Hal Davis Scrapbooks.

57. Jack Carberry, "The Second Guess," *Denver Post*, March 9, 1948.

58. Adolph H. Grundman, "Don Angelo Barksdale," *Biographical Dictionary of American Sports: 1992–1995, Supplement*, ed. David L. Porter (Westport CT: Greenwood Press, 1995), 241–42; Morris Silver, interview with the author, June 18, 1998.

59. Jack Carberry, "The Second Guess," *Denver Post*, February 9, 1948, Bob Kurland Scrapbooks.

60. *Daily Oklahoman*, January 7, 1948, Bob Kurland Scrapbooks.

61. Bob Graham, "In the Glare of the Sportlight," *Pawhuska Enterprise*, January 8, 1948, Bob Kurland Scrapbooks.

62. Laymund Crump, *Daily Oklahoman*, January 8, 1948, Bob Kurland Scrapbooks.

63. George Durham, "Ramblings in the Sports World," *Bartlesville Enterprise*, January 8, 1948, Bob Kurland Scrapbooks.

64. *Rocky Mountain News*, March 18, 1948, 3.

65. *Rocky Mountain News*, March 19, 1947, 41.

66. *Rocky Mountain News*, March 19, 1947, 22.

67. *Rocky Mountain News*, March 19, 1948, 22.

68. *Rocky Mountain News*, March 19, 1948, 23.

69. *Denver Post*, March 21, 1948, 1E.

70. *Denver Post*, March 28, 1948, 19.

71. *Denver Post*, March 30, 1948, 20.

72. Adolph H. Grundman, "Adolph Frederick Rupp," *American National Biography*, ed. John A. Garraty and Mark C. Carneres (New York: Oxford University Press, 1999), 19:68–70.

73. *Denver Post*, April 1, 1948, 30.

74. Ron Thomas, *They Cleared the Lane: The NBA's Black Pioneers* (Lincoln: University of Nebraska Press, 2002), 112.

75. *Daily Oklahoman*, April 1, 1948, Bob Kurland Scrapbooks.

76. Alfred Senn, *Power, Politics, and the Olympic Games* (Champaign IL: Human Kinetics, 1999), 80.

77. *Bartlesville Examiner*, July 1, 1948; *Kansas City Times*, July 3, 1948; *Rocky Mountain News*, July 10, 1948, Bob Kurland Scrapbooks.

78. *Atlanta Journal*, July 11, 1948, Bob Kurland Scrapbooks.

79. Thomas, *They Cleared the Lane*, 120–24.

80. *Kansas City Star*, August 3, 1948, Bob Kurland Scrapbooks.

81. *Waco Times-Herald*, April 12, 1948, Bob Kurland Scrapbooks.

82. *Kansas City Times*, August 11, 1948, Bob Kurland Scrapbooks.

7. BARTLESVILLE VERSUS THE BAY

1. Jack Carberry, "The Second Guess," *Denver Post*, March 21, 1949.

2. Joe Williams, "Amateur Status of Phillips 66 Is Questioned," *New York World-Telegram*, April 2, 1948, Bob Kurland Scrapbooks.

3. Richard O. Davies, *America's Obsession: Sports and Society Since 1945* (Ft. Worth: Harcourt Brace, 1994), 24–25.

4. Don Keown, "From the Press Box," *Wichita Beacon*, February 29, 1948, Bob Kurland Scrapbooks.

5. *Denver Post*, April 15, 1948, Bob Kurland Scrapbooks.

6. John Lardner, "Avery's Oilers," *Newsweek*, April 12, 1948, Bob Kurland Scrapbooks.

7. *Rocky Mountain News*, March 21, 1948, Bob Kurland Scrapbooks.

8. Jack Carberry, "The Second Guess," *Denver Post*, Bob Kurland Scrapbooks.

9. Hal Davis, "Pinch-hitting for the Second Guess," *Denver Post*, July 20, 1948, Bob Kurland Scrapbooks.

10. James Whiteside, *Colorado: A Sports History* (Niwot: University Press of Colorado, 1999), 312–13.

11. Whiteside, *Colorado: A Sports History*, 314; *National Basketball Association Program*, Hal Davis Scrapbooks.

12. The Denver Chevrolets, *Free Souvenir Program*, January 4, 1949, 3.

13. Jack Carberry, "The Second Guess," *Denver Post*, March 8, 1949.

14. Jack Carberry, "The Second Guess," *Denver Post*, March 19, 1949.

15. John Christgau, *The Origins of the Jump Shot: Eight Men Who Shook the World of Basketball* (Lincoln: University of Nebraska Press, 1999), 79–105; Leonard Cahn, "Pro and Cahn," *Rocky Mountain News*, March 26, 1950, 45; Letter, Seymour Smith to Adolph Grundman, February 29, 2000; Ed Schoenfeld, "Nibs Price's Five Big Bears," *Oakland Tribune-Parade*, January 10, 1954.

16. Leonard Cahn, "Pro and Cahn," *Rocky Mountain News*, March 21, 1949.

17. Ray Haywood, "It Says Here," *Oakland Tribune*, March 8, 1949.

18. Bob Brachman, "Fans Stunned by Bittner Win," *San Francisco Examiner*, March 21, 1949.

19. *Denver Post*, March 20, 1949, 1E.

20. *San Francisco Examiner*, March 21, 1949, 22.

294 NOTES TO PAGES 128–132

21. Hal Middlesworth, "On the Level," *Daily Oklahoman*, March 22, 1949.

22. Morris Silver, interview with the author.

23. Ray Haywood, *Oakland Tribune*, March 21, 1949, D30.

24. Ray Haywood, *Oakland Tribune*, March 28, 1949, D23.

25. Pat Frizzel, "Lou Bittner Dies at 72," *Oakland Tribune*, May 31, 1980.

26. Jack Carberry, "The Second Guess," *Denver Post*, March 21, 1949.

27. Bob Brachman, *San Francisco Examiner*, March 16, 1949, 29.

28. Jack Carberry, "The Second Guess," *Denver Post*, March 18, 1949.

29. Leonard Cahn, "Pro and Cahn," *Rocky Mountain News*, March 21, 1949.

30. Leonard Cahn, "Pro and Cahn," *Rocky Mountain News*, March 18, 1949, 26.

31. Jack Carberry, "The Second Guess," *Denver Post*, March 18, 1950.

32. *Denver Post*, March 17, 1950, 28.

33. Ray Haywood, *Oakland Tribune*, March 28, 1949, D23.

34. Jack Carberry, "The Second Guess," *Denver Post*, March 5, 1949.

35. *San Francisco Examiner*, March 12, 1950, 19.

36. George Yardley, interview with the author, May 23, 1995.

37. George Walker, interview with the author, June 30, 1997.

38. Schoenfeld, "Nibs Price Five Big Bears," January 10, 1954, Archives, Oakland Public Library; Joe Gergen, *The Final Four* (St. Louis: Sporting News, 1987), 58.

39. *San Francisco Chronicle*, January 10, 1944, Jim Pollard Scrapbooks.

40. *San Francisco Chronicle*, February 26, 1949, Jim Pollard Scrapbooks.

41. Taped interview in possession of Arilee Pollard.

42. The games were played on January 9, 1943, January 15, 1944, February 26, 1944, and March 4, 1946, and were widely covered in

the San Francisco Press. I read the accounts of the games in the Jim Pollard Scrapbooks.

43. *Rocky Mountain News*, March 20, 1950, 22.

44. *Rocky Mountain News*, March 20, 1950, 22

45. Ray Haywood, "It Says Here," *Oakland Tribune*, March 22, 1950.

46. *Rocky Mountain News*, March 20, 1950, 22.

47. *Rocky Mountain News*, March 26, 1950, 20.

48. *Denver Post*, March 27, 1950, 20.

49. *Denver Post*, November 4, 1950, 11.

50. Leonard Cahn, "Pro and Cahn," *Rocky Mountain News*, March 21, 1949; March 18, 1949.

51. *Rocky Mountain News*, March 19, 1951, 5.

52. Jack Carberry, "The Second Guess," *Denver Post*, March 18, 1951.

53. *Rocky Mountain News*, March 20, 1951, 32.

54. *Rocky Mountain News*, March 22, 1951, 39; March 23, 1951, 48.

55. *Rocky Mountain News*, March 22, 1951, 47.

56. *Rocky Mountain News*, March 22, 1951, 37.

57. *Rocky Mountain News*, March 23, 1951, 46.

58. *Rocky Mountain News*, March 24, 1951, 26.

59. *San Francisco Examiner*, March 15, 1950, 29.

60. *San Francisco Examiner*, February 5, 1951, 31.

61. *San Francisco Examiner*, February 9, 1951, 28.

62. *Rocky Mountain News*, March 24, 1951, 26.

63. *Rocky Mountain News*, March 21, 1951, 48.

64. Leonard Cahn, "Pro and Cahn," *Rocky Mountain News*, March 24, 1951.

65. Leonard Cahn, "Pro and Cahn," *Rocky Mountain News*, March 26, 1951.

66. Chester "Red" Nelson, "Sports," *Rocky Mountain News*, March 24, 1951.

67. *Denver Post*, December 18, 1951.

68. Max Brooks, interview with the author, May 19, 1995.

8. Here Come the Cats

1. *Rocky Mountain News*, March 4, 1952, 41

2. *Rocky Mountain News*, March 20, 1952, 40.

3. *Rocky Mountain News*, March 20, 1952, 40.

4. *San Francisco Examiner*, March 13 1952, 28.

5. *Rocky Mountain News*, March 21, 1952, 60.

6. *Rocky Mountain News*, March 22, 1952, 28.

7. *Rocky Mountain News*, March 23, 1952, 42.

8. Jack Carberry, "The Second Guess," *Denver Post*, March 16, 1952.

9. *Denver Post*, March 16, 1952, 2A.

10. *Denver Post*, March 16, 1952, 2A.

11. Leonard Cahn, "Pro and Cahn," *Rocky Mountain News*, March 22, 1952.

12. Dr. Forrest C. Allen, "Twelve Foot Baskets for College and Independent Teams," original manuscript, University of Kansas, Spencer Research Library, Allen Letter File.

13. Gergen, *Final Four*, 70.

14. Warren Womble, interview with the author, August 7, 1994.

15. *Rocky Mountain News*, March 30, 1952, 38.

16. *Rocky Mountain News*, March 30, 1952, 38.

17. *Rocky Mountain News*, April 1, 1952, 41.

18. *Rocky Mountain News*, April 2, 1952, 47.

19. *Rocky Mountain News*, April 2, 1952, 47.

20. *New York Times*, July 29, 1952, 25.

21. *New York Times*, July 31, 1952, 15.

22. *New York Times*, August 1, 1952, 3.

23. *New York Times*, August 3, 1952, sec. 5, 3.

24. *New York Times*, August 3, 1952, sec. 5, 5.

25. Jack McDonald, "Both Barrels," *Call-Bulletin*, n.d., Bob Kurland Scrapbooks.

26. George Walker, interview with the author.

27. Denver Central Bankers, Press, Radio, and Television Information, 1952–53, mimeograph, in the possession of Larry Varnell.

28. Chuck Darling, interview with the author, May 4, 1994.

29. *Rocky Mountain News*, March 19, 1953, 23. Tom Scott coached

only one year for Phillips and returned to North Carolina, where he served as a basketball coach and athletic director at Davidson College.

30. *Denver Post*, March 20, 1953, 36.

31. *Denver Post*, March 21, 1953, 11

32. Chester "Red" Nelson, "Sports," *Rocky Mountain News*, March 19, 1953.

33. *Rocky Mountain News*, March 22, 1953, 1B.

34. Leonard Cahn, "Pro and Cahn," *Rocky Mountain News*, March 23, 1953.

35. Jack Carberry, "The Second Guess, " *Denver Post*, March 22, 1953.

36. *Denver Post*, March 19, 1954, 30–31.

37. Warren Womble, interview.

38. *Denver Post*, March 21, 1954, 1B.

39. Fon Johnson, interview with the author, April 1, 1999.

40. *Denver Post*, March 21, 1954, 1B.

41. Leonard Cahn, "Pro and Cahn," *Rocky Mountain News*, March 20, 1954.

42. Leonard Cahn, "Pro and Cahn," *Rocky Mountain News*, March 22, 1954.

9. FROM BARTLESVILLE TO SEATTLE

1. Brochure, Denver Central Bankers Basketball team, 1954–55, 21, mimeograph in the possession of Larry Varnell.

2. Fred Casotti, "University of Colorado Final Four Years" in *Rocky Mountain Basketball*, (Englewood CO: Westcliffe Publishers, 1989), 38–41.

3. James P. Banks, "AAU Roundup," *Sports Review* (1955): 63–68.

4. *Rocky Mountain News*, March 23, 1955, 57; March 24, 1955, 60–61.

5. *Denver Post*, March 25, 1955, 34.

6. *Rocky Mountain News*, March 25, 1955, 76–80.

7. *Rocky Mountain News*, March 26, 1955, 70.

8. Leonard Cahn, "Pro and Cahn," *Rocky Mountain News*, March 27, 1955.

9. Leonard Cahn, "Pro and Cahn," *Rocky Mountain News*, March 28, 1955.

10. *Denver Post*, March 27, 1955, 1B.

11. Larry Zimmer, "Regional Basketball on Radio and TV," *Rocky Mountain Basketball* (Englewood CO: Westcliffe Publishers, 1989), 47.

12. Burdie Haldorson Scrapbooks.

13. Burdie Haldorson, interview with the author.

14. Al Browning, "What If?" *Tuscaloosa News*, February 8, 1981, in Johnny Dee Scrapbooks.

15. Jim Vickers, interview with the author, July 12, 2001.

16. Vickers, interview with the author; Dick Boushka, interview with the author, August 9, 1995.

17. Rick Plumlee, "Two Shocker Legends," *Wichita Eagle*, February 7, 1993; Cleo Littleton, interview with the author, August 8, 1995.

18. Littleton, interview with the author.

19. Plumlee, "Two Shocker Legends."

20. *Denver Post*, March 22, 1956, 61.

21. *Denver Post*, March 22, 1956, 63.

22. *Denver Post*, March 23, 1956, 43–44.

23. Leonard Cahn, "Pro and Cahn," *Rocky Mountain News*, March 24, 1956.

24. *Denver Post*, March 23, 1956, 43–44.

25. *Rocky Mountain News*, March 24, 1956, 38.

26. Warren "Bud" Howard, interview with the author, August 13, 1998.

27. Frank Fidler, interview with the author, August 9, 1998.

28. *Seattle Post-Intelligencer*, March 25, 1956, 32.

29. *Denver Post*, March 25, 1956, 1B.

30. Jack Carberry, "The Second Guess," *Denver Post*, March 23, 1956.

31. Jack Carberry, "The Second Guess," *The Denver Post*, March 21, 1956.

32. Jack Carberry, "The Second Guess," *Denver Post*, March 25, 1956.

33. Jack Carberry, "The Second Guess," *Denver Post*, March 26, 1956.

34. *Denver Post*, April 3, 1956, 26.

35. *Denver Post*, April 4, 1956, 41.

36. *Denver Post*, April 5, 1956, 60.

37. *Seattle Post-Intelligencer*, April 6, 1956, 19.

38. *Denver Post*, April 5, 1956, 60.

39. Bill Russell and William McSweeny, *Go Up for Glory* (New York: Berkeley, 1966), 44–45.

40. George Durham, "On to Australia," PHILNEWS, May 1956; K. S. Adams "As I See It," PHILNEWS, May 1956, 3.

41. Russell and McSweeney, *Go Up for Glory*, 45.

42. The *New York Times* provided excellent coverage of the games.

10. Parity Prevails

1. *Denver Post*, March 24, 1956, 10.

2. *Wall Street Journal*, January 24, 1957, 1.

3. Johnny Dee, interview with the author, October 2, 1994.

4. *Rocky Mountain News*, March 27, 1957, 46.

5. *Rocky Mountain News*, March 28, 1957, 46.

6. R. C. Owens, interview with the author, July 20, 2001.

7. *Rocky Mountain News*, March 29, 1957, 70.

8. Leonard Cahn, "Pro and Cahn," *Rocky Mountain News*, March 30, 1957.

9. Phil Vukicevich, interview with the author, June 17, 1998; Albert "Cappy" Lavin, interview with the author, June 17, 1998.

10. *San Francisco Examiner*, October 23, 1964; Terry Pluto, *Tall Tales* (New York: Simon and Schuster, 1992), 163–64.

11. Lavin, interview with the author.

12. Vukicevich, interview with the author.

13. Chester "Red" Nelson, "Sports," *Rocky Mountain News*, March 29, 1957.

14. Ken Flower, interview with the author, April 16, 1999.

15. *Rocky Mountain News*, March 30, 1957, 38.

16. *Rocky Mountain News*, March 31, 1957, 76.

17. *Denver Post*, March 31, 1957, 113.

18. Jack Carberry, "The Second Guess," *Denver Post*, March 31, 1957.

19. Chester "Red" Nelson, "Sports," *Rocky Mountain News*, March 19, 1957.

20. Jack Carberry, "The Second Guess," *Denver Post*, Johnny Dee Scrapbooks.

21. Leonard Cahn, "Pro and Cahn," *Rocky Mountain News*, December 2, 1957.

22. *Rocky Mountain News*, March 27, 1958, 70.

23. *Rocky Mountain News*, March 28, 1958, 78.

24. *Rocky Mountain News*, March 29, 1958, 42.

25. *Rocky Mountain News*, March 29, 1958, 42.

26. Jack Carberry, "The Second Guess," *Denver Post*, March 30, 1958.

27. Womble, interview with the author.

28. Womble, interview with the author.

29. *Rocky Mountain News*, March 30, 1958, 74.

30. Leonard Cahn, "Pro and Cahn," *Rocky Mountain News*, March 31, 1958.

31. Jack Carberry, "The Second Guess," *Denver Post*, March 31, 1958.

32. *Denver Post*, March 31, 1958, 50.

33. *Denver Post*, March 25, 1958, 21.

34. George Durham, "Basketball behind the Iron Curtain," PHILNEWS, July 1958, 6–8.

35. Harry Farrar, "Sports Diary," *Denver Post*, March 28, 1988.

36. Jack Carberry, "The Second Guess," *Denver Post*, January 6, 1958.

37. Frank Haraway, "McCracken, Gruenig Always Stars," *Denver Post*, February 26, 1968.

38. *Rocky Mountain News*, March 9, 1959, 49.

39. Chuck Garrity, "Pro, Amateur Scouts Courting Howell," *Denver Post*, March 17, 1959, 25.

40. Furman Bisher, "A Scholarship for Jackie," *Grass Roots and Schoolyard*, ed. Nelson Campbell (Lexington MA: Stephen Greene Press, 1988), 153–60.

41. *Rocky Mountain News*, March 19, 1959, 63.

42. *Denver Post*, March 20, 1959, 39.

43. *Rocky Mountain News*, March 20, 1959, 102.

44. Leonard Cahn, "Pro and Cahn," *Rocky Mountain News*, March 21, 1959.

45. *Denver Post*, March 20, 1959, 32.

46. *Basketball Hall of Fame: Class of 1994 Yearbook*, 61.

47. Alex Hannum, interview with the author, April 1, 1999; Jim Vickers, interview.

48. Hannum, interview with the author.

49. Dan Boldebuck, interview with the author, April 8, 1997; Boushka, interview with the author; *Rocky Mountain News*, March 23, 1959, 1.

50. Boushka, interview with the author.

51. *Rocky Mountain News*, March 21, 1959, 50.

52. *Rocky Mountain News*, March 22, 1959, 52.

53. Pete Lightner, "The Morning After," *Wichita Eagle*, March 24, 1959.

54. Pete Lightner, "The Morning After," *Wichita Eagle*, March 22, 1959.

55. Jack Carberry, "The Second Guess," *Denver Post*, March 23, 1959.

11. DENVER'S LAST HURRAH

1. Leonard Cahn, "Pro and Cahn," *Rocky Mountain News*, March 21, 1960.

2. Leonard Cahn, "Pro and Cahn," *Rocky Mountain News*, March 5, 1960.

3. Bob Boozer, interview with the author, July 25, 2001.

4. Royal Brougham, "The Morning After," *Seattle Post-Intelligencer*, March 28, 1960.

5. *San Francisco Examiner*, March 18, 1956, 14.

6. Fidler, interview with the author.

7. Chester "Red" Nelson, "Sports," *Rocky Mountain News*, March 22, 1960.

8. *Rocky Mountain News*, March 24, 1960, 70.

9. *Rocky Mountain News*, March 25, 1960, 98.

10. *Basketball Hall of Fame: Class of 1994 Yearbook*, 70.

11. *Rocky Mountain News*, March 25, 1960, 98.

12. *Rocky Mountain News*, March 26, 1960, 60.

13. *Rocky Mountain News*, March 26, 1960, 56.

14. *Rocky Mountain News*, March 27, 1960, 56.

15. Bruce Jenkins, *A Good Man: The Pete Newell Story* (Berkeley CA: Frog, 1999), 192–96.

16. *Rocky Mountain News*, April 1, 1960, 96.

17. *Rocky Mountain News*, April 2, 1960, 60.

18. *Rocky Mountain News*, April 3, 1960, 64.

19. *Denver Post*, April 4, 1960, 45.

20. Leonard Cahn, "Pro and Cahn," *Rocky Mountain News*, April 4, 1960, 56.

21. Jenkins, *A Good Man*, 197.

22. Jack Carberry, "The Second Guess," *Denver Post*, April 4, 1960.

23. Arthur Daley, "Sports of the Times," *New York Times*, August 28, 1960.

24. *New York Times*, September 4, 1960, sec. 5, 1.

25. Jenkins, *A Good Man*, 204.

26. Bob Boozer, interview with the author.

27. *New York Times*, September 9, 1960, 21.

28. *New York Times*, September 11, 1960, sec. 5, 1.

29. Jenkins, *A Good Man*, 206.

30. Jack Carberry, "The Second Guess," *Denver Post*, March 27, 1960.

12. The National Industrial Basketball League Collapses

1. Chester "Red" Nelson, "Sports," *Rocky Mountain News*, March 25, 1960.

2. Harry Farrar, "Sports Diary," *Denver Post*, March 27, 1960.

3. Chuck Garrity, "Changes Due for D-C, But Dee Denies Big Rift," *Denver Post*, March 25, 1960.

4. Vickers, interview with the author.

5. Bob Collins, "Sports," *Rocky Mountain News*, March 1, 1961.

6. Chester "Red" Nelson, "Sports," *Rocky Mountain News*, March 7, 1961.

7. *Rocky Mountain News*, March 5, 1961, 56.

8. *Denver Post*, March 20, 1961, 39.

9. *Denver Post*, March 20, 1961, 39.

10. Leonard Cahn, "Pro and Cahn," *Rocky Mountain News*, March 25, 1961.

11. *Rocky Mountain News*, March 24, 1961, 88.

12. *Rocky Mountain News*, March 25, 1961, 9–10.

13. *Denver Post*, March 26, 1961, B1.

14. *Denver Post*, May 27, 1961, 34.

15. *Denver Post*, May 30, 1961, 34.

16. Chuck Garrity, "Sportalk," *Denver Post*, March 27, 1961.

17. *Denver Post*, March 30, 1962, 50.

18. *Denver Post*, March 29, 1962, 71.

19. *Denver Post*, April 1, 1962, 55.

20. Chester "Red" Nelson, "Gaddin' About With Nelson," *Rocky Mountain News*, April 1, 1962.

21. *Rocky Mountain News*, April 2, 1962, 57.

22. Chuck Garrity, "Sportalk," *Denver Post*, April 16, 1962.

23. Harry Farrar, "Sports Diary," *Denver Post*, July 2, 1963; *Rocky Mountain News*, March 8, 1964, 63.

24. Bob Collins, "Sports," *Rocky Mountain News*, March 20, 1963.

25. Leonard Cahn, "Pro and Cahn," *Rocky Mountain News*, March 25, 1963.

26. Leonard Cahn, "Pro and Cahn," *Rocky Mountain News*, March 23, 1963.

27. Leonard Cahn, "Pro and Cahn," *Rocky Mountain News*, March 24, 1963.

28. Leonard Cahn, "Pro and Cahn," *Rocky Mountain News*, March 25, 1963.

29. Ralph Moore, "Empty Seats, 'Home' Setback in AAU Leave Sour Taste," *Denver Post*, March 25, 1963.

30. Chuck Garrity, "Sportalk," *Denver Post*, March 25, 1963.

31. *Rocky Mountain News*, March 16, 1964, 78.

32. Leonard Cahn, "Pro and Cahn," *Rocky Mountain News*, March 16, 1964.

33. Leonard Cahn, "Pro and Cahn," *Rocky Mountain News*, March 25, 1964.

34. Cahn, "Pro and Cahn," March 25, 1964.

35. Leonard Cahn, "Pro and Cahn," *Rocky Mountain News*, March 26, 1964.

36. Leonard Cahn, "Pro and Cahn, "*Rocky Mountain News*, March 30, 1964.

37. Chester "Red" Nelson, "Sports," *Rocky Mountain News*, March 27, 1964.

38. *New York Times*, April 3, 1964, 36.

39. *New York Times*, April 4, 1964, 21.

40. *New York Times*, April 5, 1964, sec. 5, 1.

41. *New York Times*, April 6, 1964, 40.

42. *New York Times*, April 6, 1964, 40.

43. *New York Times*, April 5, 1964, sec. 5, 2.

44. Arthur Daley, "Sports of the Times," *New York Times*, April 5, 1964.

45. *New York Times*, October 24, 1964, 21.

13. The Dribble Derby Passes into History

1. "Double Dribbles," Tournament Program, March 21–24, 1965, 9.

2. *Denver Post*, March 23, 1965, 39.

3. Gary Thompson, interview with the author, August 15, 2001.

4. *Denver Post*, March 24, 1965, 63.

5. *Denver Post*, March 25, 1965, 49.

6. Harry Farrar, "Sports Diary," *Denver Post*, March 28, 1965.

7. Chuck Garrity, "Sportalk," *Denver Post*, March 22, 1965.

8. Harry Farrar, "Sports Diary," *Denver Post*, March 25, 1965.

9. Harry Farrar, "Sports Diary," *Denver Post*, March 24, 1965; Mark Schreiber, "We Salute Bill Greim . . . World Leader in Sports," Tournament Program, March 20–23, 1966, 3; L. W. "Pete"

Seipel, "Down Through the Years—Denver AAU Story," Tournament Program, March 20–23, 1966, 12.

10. *Rocky Mountain News*, March 21, 1966, 56.

11. *Denver Post*, March 22, 1966, 46.

12. *Denver Post*, March 22, 1966, 77.

13. *Denver Post*, March 24, 1966, 67.

14. *Denver Post*, March 20, 1966, 68.

15. Leonard Cahn, "Pro and Cahn," *Rocky Mountain News*, March 25, 1967; *Rocky Mountain News*, March 27, 1967, 62.

16. *Rocky Mountain News*, March 30, 1967, 66.

17. *Rocky Mountain News*, March 31, 1967, 84–85.

18. Whiteside, *Colorado: A Sports History*, 315, 326.

19. *Denver Post*, March 26, 1968, 42.

20. *Denver Post*, March 27, 1968, 82.

21. *Denver Post*, March 28, 1968, 72.

22. Chester "Red" Nelson, "Sports," *Rocky Mountain News*, March 27, 1968.

23. Kareem Abdul-Jabbar and Peter Knobler, *Giant Steps* (New York: Bantam Books, 1983), 170–72.

24. *Rocky Mountain News*, April 5, 1968, 58.

25. *Rocky Mountain News*, April 6, 1968, 70.

26. *Rocky Mountain News*, April 7, 1968, 71.

27. *Rocky Mountain News*, April 8, 1968.

28. *New York Times*, January 8, 1968, 41.

29. *New York Times*, October 14, 1968, 64.

30. *New York Times*, October 17, 1968, 59.

31. *New York Times*, October 20, 1968, 2.

32. *New York Times*, October 24, 1968, 60.

33. *New York Times*, October 26, 1968, 68.

34. Arthur Daley, "Sports of the Times," *New York Times*, October 27, 1968.

35. Chester "Red" Nelson, "Sports," *Rocky Mountain News*, March 27, 1964.

Bibliographic Essay

NEWSPAPERS, MAGAZINES, PRESS GUIDES, AND YEARBOOKS
Most of my research required a careful reading of the accounts of
each tournament by the *Kansas City Star*, the *Kansas City Times*, the
Denver Post, and the *Rocky Mountain News*. For specific tournaments
I read the *St. Joseph Gazette*, the *Wichita Eagle*, the *San Francisco
Examiner*, the *Bartlesville Examiner*, and the *Seattle Post-Intelligencer*.
The *Converse Basketball Yearbook* and the *Spalding Official Basketball
Guide* provided useful reviews of the AAU tournament. Between 1946
and 1950 *Basketball Illustrated* provided yearly reviews of the AAU
tournament. It was renamed *Sports Review-Basketball* in 1950 and
provided previews of each season and thumbnail sketches of each
team. The National Industrial Basketball League published a yearly
press, radio, and television brochure. Pete Seiple, the second tournament director, allowed me to use his collection of tournament
programs for the years between 1935 and 1968.

SPORTS HISTORY: GENERAL WORKS
Useful general surveys of American sport include Benjamin G.
Rader, *American Sports: From the Age of Folk Games to the Age of
Televised Sports*, 4th ed. (Englewood Cliffs NJ: Prentice-Hall, 1999);
Elliott J. Gorn and Warren Goldstein, *A Brief History of American
Sports* (New York: Hill and Wang, 1993); and Richard O. Davies,
America's Obsession: Sport and Society Since 1945 (Ft. Worth: Harcourt
Brace and Company, 1994). An especially helpful survey for my

work has been James Whiteside's *Colorado: A Sports History* (Niwot: University Press of Colorado, 1999).

BASKETBALL: GENERAL WORKS

Robert W. Peterson's *Cages to Jump Shots: Pro Basketball's Early Years* (New York: Oxford University Press, 1990) is very good on basketball's evolution and offers a contrast to the amateur game. Alexander M. Weyand's *The Cavalcade of Basketball* (New York: Macmillan, 1960) is not a history but a summary of tournaments, All-America teams, and all-star teams in college, AAU, and professional basketball. George Sherman's *The Lure and Lore of Basketball in Missouri* (Virginia Beach: Donning, 1994) includes a discussion of the Hillyard basketball program. Forrest C. Allen's *My Basketball Bible* (Kansas City: Smith-Grieves, 1924) is an instructional book that gives the reader an idea of how one of America's coaching pioneers approached the game in the 1920s. Joe Gergen's *The Final Four* (St. Louis: Sporting News, 1987) and Peter C. Bjorkman's *Hoopla: A Century of College Basketball* (Indianapolis: Masters Press, 1996) trace the college game. Jeff Tuttle's master's thesis, "High—Test Hoops: Industrial Basketball and the Phillips Petroleum Company" (University of San Diego, 1995), is an excellent history of the Phillips basketball program and made good use of personal interviews.

Elmer Sark's unpublished manuscript, "The History of Phillips 66 Basketball," is a helpful collection of team pictures and records. Richard Green's "The Peacemaker" in the *Journal of Chickasaw History* traces the basketball career of Jesse "Cab" Renick. There are a number of interesting articles on Colorado basketball in the Denver Organizing Committee's *Rocky Mountain Basketball: Naismith to Nineteen Ninety* (Englewood CO: Westcliffe Publishers, 1989). John Christgau's *The Origin of the Jump Shot: Eight Men Who Shook the World of Basketball* (Lincoln: University of Nebraska Press, 1999) is a valuable study. Nelson Campbell's *Grassroots and Schoolyard* (Lexington: Stephen Greene Press, 1988) is a collection of articles on basketball. Good reference works include Ronald I. Mendell's *Who's Who in Basketball* (New Rochelle: Arlington House, 1973) and David

L. Porter's *Basketball and Other Sports* (Westport: Greenwood Press, 1989), as well as his update, *Biographical Dictionary of American Sports, 1992–1995* (Westport: Greenwood Press, 1995). In 1960 Bud Maloney, who covered the tournament for the *Rocky Mountain News*, compiled and edited *The Official History of the National* AAU *Basketball Tournament in Denver*. While he wrote only three pages of text, he compiled lists of high scorers and tournament results. It was an invaluable resource. Ron Thomas's *They Cleared the Lane: The* NBA*'s Black Pioneers* (Lincoln: University of Nebraska Press, 2002) includes good material on Don Barksdale and John McLendon.

While there is no history of Olympic basketball, the *New York Times* provided coverage of the Olympic basketball games. Good general histories of the Olympics are Allen Guttmann's *The Olympics: A History of the Modern Games* (Urbana and Chicago: University of Illinois Press, 1992) and Alfred E. Senn's *Power, Politics, and the Olympic Games* (Champaign IL: Human Kinetics, 1999).

For the 1936 Olympics, the first to include basketball, the Forrest C. Allen Papers at the Spencer Research Library at the University of Kansas helped me to understand how men's basketball became part of the Olympic program. The best general history of the 1936 Olympics is Richard Mandell's *The Nazi Olympics* (New York: Macmillan, 1971, rpt. Urbana: University of Illinois Press, 1987). An outstanding biography of the most notable athlete of the Berlin Games is William I. Baker's *Jesse Owens: An American Life* (New York: Free Press, 1986). Another biography, which has some material on the 1960 United States Olympic Trials in Denver and the Olympic Tournament in Rome, is Bruce Jenkins's *A Good Man: The Pete Newell Story* (Berkeley: Frog, 1999). There is a short discussion of the 1956 Olympics in Bill Russell and William McSweeny's *Go Up for Glory* (New York: Berkeley, 1996). In Kareem Abdul-Jabbar and Peter Knobler's *Giant Steps* (New York: Bantam Books, 1983) the UCLA star explains why he decided against playing in the 1968 Olympics.

Index